WALL-PAINTING IN ROMAN BRITAIN

WALL-PAINTING IN ROMAN BRITAIN

By

NORMAN DAVEY AND ROGER LING

ALAN SUTTON
1982

Alan Sutton Publishing Limited
17a Brunswick Road
Gloucester GL1 1HG

Published by arrangement with
Society for the Promotion of Roman Studies

British Library Cataloguing in Publication Data

Davey, Norman
  Wall-painting in Roman Britain.
  1. Mural painting and wall decorating, Roman
  — Great Britain
  I. Title II. Ling, Roger
  759.9362'04   ND2575

  ISBN 0-904387-96-8

Typesetting & origination by
Alan Sutton Publishing Limited

Printed in Great Britain by
Page Bros (Norwich) Limited

CONTENTS

LIST OF PLATES

C.   *Appendix*

LIST OF FIGURES

LIST OF ABBREVIATIONS

Affreschi	*Affreschi romani dalle raccolte dell' Antiquarium Comunale* (1976)
AJA	*American Journal of Archaeology*
Andreae and Kyrieleis	B. Andreae and H. Kyrieleis, (eds.), *Neue Forschungen in Pompeji* (1975)
Ant. Denkm.	*Antike Denkmäler*
Antiq. Journ.	*Antiquaries Journal*
Ant. K.	*Antike Kunst*
Augusti	S. Augusti, 'La tecnica dell' antica pittura parietale pompeiana', in A. Maiuri ed., *Pompeiana. Raccolta di studi per il secondo centenario degli scavi di Pompei* (1950), pp. 313–54
Arch. Anz.	*Archäologischer Anzeiger. Beiblatt zum Jahrbuch des Deutschen Archäologischen Instituts*
Arch. Camb.	*Archaeologia Cambrensis*
Arch. Cant.	*Archaeologia Cantiana*
Arch. Journ.	*Archaeological Journal*
Aurigemma	*L'Italia in Africa: Tripolitania, i. S. Aurigemma, I monumenti d'arte decorativa, ii. Le pitture d'età romana* (1962)
BABesch	*Bulletin van de Vereeniging tot Bevordering der Kennis van de Antieke Beschaving*
Barbet 1973	A. Barbet, 'Remontage des peintures murales romaines', in P. M. Duval (ed.), *Recherches d'archéologie celtique et gallo-romaine* (1973), pp. 67–81
Barbet 1974 a	A. Barbet, *Recueil général des peintures murales de la Gaule, i. Narbonnaise 1. Glanum* (1974)
Barbet 1974 b	A. Barbet, 'Peintures murales de Mercin-et-Vaux (Aisne): étude comparée' i, *Gallia* xxxii (1974), pp. 107–35
Barbet 1975	A. Barbet, 'Peintures murales de Mercin-et-Vaux (Aisne): étude comparée' ii, *Gallia* xxxiii (1975), pp. 95–115
Barbet 1977	A. Barbet, 'A propos de la collection de peintures romaines du Louvre' i, *Revue archéologique* 1977, pp. 109–14
Barbet 1978	A. Barbet, 'A propos de la collection de peintures romaines du Louvre' ii, *Revue archéologique* 1978, pp. 83–112
Barbet and Allag	A. Barbet and C. Allag, 'Techniques de préparation des parois dans la peinture murale romaine', *MEFRA* lxxxiv (1972), pp. 935–1069

Barbet *et al.* 1977   A. Barbet, Y. Davreu, A. Le Bot, D. Magnan, 'Peintures murales romaines d'Alesia, l'hypocauste no. 1', *Gallia* xxxv (1977), pp. 173-99

Becatti   *Scavi di Ostia*, iv. G. Becatti, *Mosaici e pavimenti marmorei* (1961)

Beyen i   H.G. Beyen, *Die pompejanische Wanddekoration vom zweiten bis zum vierten Stil*, i (1938)

Blagg   T.F.C. Blagg, 'Schools of stonemasons in Roman Britain', in Munby and Henig, pp. 51-73

Blake   M.E. Blake, 'The pavements of the Roman buildings of the Republic and early Empire', *MAAR* viii (1930)

Boll. d'Arte   *Bollettino d'Arte*

Boll. ICR   *Bollettino dell' Istituto Centrale del Restauro*

Boon 1957   G.C. Boon, *Roman Silchester* (1957)

Boon 1974   G.C. Boon, *Silchester, the Roman Town of Calleva* (1974)

Borda   M. Borda, *La pittura romana* (1958)

Branigan   K. Branigan, *Latimer* (1971)

Bull. Comm.   *Bullettino della Commissione Archeologica Comunale di Roma*

Cagiano de Azevedo 1949   M. Cagiano de Azevedo, 'Il restauro degli affreschi della Casa di Livia', *Boll. d'Arte* xxxiv (1949), pp. 145-9

Cagiano de Azevedo 1958   M. Cagiano de Azevedo, 'Affresco', *EAA* i (1958), pp. 100-2

CIG   *Corpus Inscriptionum Graecarum*

CIL   *Corpus Inscriptionum Latinarum*

Cunliffe   B.W. Cunliffe, *Excavations at Fishbourne* (1971)

Curtius   L. Curtius, *Die Wandmalerei Pompejis* (1929)

Dacos   N. Dacos, *La découverte de la Domus Aurea et la formation des grotesques à la Renaissance* (1969)

Dar.-Sag.   C. Daremberg and E. Saglio, *Dictionnaire des antiquités grecques et romaines d'après les textes et les monuments* (1877-1919)

Davey 1945   N. Davey, 'Examination of the materials of construction from the Park Street villa', *Arch. Journ.* cii (1945), pp. 103-9

Davey 1972   N. Davey, 'The conservation of Romano-British painted plaster', *Britannia* iii (1972), pp. 251-68

de Vos 1969   M. de Vos, 'Due monumenti di pittura postpompeiana a Roma', *Bull. Comm.* lxxxi (1968-69), pp. 149-70

de Vos 1975   M. and A. de Vos, 'Scavi nuovi sconosciuti (I 11, 14; I 11, 12): pitture memorande di Pompei. Con una tipologia provvisoria dello stile a candelabri', *Meded. Rome* xxxvii (1975), pp. 47-85

Dorigo   W. Dorigo, *Late Roman Painting* (1971)

Drack   W. Drack, *Die römische Wandmalerei der Schweiz* (1950)

EAA   *Enciclopedia dell' arte antica, classica e orientale*

Elia   O. Elia, *Pitture di Stabia* (1957)

Engemann   J. Engemann, *Architekturdarstellungen des frühen zweiten Stils* (1967)

Espérandieu   E. Espérandieu, *Recueil général des bas-reliefs, statues et bustes de la Gaule romaine* (1907-38)

Faventinus	Faventinus, *De Diversis Fabricis Architectonicae*
Frere	S.S. Frere, *Verulamium Excavations,* i (1972)
Frizot 1975	M. Frizot, *Mortiers et enduits peints antiques. Étude technique et archéologique* (1975)
Frizot 1977	M. Frizot, *Stucs de Gaule et des provinces romaines. Motifs et techniques* (1977)
Grabar	A. Grabar, *The Beginnings of Christian Art* (1967)
Hinks	R.P. Hinks, *Catalogue of the Greek, Etruscan and Roman Paintings and Mosaics in the British Museum* (1933)
Inv. mos.	*Inventaire des mosaiques de la Gaule et de l'Afrique* (1909–15)
JBAA	*Journal of the British Archaeological Association*
JRS	*Journal of Roman Studies*
Kapossy	B. Kapossy, *Römische Wandmalereien aus Münsingen und Hölstein (Acta Bernensia* iv) (1966)
Klinkert	W. Klinkert, 'Bemerkungen zur Technik der pompejanischen Wanddekoration', *Röm. Mitt.* lxiv (1957), pp. 111–48
Lethaby	W.R. Lethaby, *Londinium, Architecture and the Crafts* (1923)
Levi	D. Levi, *Antioch Mosaic Pavements* (1947)
Linfert 1973	A. Linfert, 'Römische Wandmalereien aus der Grabung am Kölner Dom', *Kölner Jahrbuch für Vor- und Frühgeschichte* xiii (1972–73), pp. 65–76
Linfert 1975	A. Linfert, *Römische Wandmalerei der nordwestlichen Provinzen* (1975)
Ling	R.J. Ling, 'Stucco-work in pre-Augustan Italy', *PBSR* xl (1973), pp. 11–57
Liverpool AAA	*Liverpool Annals of Archaeology and Anthropology*
Liversidge 1958	J. Liversidge, 'Wall painting in Roman Britain: a survey of the evidence', *Antiquity and Survival* ii (1957–58), pp. 373–86
Liversidge 1962	J. Liversidge, 'Cirencester: Romano-British wall-paintings from the Dyer Court excavations 1957', *TBGAS* lxxxi (1962), pp. 41–50
Liversidge 1968	J. Liversidge, *Britain in the Roman Empire* (1968)
Liversidge 1969	J. Liversidge, 'Furniture and interior decoration', in A.L.F. Rivet (ed.), *The Roman Villa in Britain* (1969), pp. 127–72
Liversidge 1976	J. Liversidge, 'Winterton wall-painting', in I.M. Stead, *Excavations at Winterton Roman Villa* (1976), pp. 272–87
Liversidge 1977	J. Liversidge, 'Recent developments in Romano-British wall-painting', in Munby and Henig, pp. 75–103
Lysons 1797	S. Lysons, *An Account of Roman Antiquities discovered at Woodchester in the County of Gloucester* (1797)
Lysons 1813–17	S. Lysons, *Reliquiae Britannico-Romanae,* i (1813), ii (1817), iii (1817, actually later)
MAAR	*Memoirs of the American Academy in Rome*
Meates 1955	G.W. Meates, *Lullingstone Roman Villa* (1955)
Meates 1962	G.W. Meates, *Lullingstone Roman Villa* (Ministry of Works guide-book, 1962)
Meates 1979	G.W. Meates, *The Roman Villa at Lullingstone, Kent,* i (1979)

Meded. Rome	*Mededelingen van het Nederlands Instituut te Rome*
MEFRA	*Mélanges de l'École Française de Rome. Antiquité*
Mielsch 1975 a	H. Mielsch, *Römische Stuckreliefs (Röm. Mitt. Ergänzungsheft* xxi) (1975)
Mielsch 1975 b	H. Mielsch, 'Verlorene römische Wandmalereien', *Röm. Mitt.* lxxxii (1975), pp. 117–33
Mielsch 1978	H. Mielsch, 'Zur stadtrömischen Malerei des 4. Jahrhunderts n. Chr.', *Röm. Mitt.* lxxxv (1978), pp. 151–207
Mon. Ant.	*Monumenti antichi pubblicati per cura della Accademia Nazionale dei Lincei*
Mon. pitt. ant.	*Monumenti della pittura antica scoperti in Italia*
Mora	P. Mora, 'Proposte sulla tecnica della pittura murale romana', *Boll. ICR* 1967, pp. 63–84
Morricone Matini	M.L. Morricone Matini, 'Mosaici romani a cassettoni del I secolo a.C.', *Archeologia classica* xvii (1965), pp. 79–91
Mosaique i	*La mosaique gréco-romaine* (1965)
Mosaique ii	*La mosaique gréco-romaine, ii* (1975)
Munby and Henig	J. Munby and M. Henig (eds.), *Roman Life and Art in Britain* (1977)
Neal 1974	D.S. Neal, *The Excavation of the Roman Villa in Gadebridge Park, Hemel Hempstead* (1974)
Neal 1976	D.S. Neal, 'Three Roman buildings in the Bulbourne valley', *Hertfordshire Archaeology* iv (1974–76), pp. 1–135
Noll *et al.* 1973	W. Noll, L. Born, R. Holm, 'Chemie, Phasenbestand und Fertigungstechnik von Wandmalereien des römischen Köln', *Kölner Jahrbuch für Vor- und Frühgeschichte* xiii (1972–73), pp. 77–88
Noll *et al.* 1975	W. Noll, L. Born, R. Holm, 'Die römische Wandmalereien der Kölner Domgrabung von 1969 in naturwissenschaftlicher Sicht', in Linfert 1975, pp. 49–60
Not. Scav.	*Atti della Accademia dei Lincei. Notizie degli scavi di antichità*
Palladius	Palladius Rutilius, *De Re Rustica*
Parlasca	K. Parlasca, 'Wandmalereien', in W. Krämer, *Cambodunum-forschungen 1953*, i (1957), pp. 93–102
PSBR	*Papers of the British School at Rome*
PDNHAS	*Proceedings of the Dorset Natural History and Archaeological Society*
Peters	W.J.T. Peters, 'La composizione delle pareti dipinte nella Casa dei Vetti a Pompei', *Meded. Rome* xxxix (1977), pp. 95–128
Pliny, *NH*	Pliny, *Naturalis Historia*
Praschniker and Kenner	C. Praschniker and H. Kenner, *Der Bäderbezirk von Virunum* (1947)
RCHM	Royal Commission on Historical Monuments (England)
Reinach	S. Reinach, *Répertoire de peintures grecques et romaines* (1922)
Reusch	W. Reusch (ed.), *Frühchristliche Zeugnisse im Einzugsgebiet von Rhein und Mosel* (1965)

Röm. Mitt. | *Mitteilungen des Deutschen Archäologischen Institutes Römische Abteilung*

Schefold | K. Schefold, *Vergessenes Pompeji* (1962)

Sear | F.B. Sear, *Roman Wall and Vault Mosaics (Röm. Mitt. Ergänzungsheft,* xxiii) (1977)

Smith 1859 | C.R. Smith, *Illustrations of Roman London* (1859)

Smith 1969 | D.J. Smith, 'The mosaic pavements', in A.L.F. Rivet (ed.), *The Roman Villa in Britain* (1969), pp. 71-125

Smith 1976 | D.J. Smith, *The Roman Mosaics from Rudston, Brantingham and Horkstow* (1976)

Smith 1977 | D.J. Smith, 'Mythological figures and scenes in Romano-British mosaics', in Munby and Henig, pp. 105-93

Spinazzola | V. Spinazzola, *Pompei alla luce degli scavi nuovi di Via dell' Abbondanza (anni 1910-23)* (1953)

Strocka | *Forschungen in Ephesos,* viii, 1. V.M. Strocka, *Die Wandmalerei der Hanghäuser in Ephesos* (1977)

Strong and Brown | D. Strong and D. Brown (eds.), *Roman Crafts*

Tacitus, *Ann* | Tacitus, *Annales*

TBGAS | *Transactions of the Bristol and Gloucestershire Archaeological Society*

Toynbee 1962 | J.M.C. Toynbee, *Art in Roman Britain* (1962)

Toynbee 1964 | J.M.C. Toynbee, *Art in Britain under the Romans* (1964)

Trans. Thoroton Soc. | *Transactions of the Thoroton Society of Nottinghamshire*

Tran Tam Tinh | V. Tran Tam Tinh, *Catalogue des peintures romaines (Latium et Campanie) du musée du Louvre* (1974)

Van Essen | C.C. Van Essen, 'Studio cronologico sulle pitture parietali di Ostia', *Bull. Comm.* lxxvi (1956-58), pp 155-81

VCH | *The Victoria History of the Counties of England*

Vitruvius | Vitruvius, *De Architectura*

Von Gonzenbach | V. Von Gonzenbach, *Die römischen Mosaiken der Schweiz* (1961)

Wacher | J.S. Wacher, *The Towns of Roman Britain* (1975)

WAM | *Wiltshire Archaeological Magazine*

Wilpert 1903 | J. Wilpert, *Die Malereien der Katakomben Roms* (1903)

Wilpert 1929-36 | J. Wilpert, *I sarcophagi cristiani antichi* (1929-36)

Winkes | R. Winkes, *Clipeata imago* (1969)

Wirth | F. Wirth, *Römische Wandmalerei vom Untergang Pompejis bis ans Ende des dritten Jahrhunderts* (1968)

YAJ | *Yorkshire Archaeological Journal*

Y Cymmr. | *Y Cymmrodor*

PREFACE

Systematic recovery of fallen painted wall-plaster from the ruins of Romano–British buildings began only after the Second World War. The excavation of the Lullingstone villa under Lt. Col. G.W. Meates first demonstrated the possibilities, and Mr. C.D.P. Nicholson pioneeered its re-assembly. When the Verulamium excavations in 1955 and 1956 and in subsequent seasons revealed large sheets of fallen plaster, Dr. Norman Davey devised new methods of lifting and of subsequent treatment and mounting. At Verulam the task was facilitated by the fact that many of the painted walls had been built of clay and had not been greatly fragmented when they fell over. Nevertheless the time which has to be devoted to the task of re-assembly, after the digging has finished, has proved daunting to the normal excavator and calls for a specialist team with a well-equipped laboratory.

British archaeology has been very fortunate in the services rendered by Dr. Davey, whose archaeological interests and professional position at the Government's Building Research Station at Watford combined to give him both the incentive and the expertise to undertake experiments and the long laborious work which he has continued during his retirement. The growth of Government involvement in Rescue archaeology during the Sixties meant that the Ministry of Works (now the Department of the Environment) itself became responsible for much more plaster recovered from a wide variety of sites; and the problem of its treatment was solved by providing Dr. Davey with the facilities of a laboratory which was eventually moved to his own garden.

The enormous achievement of Norman Davey has hitherto received little notice; but it would be no exaggeration to state that he has provided a whole new dimension to Romano–British archaeology by recreating the nature of painted walls and ceilings to complement the conventional plans and pavements. In doing so he has made apparent a fresh channel of impact whereby classical art and culture affected Romano–British life.

By the late Seventies, Davey had restored some eighty panels, and the time was felt to be ripe for a full publication. In this volume Norman Davey himself describes his methods and the ancient technical features which he has observed, and Dr. Roger Ling has provided a commentary on the art-historical aspects of the results. His wide learning puts the paintings in their Roman context. Ideally such a publication should be all in colour. In practice, costs make this impossible; but 15 coloured plates are provided, and a microfiche allows the possibility of appreciating the schemes of others.

The Editorial Committee of *Britannia* expresses its gratitude to the Department of the Environment for making this publication possible.

SHEPPARD FRERE

GLOSSARY

aedicula (-ae)	pavilion, especially the unreal type of architectural structure used in Roman painting to frame a figure, picture or other motif
architrave	horizontal beam resting on column-capitals, the lower part of the entablature in classical architecture
astragal	small rounded architectural moulding, often decorated with a bead-and-reel
ballista	artillery engine
basilica (-ae)	public hall at the civic centre of a town or in a military head-quarters, generally three-aisled, and used among other things for the administration of justice
breccia	a type of rock consisting of angular stones cemented in a matrix
calathus (-i)	cylindrical basket, flaring towards the rim
caldarium (-a)	hot room in baths
candelabrum (-a)	lamp-stand, or similar ornament in painting
clavus (-i)	a stripe or stripes, generally of purple, running down the front of a Roman tunic; originally worn as a badge of rank, later more widely used
colonia (-ae)	settlement of Roman legionary veterans, or town granted the status of such a settlement
contubernium (-a)	living-quarters of ordinary soldiers in barrack-blocks
cyma recta	architectural moulding with a profile of double curvature, in which the projecting half is concave; the opposite type, in which the projecting half is convex, is called 'cyma reversa'
dado	the lower part of a wall, and especially the clearly-differentiated base-zone in a tripartite scheme of wall-painting
decurion	member of town council
Durchblick (-e)	literally 'view through', a term used by German art-historians to describe each of the apparent openings, often decorated with perspectival architecture, between the main fields (often called 'Vorhänge', or 'hangings') in Roman wall-decorations
echinus (-i)	the convex moulding, circular in plan, which forms the lower part of a column-capital

exedra (-ae)	recess; room, whether rectangular or semicircular, open at one side
fascia (-ae)	broad band
forum (-a)	public square at the centre of a town
fresco	technique of painting without an organic medium on damp plaster
frigidarium (-a)	cold room in baths
giallo antico	type of marble, predominantly yellow in colour
giornata (-e) di lavoro	literally 'day's work', in fresco-painting an area of fresh plaster laid for one session of work
gorgoneion (-a)	head of gorgon, a mythical creature whose face turned viewers to stone; used as a decorative motif in Roman art
guilloche	an ornament used in architectural carving and mosaic pavements which imitates braided ribbons
hoplomachus (-i)	one of the classes of Roman gladiators, a combatant who fought in heavy armour
imago (-ines) clipeata (-ae)	a portrait- or other bust painted or modelled upon a shield; such shields were often dedicated in temples or public places
imbrication	arrangement of overlapping elements like the scales of a fish or pine-cone
insula (-ae)	city-block
lacerna (-ae)	type of mantle, open at the front, and fastened with a brooch under the throat
lozenge	diamond shape
maenad	female devotee of the god Bacchus (Dionysus)
mansio (-nes)	posting-station of Imperial courier-service
mausoleum (-a)	monumental chamber-tomb
modillion	in architecture a bracket on the underside of a cornice, especially in the Corinthian order
municipium (-a)	a town whose magistrates had been granted Roman citizenship
Nebenzimmer	a subsidiary room
nimbus (-i)	disc shown round heads of figures in Roman and Christian art, used at first for gods of light, then increasingly for other gods, personifications, members of the Imperial family, saints, etc.
nymphaeum (-a)	fountain-house, or room containing an ornamental flow of water
onkos (-oi)	the lofty hair-style of a theatrical, especially tragic, mask
orans (-ntes)	an orant (praying figure), represented in art frontally with arms extended to the sides
ordo	city council, usually about a hundred strong
palladium	sacred image of Minerva (Athena), carried by Aeneas from Troy
paratactic	a term used to describe an arrangement of elements in series, side by side, as in wall-decorations which lack the normal centralised scheme
patera	sacrificial plate

pedum (-a)	a throwing-stick like a shepherd's crook, carried in Roman art by rustic characters and especially by satyrs
peristyle	colonnade round a courtyard
pisé	stiff clay rammed between shuttering as a building-material
podium (-a)	a raised platform, especially one supporting columns in front of a wall
Praetorium (-a)	quarters of commandant in fort or fortress
principia	headquarters building in a fort or fortress
predella	in Roman wall-painting a narrow frieze (decorated with figures or ornaments) between the dado and the main zone
samian	red-gloss table-pottery made in Gaul
sarcophagus (-i)	stone or terracotta coffin
satyrs	spirits of the woods and hills, who formed part of the circle of the god Bacchus (Dionysus)
serpentine	type of rock, generally dark green in colour
socle	the base-zone in a wall-decoration: cf. *dado*
spirtling	the practice of spraying a painted surface with splashes of colour to secure an effect of mottled stone
tablinum (-a)	a large room behind the main hall *(atrium)* in the traditional Roman-Italian house; originally the chief bedroom, later the main reception-room
Tapetenmuster	literally 'wallpaper pattern', a term used by German art-historians to describe painted designs based on a network of simple geometric shapes (squares, circles, octagons and hexagons, etc.)
telamon (-es)	male figure serving as an architectural support, the counterpart of the female caryatid
tempera	technique of painting with organic medium to bind pigments to the surface
tepidarium	warm room in baths
terminus ante quem	'date before which', a fixed chronological point used in dating a building or period of occupation
thyrsus (-i)	a wand, generally surmounted by a pine-cone and decked with ribbons, carried by devotees of the god Bacchus (Dionysus)
tondo	a roundel, especially one containing a relief or painting
torus (-i)	an architectural moulding, convex in profile, larger than an astragal
trompe l'oeil	in art-historical parlance a type of representation, especially in painting, which gives such an illusion of reality as to 'deceive the eye'
vicus (-i)	civilian settlement outside a fort or fortress
Vorhang (-hänge)	a 'hanging' or 'curtain': see *Durchblick*

ACKNOWLEDGEMENTS

A book like this could not have been written without the help of innumerable friends, colleagues and institutions. We are grateful above all to the staff of the Ancient Monuments division of the Department of the Environment, the body which has funded to a greater or less degree almost all of the excavations from which the wall-plaster has been recovered, and which has financed the programme of conservation which forms the basis of this study. Special thanks are due to Dr. M.R. Apted, Miss S.A. Butcher, and Messrs. J.W.G. Musty and J. Price, and to Mr. L. Biek, who has contributed the table of analyses (table X) besides providing very valuable and detailed comments on Section 6 of the Introduction.

In general terms the writers owe an enormous debt to Miss Joan Liversidge, who through her writings has laid the foundations for the study of wall-painting in Roman Britain, and who in personal contacts has always been ready to help. Our friend Alix Barbet has performed similar services in respect of the Continental material. Special gratitude is also due to Professor S.S. Frere, who provided the initial stimulus for the programme of conservation and who has continued to give invaluable assistance during the birth-pangs of the present book. Finally we must single out Mr. D.S. Neal, whose wide knowledge of wall-paintings and mosaics in Britain has been consistently placed at our disposal.

Others who have helped in various ways, whether by providing information about excavations, by allowing access to material, by furnishing illustrations, or by commenting on parts of the text, may be listed: Sarah Adams, R.M. Alcock, Dr. J.J.G. Alexander, Claudine Allag, the Ashmolean Museum, J. Bakewell, Katherine Barclay, Dr. L.H. Barfield, T.F.C. Blagg, G.C. Boon, R.J. Brewer, James Brown, H.P.A. Chapman, Pamela V. Clarke, Dr. J.R. Collis, Philip and Nina Crummy, C.M. Daniels, D. Gareth Davies, G.M.R. Davies, Josephine Dool, Dr. W. Drack, Patricia Drummond, Hélène Eristov, B. Featherstone, M. Fuchs, J. Goldsmith, Lt.-Col. G.E. Gray, Barbara Green, C.J.S. Green, E. Greenfield, D. Griffiths, Elizabeth Hartley, A. Havercroft, L.C. Hayward, Dominique Heckenbenner, Carolyn Heighway, Brenda Heywood, J. Hopkins, R. Hudson, the John Rylands University Library (Manchester), Catherine Johns, D.E. Johnston, R.F.J. Jones, Jeny Keighley, Margaret Knowles, Madge Langdon, J.M. Lewis, Susan Little, Dr. Glenys Lloyd-Morgan, Carole Long, Dr. I.H. Longworth, G.I. McCabe, Jean E. Mellor, T.J. O'Leary, W.D. Park, Mary Parris, R.N.R. Peers, A.D. Phillips, Cynthia Poole, P.B. Rawson, Susan Read, Valery Rigby, D.J. Rudkin, Margaret Rule, J.H. Rumsby, R.A. Rutland, C. Saunders, A. Saville, the Shepherd Building Group, J. Sheppard, the Society of Antiquaries of London, Dr. I.M. Stead, M.J. Stone, T.J. Strickland, J.T. Sturge, E.J. Swain, Prof. J.M.C. Toynbee, the Trustees of the British Museum, David and Linda Viner, J.S. Wacher, B. Walters, Frances J. Weatherhead, Dr. G.A. Webster, A.J. White, Dr. J.P. Wild. To any one whose name has been accidentally omitted we offer our sincere apologies.

We must also thank all those who have helped in the production of drawings: notably Frank Gardiner and his staff in the Ancient Monuments Drawing Office (Christine Boddington, Yvonne Brown, Diane Dixon, Judith Dobie, David Honour, Jim Thorn, and Margaret

Tremayne) and Tina Baddeley, who came like manna from heaven when one of the authors found that he had bitten off more than he could chew.

We must also express our indebtedness to the Southwell Cathedral Council and to the Dean and Chapter of York.

Finally a special word of thanks is due to Dr. Lesley A. Ling, who has read the whole of the text and made numerous valuable suggestions, besides acting as companion and chauffeuse on visits to sites and museums all over Britain.

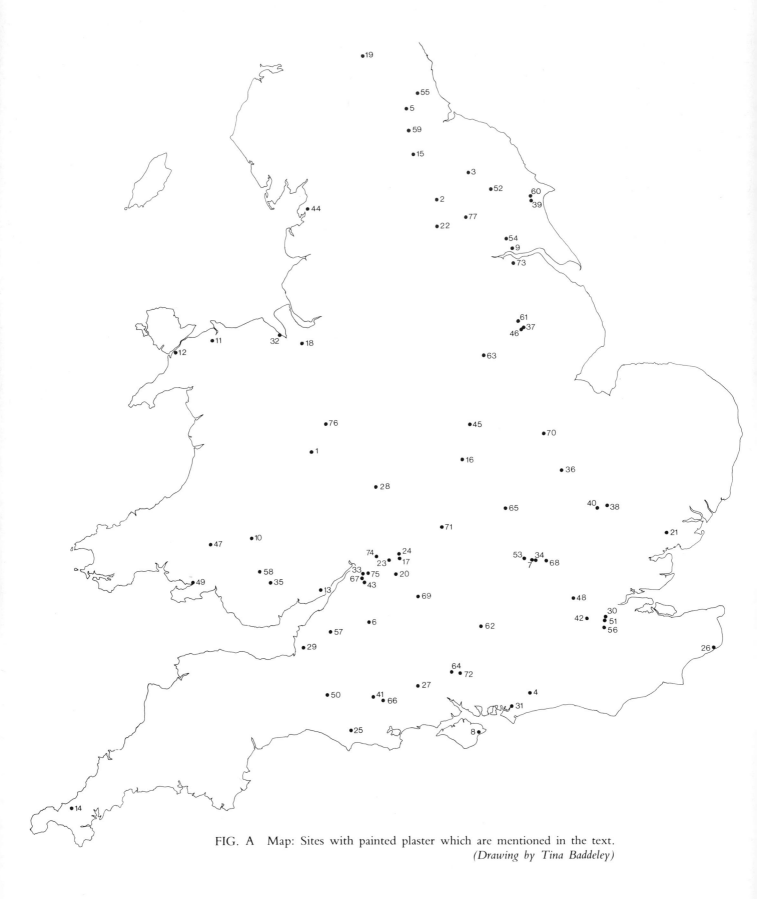

FIG. A   Map: Sites with painted plaster which are mentioned in the text.
(Drawing by Tina Baddeley)

FIG. A. KEY TO SITES WITH PAINTED PLASTER MENTIONED IN THE TEXT

1	Acton Scott	40	Ickleton
2	Aldborough	41	Iwerne Minster
3	Beadlam	42	Keston
4	Bignor	43	Kingscote
5	Binchester	44	Lancaster
6	Box	45	Leicester
7	Boxmoor	46	Lincoln
8	Brading	47	Llys Brychan
9	Brantingham	48	London
10	Brecon Gaer	49	Loughor
11	Caerhun	50	Lufton
12	Caernarvon	51	Lullingstone
13	Caerwent	52	Malton
14	Camborne	53	Northchurch
15	Catterick	54	North Newbald
16	Caves Inn	55	Old Durham
17	Chedworth	56	Otford
18	Chester	57	Pagans Hill
19	Chesters	58	Penydarren
20	Cirencester	59	Piercebridge
21	Colchester	60	Rudston
22	Collingham	61	Scampton
23	Comb End	62	Silchester
24	Compton Abdale	63	Southwell
25	Dorchester (Poundbury)	64	Sparsholt
26	Dover	65	Stanton Low
27	Downton	66	Tarrant Hinton
28	Droitwich	67	Uley
29	East Brent	68	Verulamium
30	Farningham	69	Wanborough
31	Fishbourne	70	Water Newton
32	Flint	71	Wigginton
33	Frocester Court	72	Winchester
34	Gadebridge	73	Winterton
35	Gelligaer	74	Witcombe
36	Godmanchester	75	Woodchester
37	Greetwell	76	Wroxeter
38	Hadstock	77	York
39	Harpham		

INTRODUCTION

1. THE NATURE OF THE EVIDENCE

The study of wall-painting in Roman Britain is still in its infancy. Before the 1950s almost nothing was known about the schemes of decoration or figure-subjects employed, still less about their chronological sequence. Fragments of painted wall-plaster had been found, often in profusion, in most excavations; but the difficulty of dealing with the material, and the lack of comparative data in the province, prevented excavators from interpreting the role of their fragments in the decoration as a whole. On the rare occasions when a reconstruction was attempted, restorers were hampered by not knowing what to expect: thus the Silchester 'dado' (see Catalogue No. 33) was probably created from the fragments of an all-over pattern of the kind more normally found in ceilings. Occasionally, where stone walls or wall-footings still stood to a certain height, the lower parts of painted decorations were preserved *in situ*; but these were not always drawn and photographed, and it was never possible to remove or conserve them. The few early drawings and photographs which we have, for example Lysons's drawings at Comb End and Witcombe, Artis's drawing at Water Newton, and Gray's photographs at Iwerne Minster, are of inestimable value and have been included in the appendix to our catalogue.

The situation was totally changed by the excavations at Lullingstone and Verulamium in the 1950s. At Lullingstone the so-called Deep Room, discovered in 1949, contained thousands of fragments of wall-plaster, most of which had collapsed from the room above; the excavator, Lt.-Col. G.W. Meates, quickly realised the significance of the material and to his everlasting credit grasped the nettle: 'the plaster must be carefully collected, every fragment, however unimportant it might seem; for the pieces would fit together and might some time, with the utmost skill and patience, be reassembled.'[1] It was thanks to this bold decision, and to the skill and patience, in the most unfavourable circumstances, of Mr. C.D.P. Nicholson that the famous Christian paintings gradually began to emerge from the gigantic jigsaw puzzle. The work continued through the 1950s and, resumed by others after Nicholson's death, is still barely completed in 1979 (see No. 27).

The Verulamium excavations, under the direction of Mr. (now Professor) S.S. Frere, were occasioned by the construction of a road which was to cut through several *insulae* of the Roman city. Already in the first year of work (1955) Professor Frere encountered wall-paintings which had fallen together with the timber-framed clay walls which they had decorated (Building XXII, 1). One of the present writers (N.D.) was invited to supervise the lifting of the plaster and to carry out reconstruction and restoration of the fragments, a task which was performed at the Building Research Station at Garston, Herts. Further, similar discoveries during the following five years led to the reconstruction of a unique series of wall- and ceiling-decorations which were found more or less complete where they had collapsed, notably those of the courtyard house XXI, 2, where the 'barley-stalk' ceiling of corridor 3 had come down first and

[1] Meates 1955, p. 73.

was sealed by the red decoration of the south-west wall (see No. 41, B-D). An account of the lifting the reconstruction of the Verulamium decorations is given below, pp. 65-73.

The results achieved at Lullingstone and Verulamium paved the way for the work of the 1960s and 1970s. Excavators have become increasingly aware of the value of wall-plaster and of their duty to collect it carefully; at the same time the spate of rescue excavation caused by inner-city and other developments during the period has swollen the volume of available material. Fragments from sites all over England have been assembled to form areas or details of decorations, thus immeasurably enlarging our knowledge of schemes and motifs. One or two areas of wall-decoration have also been found in position. In 1962 the lower part of a decoration was uncovered at Cirencester and a section removed for exhibition in Corinium Museum (No. 9). In 1971 paintings were found preserved to a height of two metres in three rooms of a house at Dover which was consequently named the Painted House; here the excavators have bravely resolved to preserve the paintings *in situ* and have built a museum over the site (No. 14).

Now at last the time has arrived when a corpus can be compiled and some tentative ideas can be formed on general aspects of Romano-British painting. The core of the present work is the catalogue, which includes all the more important restored decorations or pieces of decorations, as well as the paintings found in position on walls and groups of fragments awaiting study. An attempt has also been made to evaluate fragments found before the modern programme of restoration was established, especially where these fragments provide parallels for the restored pieces or shed further light on the evolution of schemes or the organisation of work in the province. This naturally involves a very selective approach: many interesting figured or representational pieces, for example from Box, Brading, Caerwent, Ickleton, and London,[2] have been omitted because they are undatable or contribute little to our understanding of style or decorative scheme. They, and some non-representational pieces, will be cited, where necessary, in footnotes. One or two fragments, though artistically interesting, must be omitted because of doubts over their provenance: a fragment in Newport Museum which has become associated with the Caerwent material, and another in the Museum of London showing female dancers, are both stylistically and technically related to Roman-Italian paintings and may well have reached Britain as souvenirs of the Grand Tour.[3]

Besides the deliberate omissions there may well be many accidental omissions. The present writers recognise that, with the volume of material which has emerged from the ground in the last generation and is in most cases still unpublished or even unstudied, they are bound to have overlooked items which they would otherwise have wished to include. Short of examining thousands of boxes stored in museum-basements all over Britain, it would be impossible to track down all the necessary information. It is to be hoped that work of this sort will be carried on during the coming years and that the present compilation will serve as a nucleus to which further material may be added.

2. DATING

The dates given in the catalogue are based, as far as possible, upon archaeological evidence, either supplied by the excavator or gleaned from publications. Fortunately we are dealing mainly with recent, scientifically-conducted excavations, and mainly with plaster which was found within the room that it decorated rather than in a residual context; so broad dates can be supplied by associated coins or pottery, or by the phases of construction or destruction within which a decoration can be bracketed.

It is not possible to discuss each case in detail: reference can generally be made to the excavation-reports. But three or four examples may be cited. The first-phase plaster from Boxmoor (No. 2) belongs to a timber building which is dated to the late first or early second

[2] See e.g. Liversidge 1968, pp. 88-92, figs. 35, 36, pl. 16 *b* (Caerwent, London); Liversidge 1969, p. 144, pl. 4.6, colour pls. 4.3-5 (Box, Brading, Ickleton).

[3] Caerwent: Liversidge 1968, pl. 16 *a* (arm of girl holding leafy twigs). London: Lethaby, p. 171, fig. 117. We are indebted to Messrs. G.C. Boon and H. Chapman for information on these two pieces.

centuries on the strength of sherds of Flavian and Trajanic samian ware which were sealed in the occupation-material and collapsed daub.[4] The Brantingham paintings (No. 4) are dated after 330 by a coin sealed beneath a mortar layer contemporary with the wall of the room; there was also early fourth-century pottery below the mosaic pavement and further coins of c. 330-335 under another mosaic from the site.[5] At Winchester the painted building south of the Forum (No. 48) was not erected before the late second century, since a coin of Trajan and a samian stamp of the potter Paternus, active c. 160-190, were sealed beneath the floor; and it was probably abandoned towards the end of the third century, because the latest occupation-level contained nineteen coins of the period 270-290 and the destruction rubble an issue of Carausius of 287-293.[6] The Dorchester mausoleum (No. 13) was evidently in use in the second half of the fourth century, since the layer above the floor yielded pottery and glassware of this period, a slightly worn coin of Valentinian I (364-375), and an issue of Magnentius (350-353) which had been turned into a Christian amulet. From the destruction-rubble came a coin of 388-402.[7]

In Britain there are few dating-points as firmly fixed or as easily identified in the archaeological record as the events used to date paintings at Pompeii — especially, of course, the earthquake of 62 and the final destruction of 79.[8] An exception is the rebellion of Boudicca, which led to the destruction of Colchester, Verulamium and London in 60 or 61.[9] Paintings from insula XIX at Verulamium (No. 40) are neatly dated before this event, because they are scaled by a layer of burning, which is in turn sealed by a floor overlaid by a deposit of the Flavian period (dated by samian of c. 70-90 and a coin of Vespasian); moreover a beam-slot associated with the new building contained a late Neronian coin in mint-condition.[10] Since the painted building, which had stone-founded walls, is hardly likely to ante-date the founding of the municipium, which in its turn is hardly likely to ante-date that of the colonia at Colchester,[11] we can place the paintings with some confidence between 49 and 60/61. At Colchester, after the Boudiccan fire, a new ditch was dug on the west side of the colonia, and only when this ditch was filled (c. 75) was the house built which yielded the gladiatorial painting (No. 10).[12]

Another useful fixed point, though itself dated by archaeological rather than literary evidence, is the fire which swept parts of central Verulamium in the Antonine period. Study of the samian in the burnt deposits has pin-pointed this to the years c. 155-160.[13] We thus have a convenient terminus ante quem for the wall-paintings in the timber buildings in insula XXVIII which were destroyed by the fire (Nos. 43; 44).

It should be stressed, however, that dates of construction and destruction are merely termini. A wall-decoration may be contemporary with the wall to which it was applied, or it may be considerably later. Re-decorations could be frequent: for instance, in the pre-Boudiccan phase in Verulamium, insula XIX, already mentioned, there seem to have been two layers of decoration; in the presumed mansio at Catterick there were three layers of painting in a building whose life extended from mid Hadrianic times to the early third century (see No. 5); and in the fort at Lancaster there were five phases of decoration in a bath-house occupied for no more than eighty years or so.[14] Normally each new decoration was applied over its predecessor (see below,

[4]Neal 1976, p. 59.

[5]Britannia, iv (1973), pp. 89, 95. Cf. YAJ, xxxvii (1951), p. 517.

[6]Antiq. Journ., xlix (1969), p. 315.

[7]PDNHAS, xcii (1970), p. 138; C.J.S. Green, The Funerary Wall Paintings and Cemetery at Poundbury, Dorchester, Dorset (B.A. dissertation, London, 1971), p. 4.

[8]On the value of the earthquake as a dating terminus see M. De Vos, in Meded. Rome, xxxix (1977), pp. 37-42.

[9]Tacitus, Ann., xiv, 29 ff., dates the rebellion to 61; R. Syme, Tacitus (1958), p. 765 f., suggests that it spans two years, 60 and 61.

[10]Information from Mr. C. Saunders.

[11]Cf. Frere, p. 19.

[12]Britannia, viii (1977), p. 96 f.

[13]Frere, pp. 97 f., 256, 262.

[14]R.J. Ling, in G.D.B. Jones and D.C.A. Shotter, eds., Roman Lancaster, forthcoming. There is an example of six different plaster-surfaces from the fourth-century phase of the praetorium in the fort at Binchester (information from Mr. R.F.J. Jones); and in a pre-Boudiccan building on the site of the London Forum there seem to have been four layers of painted plaster in a phase which could have lasted only about ten years (Britannia, viii (1977), pp. 9, 15).

p.56), and one can assume that a coat of plaster which rested directly on the fabric of the wall belongs to the original phase; but in the case of fragments it is often difficult to tell whether this was the case. Dates in the catalogue are often, therefore, given in very broad terms (e.g. Bignor, No. 1; Leicester, No. 23).

Sometimes, especially in the case of old excavations, there is no clear dating evidence for phases or deposits. Here, unless we can appeal to the stylistic dating of an associated mosaic pavement (Rudston, No. 31; Caerwent, Appendix, No. 4), it is safest to leave the question open.

It is, on the whole, dangerous to place too much dependence for dating upon resemblances with paintings in Rome or the other provinces: Britain was, after all, remote from the heartland of the Empire, and separated by a sea-voyage from even the nearest province, Gaul. Even Drack's attempt to build up a stylistic chronology for painting in Switzerland, an area much closer to the metropolis, seems a little too bold; the parallels adduced are often unconvincing, and some of the conclusions (e.g. the idea that 'Tapetenmuster' disappeared in the second, to be revived in the third century) have tended to be disproved by more recent discoveries.[15] But it is striking how much painting in Britain, as in Switzerland,[16] has a classical 'feel' to it. Certain especially sophisticated decorations, such as those at Dover (No. 14) and Tarrant Hinton (No. 38), show a clear relationship to metropolitan work; and in these examples it is worth comparing style and design to those of paintings in Rome, provided that such comparisons are used with discretion. Normally stylistic parallels must take second place to independent dating criteria, and, where they *are* adduced, due allowance must be made for a time-lag between developments on the Continent and their arrival in Britain.

3. STYLES AND PATTERNS

Despite the external dating evidence, relatively much more abundant than that available to Drack for the material in Switzerland (he was writing in the 1940s), it is still too soon to establish a detailed framework for the chronology of British wall-paintings. Too few examples are closely dated, and too few show the sort of diagnostic features which can be used to date by style. Schemes of decoration give general guidance, but no more. As the Continental material shows, schemes based upon architectural frameworks could co-exist with simple two-dimensional panel-decorations: thus in Rome architectural decorations appeared alongside striped and linear decorations not only during the Severan period but also probably through the rest of the third century.[17] For an earlier period the contemporaneity of illusionistic and simple schemes has been noted in the Rhineland and in Hadrian's Villa at Tivoli; while even in Pompeii the simple paintings of the 'Nebenzimmer' outnumbered the elaborate architectural schemes which formed the basis for the identification of the four styles.[18]

Nevertheless certain generalisations about styles and patterns are possible, and it is worthwhile surveying British paintings in rough chronological order. One very general rule is that the most technically accomplished decorations, with coloured ground-surfaces in which the pigments are evenly applied and the surface highly burnished, are typical of the first and second centuries; while rather coarser work, in which the surface is comparatively roughly finished and much of the background is left in the natural white of the plaster, becomes more common, even for relatively elaborate decorations, in the third and fourth centuries.[19] The increasing

---

[15]Drack, pp. 12-36. He tries to fit the Swiss paintings into the Wölfflinian framework used by Wirth for Roman painting in Italy, an exercise which is rendered hazardous by the fragmentary nature of the material and by the uncertainties over its dating.

[16]*Ibid.*, p. 25.

[17]Mielsch 1978, p. 170 and n. 75; cf. Mielsch 1975 b, pp. 122-129 (Severan and post-Severan paintings).

[18]Rhineland: Linfert 1975, pp. 30-33 (citing Hadrian's Villa). Pompeii: V.M. Strocka, 'Pompejanische Nebenzimmer', in Andreae and Kyrieleis, pp. 101-14.

[19]Cf. e.g. Neal 1976, p. 29 f.

dominance of white-ground decorations, not only for minor but also for major rooms, has been noticed also in other provinces from the end of the second century onwards.[20]

(A)   Walls

The wall, as in Gaul and Germany, was normally divided into three zones: the dado, the middle or main zone, and the frieze. There is almost no evidence for an elaborately-decorated upper zone with architectural or pseudo-architectural forms, as at Pompeii and in second-century decorations in Rome and Ostia; the nearest things to exceptions are a third-century wall from Verulamium, in which traces remain of an upper zone with panels containing trellis-work fences (No. 42), and the early fourth-century wall from the *principia* at York, where a theatrical mask and bands containing imitation egg-and-dart are set in this position (No. 52, A). The general absence of an upper zone is characteristic also of the other north-western provinces.[21] The dado, in measurable examples, varies in height from about 30 cm to about 90 cm. The narrower dados are generally unbroken;[22] but the higher ones tend to be divided into panels, often with a continuous dark-coloured baseboard up to 30 cm high running along the foot. In almost every case there is an attempt to suggest a facing of coloured marble. In its simplest form the coloured surface is covered with splashes of different colours, no doubt applied by flicking the bristles of the paint-brush. Such stippling or spirtling seems to have occurred at all periods; but more elaborate forms of marbling appear alongside it at least from the second century — notably painted veins or pools of colour giving the effect of exotic breccias and alabasters (e.g. Verulamium, No. 44, A). These forms, at first relatively naturalistic, become more stylised in the third and fourth centuries, when the veins can be little more than scribbles or quick diagonal brush-strokes, and the pools tend to turn into 'fried eggs' — that is a pattern in which a blob of one colour (the 'yolk') is framed by a wavy line in another (e.g. Catterick, No. 6; Lullingstone, No. 27, (A). At the same time there is an increasing tendency, apparent already in the early second century, to set the marbled panels in surrounds of different colours. Of more elaborate decoration in the dado there is little evidence. Two or three examples (see Chester, No. 7; Dorchester, No. 13) show clumps of reeds, a motif found in this position in other provinces; but there is as yet no example in Britain of the familiar scheme in which plants are combined with storks, hunting animals, or similar creatures.[23]

The middle zone receives the main decorative emphasis and is up to three times the height of the dado. In few British examples is the reconstruction reliable enough to compute the height accurately: in the corridor of Verulamium XXI, 2 (No. 41, B, C) it is 1.82 m; in the second-phase decoration from the *mansio* at Catterick (No. 5, B) 1.40 m; in the Catterick third phase (No. 5, C) 1.18 m. In the Deep Room at Lullingstone (No. 26) it has been calculated at approximately 1.52 m. The decoration, if one leaves aside certain special cases, such as the garden paintings at Fishbourne, which are designed to appear as an extension of the actual garden,[24] can take one of three basic forms: a two-dimensional panel-scheme, an architectural system involving an illusion of depth, and a large-scale figure-scene occupying the whole surface.

Panel-schemes are the simplest and by far the commonest form, occurring right through the Roman period. They normally consist of large rectangular fields, rather higher than they are wide (e.g. Verulamium XXI, 2: 1.63 m high by 96 cm wide),[25] separated by narrow intervals often painted in a different colour: a favourite colour-scheme of the late first and second centuries is red fields and black intervals. Sometimes the intervals merge with horizontal bands at the top and bottom of the zone, forming a complete frame for each of the main fields. Panel-schemes can be carried out simply in areas or bands of plain colour (including, of course,

[20]Drack, p. 21 f.; Linfert 1975, pp. 40–42.

[21]Linfert 1975, *passim* (esp. p. 19 f.).

[22]E.g. Liversidge 1969, pls. 4.2 (Bignor), 4.9 (Farningham).

[23]See e.g. Barbet 1974 b and 1975, *passim*; Linfert 1973, p. 66, pl. 12 (1), Linfert 1975, p. 34, pl. 39.

[24]Cunliffe, ii, p. 82.

[25]The fields in the successive decorations from the *mansio* at Catterick (No. 5) are, as restored, an exception to the rule, being wider than they are high: 1.35 m x 1.10 m in the latest phase).

white), can be painted to simulate marbling as in the dado, or can, in more elaborate decorations, be enlivened with vegetal or even figural elements.

Architectural-illusionistic schemes appear first, to judge from present evidence, at the middle of the second century. They can be articulated like the two-dimensional schemes, with the architectural framework occupying the narrow spaces between broad fields: the architecture either takes the form of projecting pilasters and semi-columns (Dover, No. 14), or consists of slender perspectival *aediculae* set in the intervals (Leicester, No. 22). In either case the dado is turned into a continuous projecting podium whose upper surface acts as a sort of stylobate. Although the use of perspective and shading is never totally logical or consistent, the architectural forms in second-century paintings are relatively naturalistic and convincing; but fourth-century schemes become more pattern-like and unrealistic. A Corinthian capital may become an amorphous cluster of leaves (York, No. 52, A), and a tiled roof or coffered ceiling a series of different-coloured lozenges (Lullingstone, No. 27, A); a *trompe l'oeil* recess is reduced to an aggregation of different-coloured geometric shapes (Caerwent: Appendix, No. 4).

Large-scale figure-compositions which open up much of the wall-surface seem, as in Rome,[26] to be typical of the third and fourth centuries. An early example, if it does not belong to the ceiling rather than the wall, is the painting of a swimming Cupid at Southwell, dated to the late second or early third century (No. 34, A). Other examples are probably not earlier than the late third century. The subjects are sometimes almost certainly mythological (Kingscote, No. 21; Tarrant Hinton, No. 38), sometimes of uncertain significance, like the painting in the Dorchester mausoleum, which may have shown a series of civic dignitaries (No. 13). It is not always easy to tell how space was treated in these compositions, but probably, as in the metropolitan parallels, the background was largely neutral and there was no great feeling of recession within the picture. This was certainly so in the most completely known example, the mural from Kingscote.

The evidence for the treatment of the area above the main zone is naturally more defective. We have already mentioned two decorations where there is evidence for a relatively elaborate treatment of this area (see above); but it is clear that the average decoration had no more than a frieze of horizontal stripes in various colours (e.g. Boxmoor, No. 2; Catterick, No. 5, B, C). At Catterick the frieze was surmounted by a plain white zone reaching up to the ceiling. Sometimes the stripes of the frieze are painted in yellows, greys or browns in order to give the impression of a series of plaster mouldings; this is certainly true of the third-phase decoration from the Catterick *mansio* (No. 5, C), of a decoration in Room 9 of Verulamium XXVIII, 3 (No. 44, B: a largely plain red zone above), and of decorations in Rooms 2 and 4 in Verulamium XXI, 2 (No. 41, E, F), and it may have been true of other decorations too (e.g. Scampton, No. 32).[27] There may indeed sometimes have been actual stucco cornices in this position.[28] More elaborate are the friezes with vegetal or semi-vegetal ornaments. A favourite in Britain, as on the continent,[29] is a continuous scroll, used at Verulamium in the courtyard and corridor 3 of XXI, 2 (No. 41, A, B) and in corridor 3 of XXVIII, 3 (No. 44, A, ii). In each example the zone containing the scroll filled virtually the whole space between the main zone and the ceiling: compare the restored frieze of a decoration from Alesia in France.[30] Simplified

---

[26]E.g. Borda, p. 320 and plate opposite; Mielsch 1978, pls. 92 (2, 3), 93, 97, 99, 100.

[27]It is possible that the imitation mouldings from Room 16 of the main dwelling-house at Winterton (Liversidge 1976, pl. XXXVIII) should be placed above the main zone rather than above the dado (as *ibid.*, p. 285, fig. 144). Rendered in greenish-black lines of varying width on a white ground, they seem to indicate a three-fascia architrave surmounted by a *cyma recta* frieze.

[28]Fragments of such cornices have been found in the villa at Bignor (S.S. Frere, *Britannia* xiii (1982) forthcoming); and others are mentioned in old accounts, e.g. at Headington (*JBAA* vi (1851), p. 66) and at Latimer (Branigan, p. 148). There is as yet only one example in Britain of the figured stucco cornices common on the Continent: the cornice with birds and fruit at Fishbourne (Cunliffe, ii, p. 50, fig. 26, 1; for the Continental parallels Frizot 1977, *passim*). The stucco reliefs from Gorhambury (*St. Albans and Hertfordshire Architectural and Archaeological Society Transactions*, 1961, p. 24 and pl. 4) are from large-scale figures.

[29]Barbet *et al.* 1977, pp. 191-95.

[30]*Ibid.*, pp. 176 f., 192, fig. 3.

scroll-like motifs may have occupied a similar position in decorations at Collingham (No. 12, B, C) and East Brent (No. 16, A).[31] At Leicester one area of wall-decoration from the peristyle of the house in Blue Boar Lane (No. 22, B) has a broad black-ground frieze containing a series of short candelabra, above which comes a red band decorated with double-volute ornaments. In another area of decoration from the same peristyle (No. 22, A) the black-ground frieze is divided into panels containing stylised umbrella- and dolphin- ornaments and, in one case, a theatrical mask. Both these friezes can, however, alternatively be regarded as part of the middle zone, since their colour and position equate them with the upper part of the framing bands of the main fields in a red and black scheme; only their greater height and more elaborate treatment distinguish them from the equivalent element in other decorations.

A brief chronological survey of the more closely-dated and more informative decorations will give a fuller idea of the evolution of patterns and styles in wall-painting.

For the Neronian period we have fragmentary remains of decorations at Verulamium (No. 40) and Fishbourne (No. 17). Both show painting of fine quality including naturalistic motifs: a still life in the former, and fruit and a shrimp (?) in the latter. An unusual aspect is the use at Fishbourne of yellow fields in the main zone, a feature characteristic of the late Third and Fourth Styles at Pompeii (c. 60-79) and also of second-century decorations at Ostia but rarely found in Britain (for two exceptions in Flavian times see below). The Verulamium still life may perhaps have been set at the middle of a red field, like analogous subjects in the House of the Vettii at Pompeii; but other positions are possible.

The Flavian and Trajanic periods (69-117) see the dominance of red fields. Of the better-quality decorations only those of the Flavian palace at Fishbourne (see No. 18) employ yellow: a yellow wall at Cirencester, dated to the early second century, is (despite its delicate dado-ornament) a much simpler, more run-of-the-mill piece of work (No. 9). It is at this stage that the first schemes of red fields and black intervals appear. The simplest form is exemplified by a Flavian wall-painting at Cirencester (No. 8), in which the black intervals are undecorated, while the red fields are enclosed by either green or yellow bands edged by white lines; the dado, which is unbroken, is coloured pink with black, white, red and blue splashes. Another Flavian decoration, this time from Boxmoor, Herts. (No. 2), is a slightly more ornate version of the same thing: the pink dado is now divided into panels by black stripes, and the surviving black interval carries a simple candelabrum. In both decorations the red fields have yellow lines set a short distance inside their edges, with ⊥ -shaped formations of spots set diagonally at the corners. The whole formula — pink, speckled dado; red fields with green border-bands between white lines and with inner border-lines of yellow; black intervals decorated with candelabra — reappears with modifications, usually towards greater elaboration, in several contemporary decorations in the other north-western provinces.[32]

A simpler, cruder version of the red and black scheme has been identified in a Flavian building in the fortress at Chester (No. 7). Here the red fields lacked borders and were thus directly contiguous with the black intervals and with the dado below. At the same time the dado was closer to the Continental parallels in that it was divided into two registers, a pink baseboard and the dado proper (white rather than black, however), and that it contained clumps of reeds (see above).

Further north the red and black scheme seems to have been applied in a building in the fort at Malton (No. 28). Although the fragments, which are still being reconstructed, were found in association with pottery which was Flavian in character, they show signs of greater elaboration than the Boxmoor and Cirencester paintings and may be slightly later in date, perhaps Trajanic. Not only were the candelabra in the intervals richly modelled in yellow and white with green leaves, but the red panels were apparently decorated with naturalistic garlands, recalling a motif of the Second Pompeian Style;[33] and the dado seems to have been divided into different-

[31]So too may the chain of intersecting semicircles containing stylised plant-ornaments from Caerwent VII N: *Archaeologia* lx (1906-07), p. 453, pl. XLIII.

[32]Barbet 1974 b, *passim*; Linfert 1973, pp. 71-73; Linfert 1975, pp. 15 ff.

[33]Beyen i, figs. 6, 12, 15a, 87-89; Schefold, pls. 3(1), 24, 26, 27.

coloured panels, including red lozenges set in blue rectangles. For the combination of a vari-coloured, lozenge-panelled dado with a fairly ornate red and black candelabrum-scheme one can compare a restored decoration from the villa at Müngersdorf near Cologne.[34]

A variant on the red and black formula is represented by a particularly fine decoration, fragments of which have been found at Colchester (No. 10). Here both intervals and fields had a red ground, while black was used for borders. The candelabrum in the interval was a particularly sturdy organic structure in white, cream and pink. Fragments of a panel containing skilfully painted gladiators on a green ground are perhaps to be set at the centre of one of the main fields, thus recalling the role of picture-panels in the Pompeian Fourth Style — a role which may have been reflected in the Neronian still life at Verulamium (No. 40) and a Flavian landscape at Fishbourne (No. 18), but which is only once afterwards attested in Britain (Leicester, No. 24, B).[35]

Simpler decorations of the Flavian period include a dark blue trellis-pattern at Farningham, Kent (a pattern for which there are more delicate and more richly ornamented precedents in Neronian and Vespasianic wall-paintings in Italy, and which has a number of successors in Britain)[36] and what were possibly largely white-ground decorations carrying green and yellow leaf-designs at Chester, Caerhun and Flint.[37] Slightly later, in the early second century, a very simple wall in Room 1 of Verulamium XXVIII, 3B had merely red, green and black bands on a white ground.[38]

The Hadrianic period (117-138) is sparsely represented in British paintings. While contemporary work in Italy shows a precise and delicate style with fine, often mannered ornaments,[39] the British evidence — at least that which can be dated — consists of three very simple decorations. The first-phase plaster from the *mansio* at Catterick (No. 5, A) remains largely hidden beneath the second-phase plaster, but seems to have consisted, like its successor, of a series of large fields outlined by coloured bands on a white ground, with plant-forms growing in the intervals. An unusual feature was the presence of plants growing in the white zone above the frieze. Still simpler was a decoration in Verulamium XXVIII, 3A, a building probably erected *c*. 130-135; this consisted merely of white panels marbled with red and black brush-flecks and outlined with red and black bands.[40] The only red-ground decoration of the period is represented by fragments from the Middleborough site at Colchester, which could be either Hadrianic or early Antonine (No. 11). Here the familiar pale green border edged with white lines was used to delineate the main fields, but there were no black intervals and no candelabra: the borders floated, as it were, upon a continuous surface of red. The dado, as at Malton, was divided into panels set in surrounds of a different colour (yellow in grey).

Much more ornate successors of the Flavio-Trajanic red and black schemes are found in the Antonine period (138-193). A timber-framed house at Verulamium (XXVIII, 3) decorated

[34]J. Klinkenberg, in F. Fremersdorf, *Der römische Gutshof Köln-Müngersdorf* (1933), pp. 55-61, pl. A. The villa was built in the mid first century; the painting was carried out some time between then and the end of the third century.

[35]Contrast the situation in Germany, where mythological picture-panels are attested in the second century at Trier and Echzell: e.g. Barbet 1974 b, p. 133 f. (with bibl.); D. Baatz, 'Römische Wandmalereien aus dem Limeskastell Echzell Kr. Büdingen (Hessen)', *Germania* xlvi (1968), pp. 40-52. Cf. Linfert 1975, pp. 33 ff.

[36]Liversidge 1969, p. 134, pl. 4.9. Precedents in Italy: Elia, pls. XXXVII, XXXVIII; Barbet and Allag, pp. 1000, 1003-6, figs. 29 (b, c), 31. Successors in Britain: London (Hinks, p. 52, no. 74, fig. 61), Lullingstone (Meates 1955, p. 99, fig. 7 *a*; Meates 1962, pp. 12, 15), Gadebridge (J. Liversidge, in Neal 1974, pp. 200-202, figs. 89 *a*, 90, pl. XXI *b*), Stanton Park, Wilts (information from M.J. Stone). Cf. *JBAA* x (1853), p. 357 (Wendens Ambo, Essex); *WAM* vii (1862), p. 64 (North Wraxall, Wilts); RCHM *Roman London* (1928), p. 113 (London).

[37]Chester: *Liverpool AAA* xviii (1931), p. 139, fig. 5, pl. L (124); xxiii (1936), pp. 16, 38 f., pls. IX, X (we are grateful to Dr. G. Lloyd-Morgan for showing us these fragments and other related pieces from the Paige-Cox collection in the Grosvenor Museum). Caerhun: P.K. Baillie Reynolds, *Excavations of the Site of the Roman Fort at Kanovium* (1938), 'First and second interim reports', p. 46. Flint: from a building dated perhaps *c*. 90-95 (R.J. Ling, in forthcoming publication by T.J. O'Leary).

[38]Information from Prof. S.S. Frere.

[39]H. Mielsch, 'Hadrianische Malereien der Vatikannekropole "ad Circum"', *Atti della Pontificia Accademia Romana di Archeologia, Rendiconti*, xlvi (1975), pp. 79-87.

[40]We are again indebted to Prof. S.S. Frere for information.

shortly before the fire of *c* 155–160 has yielded fragments of an example in which the red fields were apparently plain and framed by the usual green borders, but the candelabra between them had become elaborate arabesques in pink (or yellow?), purple and blue (No. 44, B). Above came an imitation stucco cornice-moulding, including dentils, surmounted by a broad red frieze.

Altogether more elaborate were the roughly contemporary decorations from the peristyle of a large courtyard house at Leicester (No. 22). Here the dado becomes a projecting podium, painted in *trompe l'oeil* as if viewed from above; the black intervals become 'Durchblicke', that is visual openings in the wall-surface, decorated with tall columnar *aediculae* shown in perspective; the horizontal black bands below and above the red fields become respectively a predella and a frieze decorated with various ornamental motifs; and the red fields themselves carry human figures framed by delicate yellow floral rods and candelabra. The result is a slightly uneasy compromise between architectural illusionism and a two-dimensional panel-system, but at the same time one which, in its richness and elaboration, is closer to contemporary metropolitan work than are most British wall-paintings.

The paintings from the courtyard and corridor 3 of Verulamium XXI, 2, perhaps datable twenty or thirty years later, are a simpler and less artistically accomplished version of the Leicester scheme (No. 41, A–C). The element of architectural illusionism is removed, giving way once more to a scheme of red fields and black intervals and a panelled dado; but the richness of ornamentation is retained. The red fields are embellished with a delicate floral framework, as at Leicester, here focussed round a central bird rather than a human figure or figures; the intervals contained ornate candelabra, of which faint traces remain; the black bands above and below the red fields were decorated with volute-ornaments. At the top of the wall came an element lacking at Leicester: a large running scroll on a red or yellow ground, peopled, at least in the courtyard, with birds and animals' heads.

Contemporary decorations in the same house recall the one-colour scheme of the house outside the north gate at Colchester (No. 11). The end-wall of corridor 2 had fields outlined by purple (?) and yellow bands on a red ground; and Room 4 fields outlined by red bands on a green ground. In each case there was a dado of marbled panels and a frieze painted in imitation of stucco mouldings.

Other Antonine decorations at Verulamium seem to have placed the emphasis on coloured marbling. There is too little of the decoration found beneath Building 1 in insula XXVIII to determine its overall design (No. 43); but part of the south-west wall of the corridor in XXVIII, 3 has been reconstructed, revealing a scheme of large marbled fields articulated by curiously isolated columns floating in purple intervals (No. 44, A). This painting again is dated shortly before the fire of *c*. 155–160.

Simple white-ground decorations of the period are represented by the second- and third-phase plaster from the *mansio* at Catterick (No. 5, B, C). In the former the dado was pink, the fields in the main zone had red frames, and the interval between them carried a plant growing from a red chalice. In the latter the dado was divided into marbled panels imitating *giallo antico* and serpentine, while the fields in the main zone were framed by green bands and separated by plain fasciae containing yellow and purple stripes. The dado-panels included lozenges, a feature found also in the dado of the Deep Room at Lullingstone, dated in the last quarter of the second century (No. 26). Here the main zone consisted of large fields outlined by stripes of red, orange and green, with stylised yellow and red date-palms at the corners.

Also in the Deep Room at Lullingstone a niche contains the first comparatively large-scale figure-subject in British painting: a group of three water-nymphs, approximately one-third life-size. Shown against a neutral white background, a feature increasingly characteristic of Roman figure-painting from the late second century onwards,[41] the nymphs are nonetheless modelled by light and shade in a fully classical style; only their drapery receives a harder, more linear treatment.

[41]Cf. the illustrations in Borda, pp. 298 ff.

The Antonine and Severan periods seem, if the meagre evidence is anything to go by, to have witnessed something of a vogue for illusionistic architecture in painting. The *aediculae* and projecting podium of the Leicester walls (see above) provide a good early example. A simpler form is illustrated by the fluted column from Boxmoor, one of a pair which evidently framed a doorway in the period 3 building (constructed in the mid second century, destroyed in the first half of the third) (No. 3). A fragment of a jutting pier and entablature at Winchester, datable to the late second or early third century (No. 48), may perhaps have belonged to a scheme of red fields and perspectival *aediculae* like that at Leicester. But the most complete evidence comes from the so-called Painted House at Dover, where three rooms preserve the lower parts of fully architectural schemes (No. 14). In each room a continuous podium, its front face veneered with representations of coloured marble, is shown supporting a series of pilasters and semi-columns articulated with a solid back-wall; the spaces between the pilasters each take the form of a white field with a coloured border, and in front of them are set various plant-forms or inanimate objects. The paintings can be ascribed to the second half of the second or to the early third century, with the balance of the comparative stylistic evidence tilting in favour of a date after 200.

The third century is for Romano-British painting, as for Romano-British mosaics, something of a Dark Age. There was no doubt a check on economic prosperity in Britain, reflecting the crisis of the Empire as a whole; but this certainly did not mean a complete cessation in the activity of interior decorators.[42] Already recent research has pin-pointed one or two mosaic pavements which can be placed in the gap,[43] and we may assume that certain paintings could join them if only the dating evidence were available. Of the items in our catalogue several — notably the fragments with 'fried-egg' marbling from a shop at Catterick (No. 6), the pieces from the villa at Collingham (No. 12), the recently excavated plaster from a suburban house at Leicester (No. 24), the pieces from the main villa-building and bath-house at Sparsholt (Nos. 36, 37), and the red and yellow decoration from Verulamium XXII, 1 (No. 42) — are vaguely dated to the third or the first half of the fourth century, and some of them may well belong within the hiatus.[44] In Rome and in the other north-western provinces the third century was the hey-day of simple linear and striped patterns on a white ground,[45] but more elaborate decorations are not excluded (cf. above, p. 30).

The picture becomes clearer again in the Tetrarchic and early Constantinian periods (*c.* 286–315). To this period belongs the important mythological figure-painting from Kingscote, the first clear example in Britain of a decoration where the whole wall-surface save the dado is opened up as a stage for a representational scene (No. 21). Although most of the forms are modelled by shading, the occasional use of hard, red contours and the largely neutral white background militate against an effect of volume and space. The faces retain the oval eyes of pre-Tetrarchic art. Also about this time (early fourth century: but see p. 207, note 1) are the paintings from the *principia* at York (No. 52). These take up the architectural formula of Antonine and Severan times, with a marbled podium supporting pairs of columns; but the heavy contours of the columns and other elements, the violent and contrasting colours (reds, yellows, greens, purples), the almost abstract treatment of the marbling patterns, and the disintegrated form of the leaf-capitals — all contribute to produce an unrealistic, non-spatial effect quite at variance with the early decorations. Richly coloured, pattern-like marbling is popular in

[42]On the apparent decline in the middle part of the third century and the subsequent revival at the end of the century see e.g. K. Branigan, *Town and Country. The Archaeology of Verulamium and the Roman Chilterns* (1973), pp. 74–7, 116 ff.); cf. Branigan, p. 180 f. But the effects of the political and economic crisis in Britain have probably been overestimated: cf. S.S. Frere, *Britannia* (1967), pp. 188, 254.

[43]Branigan, pp. 137 f., 180; cf. E.P. Johnson, 'The problem of the third century in the study of Romano-British mosaic', in *Mosaic* (Newsletter of the British Branch of the Association Internationale pour l'Étude de la|Mosaïque Antique), i (April, 1979), p. 4 f.

[44]Another candidate is the material from the villa at Droitwich, which was put up in the late second or early third century and destroyed by the end of the third century (No. 15).

[45]Wirth, pp. 134 ff., 165 ff.; Mielsch 1975 b, pp. 127–29; Drack, pp. 20–23, 31–34; Linfert 1975, pp. 40–42.

metropolitan wall-painting of this period,[46] and in Britain the panelling from the villa at Bignor (No. 1) is also datable to the late third or early fourth century. Simple white-ground decorations of course continued alongside the more elaborate and polychrome walls: the paintings in the villa at Iwerne Minster, with their panel-system delineated by lines and stripes of red, yellow and green (Appendix, No. 10), may have been applied not long after 300. Simple trellis-patterns in the Gadebridge villa belong to this and the succeeding period.[47]

To the later years of Constantine and the reigns of his sons (c. 315-361) we may ascribe the fragments from Tarrant Hinton (No. 38) and Brantingham (No. 4). The former were perhaps derived from a large figure-scene or scenes analogous to that from Kingscote; but the more plastic treatment of form, the wide semicircular eyes, and the clear indication of a ground-surface combine to indicate a slightly later date, perhaps contemporary with the paintings from the Constantinian palace at Trier. They fit well into the phase of Constantinian classicism detected in metropolitan work.[48] The Brantingham paintings are less complete and thus less easy to place; but the hardening of forms and the further enlargement of the eye, giving it an almost staring quality, foreshadow the anti-classical reaction of the second half of the century. The mural from the Dorchester mausoleum (No. 13), another example of a large-scale figure-composition occupying much of the wall, perhaps belongs to the same phase, with its linear drapery and apparently largely shadowless faces.

The second half of the century embraces the final group of paintings. Those from the Christian rooms at Lullingstone (No. 27) sum up its features: hard, linear figures, a fully pattern-like architectural framework, bright and contrasting colours (blue, purple, pink, brown, yellow, orange etc.), a total denial of volume and space. The last-phase painting in Room 7 of House VII S at Caerwent (Appendix, No. 4) represents another architectural abstraction, in which vaguely perspectival forms are employed in a pattern of juxtaposed red, yellow, pink, green and ochre surfaces. Finally a representational scene in a similar anti-classical style may perhaps be seen in Lysons's drawing of the mural at Comb End (Appendix, No. 7): here linear figures seem to act out some episode amid stylised columns on an undifferentiated white background, while to the right runs a series of rectangular shapes best interpreted as a schematic portrayal of a building.

(B) Ceilings

It is less easy to carry out a chronological survey of ceiling-paintings, since very few of the surviving examples are closely dated. The commonest treatment is a repeating pattern, based on various geometric shapes (especially roundels, octagons and squares), and rendered both in the form of linear frames and by means of floral and foliate motifs; this seems to occur at all periods, and it is not possible to establish if any particular variety was fashionable at any given time.

The earliest example, if our interpretation of the fragments is correct, would be a ceiling from the Neronian proto-palace at Fishbourne, in which tiny star-like elements were well spaced on a white ground (see No. 17). From the Flavian period there are fragments at Cirencester with curving bands of yellow, red and green which could derive from an all-over curvilinear scheme (see No. 8). Antonine, or possibly later, is the scheme of large black and grey-yellow octagons containing roundels from the baths at Wroxeter (No. 51). Late Antonine are two decorations from Hertfordshire: the monochrome decoration of square coffers, clearly designed to imitate stone or stucco vaults, from the villa at Gadebridge (No. 19), and the pattern of intersecting barley-stalk octagons peopled by birds and panthers heads on a purple-red ground from Verulamium XXI, 2 (No. 41, D). Another couple of patterns on a similar-coloured

---

[46]Borda, pp. 135-42; Mielsch 1978, pp. 163 f., 201-3 (with bibl.).

[47]Above, n. 36. Simple white-ground decorations in Verulamium V, 1 are also perhaps datable soon after 300: R.E.M. and T.V. Wheeler, *Verulamium, a Belgic and Two Roman Cities* (1936), p. 109, pl. CVIII A.

[48]Mielsch 1978, pp. 173-9.

ground, reconstructed from fragments found in Silchester XIV, 1, are probably also ascribable to the second half of the second century, the assumed period of the house's first hey-day; they too included heads of barley, here arranged in alternation with triple-leaf ornaments round focal geometric shapes, in one ceiling a square, in the other a roundel (No. 33).

This latter type of pattern, based on plant-forms radiating from roundels, reappears in a ceiling from the supposed market-hall at Leicester, dated to the late second or early third century (No. 23). It was probably also employed in ceilings from villas at Harpham, Yorks., and Greetwell, Lincs., neither of which can be dated (No. 20; Appendix, No. 8). A slightly different scheme consists of intersecting garlands forming square compartments which contain roundels, as for example on a third- or fourth-century ceiling from the villa at Witcombe, Glos. (No. 50). Intersecting garlands were, in fact, a favourite dividing motif. In addition to small-scale examples at Winterton and Cirencester, they recur on fragments from Room 8 in Caerwent VII N, where they seem to have formed both square and octagonal panels (PLS. I, II unpublished drawings in Newport Museum).

An octagonal scheme with solid frames has been reconstructed from third- or fourth-century fragments from the villa at Collingham (No. 12, A): here the colours are graded in a kind of monochrome, as at Gadebridge, to suggest a decoration in stone or stucco relief. In another example, however, — this time from Caerwent VII S (unpublished drawing) — the octagons were apparently rendered in full polychromy (grey, yellow-brown, purple and red). At Catterick, in the last phase of decoration of the *mansio*, the ceiling carried bands of yellow ochre which may again have formed an octagonal system (No. 5, D).

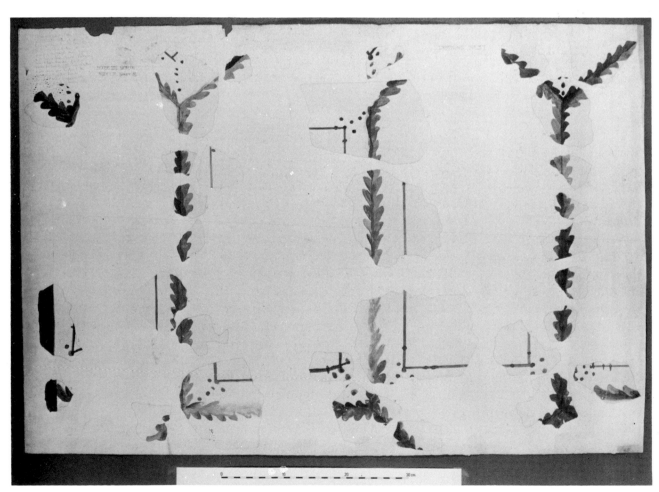

I   Fragments of painted plaster from Caerwent VII N (Room 8): watercolour drawing in Newport Museum. Scale, 1:6. *Photo: National Museum of Wales*

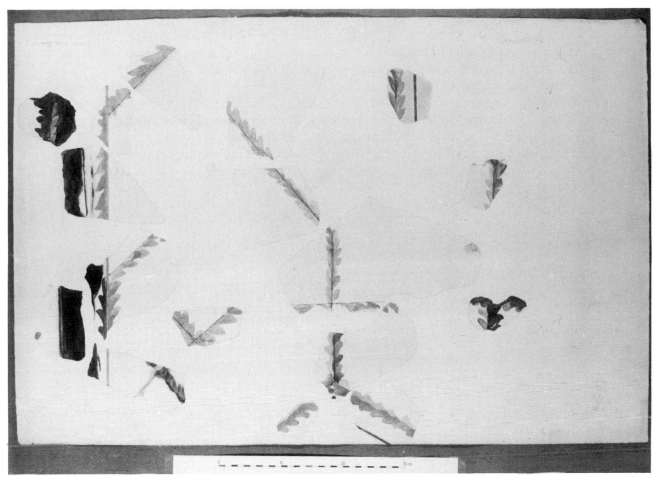

II   Fragments of painted plaster from Caerwent VII N (Room 8): watercolour drawing in Newport Museum. Scale, 1:6.
Photo: National Museum of Wales

One last repeating design may be mentioned: the pattern of roundels and connecting bands from a vault at Tarrant Hinton (No. 39). This pattern, here rendered in grey, yellow and red, with yellow or green squares in the interstices, was a favourite in Roman ceiling-decoration in Italy and the provinces, but is not otherwise known in Britain.

A different principle of design evidently underlay a ceiling-decoration from Wigginton in Oxfordshire (No. 46, A). Here, on a white ground, a roundel 77 cm in diameter probably served as the focal point of a centralised design carried out in red and green bands, a kind of decoration familiar from the vaults of the Roman catacombs in the third and fourth centuries. Once again there is no identifiable parallel, to our knowledge, in Britain.

Other forms of ceiling-decoration are representational rather than geometric or vegetal. A specialised case is the marine environment painted on the vaults of plunge-baths: that is an all-over scattering of fish and other aquatic creatures on a blue or blue-green background. This aquarium would presumably in many cases, as in metropolitan decorations,[49] have spread on to the walls as well, and it is not always easy to know from which surface a given fragment may have been derived. In our catalogue such marine pieces are noted at Southwell (No. 34), Sparsholt (No. 37, C), Winterton (No. 49) and Witcombe (No. 50), and further examples are cited under the first-named.

Finally there is a little evidence for ceiling-decorations with human figures, notably in the Dorchester mausoleum (No. 13), where fragments of figures and drapery in green, white and crimson show on the reverse the characteristic imprints of the reeds used in

---

[49]Rome, Via Portuense: *Arch. Anz.,* 1940, cols. 482-8, figs. 34-6. Ostia, Baths of the Seven Sages: Van Essen, p. 60 f., fig. 2. Dorigo, colour pl. 5. Cf. Kapossy, p. 37 (Hölstein in Switzerland).

ceiling-construction. Another site where the excavators thought that they had found fragments of figured ceiling-plaster is Kingscote, but the evidence here is more uncertain.[50]

One interesting point about the ceiling-decorations is that, with the exception of the marine paintings, the vast majority of them have a white ground. Only a handful of examples (in addition to Verulamium XXI, 2, Silchester XIV, 1, and Caerwent VII S we may cite Brantingham, No. 4, C) seem to break this rule. It is obviously difficult, in the state of our knowledge, to make generalisations about decorative ensembles in Britain, but we may suspect that there was a general desire on the part of decorators, as in Italy in most periods,[51] to maintain a pleasing colour-balance: ceilings should be fairly lightly coloured, so as not to distract from, or clash with, the stronger and richer colouring of the painted walls. The Collingham bath-house provides a case in point, since the subdued, almost monochrome treatment of the ceiling was combined with bright yellows, purples, reds and greens on the walls (No. 12). A similar rule, of course, applied to mosaic pavements. However elaborately these were decorated, their dominant tone (that of the background) was normally white, and the range of colours was almost exclusively limited to certain readily available hues of stone and terracotta — grey, black, red and yellow — which would not conflict too greatly with the polychromy of wall-paintings.[52]

While on the subject of paintings in their context, we may mention the relationship between ceiling- and floor-designs. Isolated borrowings can certainly be detected in Roman Italy,[53] but as a rule painted (and stuccoed) ceilings and mosaic pavements pursued independent courses; there is certainly no clear example of a ceiling- or vault-decoration which precisely reproduced a floor-decoration, still less reflected the actual floor-decoration beneath it. The nearest that we come to the latter is in bath-chambers where marine paintings on the vault accompanied a marine mosaic on the floor; but here the colouring and details of the two decorations would always have been rather different.[54]

Certain mosaic pavements admittedly have designs which look as if they were intended for domes. Thus at Horkstow (Lincs.) a circular design is supported at the angles by serpent-legged *telamones* who would perform their role more logically in the pendentives of a domed ceiling;[55] and a somewhat similar motif in a pavement in the Baths of the Drovers at Ostia suggests the decoration of a groined cross-vault.[56] At Horkstow, and again at Brantingham, several of the figures or scenes have coloured backgrounds, red or blue, a feature more at home in painting than in mosaic; and at Brantingham the busts represented on the floor seem actually to have echoed painted busts in the same room (though whether these were on the ceiling or on the walls is uncertain: No. 4, A, B). But in no case are we entitled to assume more than a general inspiration from ceiling-decoration. Similarly with the mosaic from Hinton St. Mary in Dorset:

[50]Information from Mr. E.J. Swain. Among the fragments from Room 1 were several of a thin crumbly plaster which was distinct from that of the figure-scene on the south wall (No. 21) and which were therefore ascribed to the ceiling. These seemed to show drapery, but it is possible that they formed part of the marbled dado.

[51]Cf. Ling, p. 46. There are, however, certain monuments, notably in the Neronian, Flavian and Antonine periods, in which the rule seems to have been forgotten.

[52]Here, of course, the relative cost of stone and polychrome glass tesserae must have been another factor. For examples of glass tesserae in Romano-British mosaics see D.S. Neal in Strong and Brown, p. 243.

[53]Ling, pp. 52-5; *idem* in F. Zevi (ed.), *Pompei 79. Raccolta di studi per il decimonono centenario dell'eruzione vesuviana* (1979), pp. 148, 158.

[54]Kapossy, pp. 9-26 (Münsingen). Cf. the villa at Witcombe, where the *frigidarium* (Room 6) had a marine mosaic pavement (*Archaeologia*, xix (1821), p. 181 f.) and one at least of the cold plunge-baths opening off it (7a) had marine paintings (see No. 50).

[55]Smith 1976, p. 25, pl. x; Smith 1977, pl. 6. XVIII *b*. Cf. mosaics at Avenches in Switzerland (Von Gonzenbach, p. 43 f., pl. 79), at Trier (K. Parlasca, *Die römischen Mosaiken in Deutschland* (1959), p. 55 f., pl. 53), and at Lambiridi in Algeria (K.M.D. Dunbabin, *The Mosaics of Roman North Africa* (1978), pp. 139f., 264, pl. 138). On carved *telamones* see L. Castiglione, 'Zur Plastik von Pompeji in der frühkolonialen Zeit', in Andreae and Kyrieleis, pp. 211-24, pls. 206-24.

[56]Becatti, pp. 42-4 (no. 64), pls. CVII, CVIII. For supporting figures at the corners of vault- and dome-decorations see K. Lehmann, 'The dome of heaven', *Art Bulletin*, xxvii (1945), pp. 1-27 (esp. 14-19).

it has been ingeniously argued that this is a direct translation of a ceiling-design;[57] but the Procrustean methods which have to be used to reconstruct the design in question, and the existence in Britain, as well as in other provinces, of numerous mosaic floors with identical or more or less closely related lay-outs,[58] speak for a rather looser relationship between floor and ceiling. There is in fact no compelling reason why the basis of the design, a central roundel supported by four semicircular panels at the sides with quarter-circles at the corners, could not have been invented by mosaicists unaided.

One ceiling-painting where the influence of mosaic pavements has been seen is the coffered piece from Gadebridge (No. 19). Certainly the guilloche used in the frames is a motif more commonly found in mosaics, and such, indeed, may be its ultimate source; but the mono-chrome treatment and the use of shading demonstrate that the immediate source is vault-decoration in stone and stucco — in both of which the guilloche is sometimes found (see pp. 177·f., notes 2, 3).

4. SUBJECTS AND MOTIFS

The range of figure-subjects which can be identified in Romano-British paintings is still, in the present state of our knowledge, very limited. But the evidence suggests an overwhelming bias towards classical culture and pursuits.

Scenes from classical mythology are almost certainly depicted in the fragmentary paintings from Kingscote (No. 21) and Tarrant Hinton (No. 38): the former perhaps shows Achilles among the daughters of Lycomedes, the latter Narcissus looking at his reflection in the pool. The problematic scene from Winterton may also have shown a classical subject, since one of the figures looks like a Cupid (No. 49, A). Other mythological subjects have been suggested at Comb End (Glos.: Appendix, No. 7) and Ickleton (Cambs.), although in both only feet are known: in the former, recorded in Lysons's drawing, we may possibly see a representation of Iphigenia in Tauris, in the latter a nymph or a maenad.[59] But this is obviously little more than guesswork.

All these examples are probably datable to the late third or fourth centuries, but evidence for the influence of classical literary culture is also found in the first or second centuries in the fragments from a presumed villa at Otford, Kent (No. 30). Here skilfully-painted small-scale figures enacted an episode or episodes, perhaps a continuous frieze of episodes, from the story of Aeneas; and the action seems to have been accompanied by a quotation or quotations from Virgil's *Aeneid*, a device which would have been lost on an owner who lacked a knowledge of the poem. The popularity of Virgil among the educated classes in Britain is, of course, corroborated by the fourth-century mosaics from Low Ham and Lullingstone, one of which shows scenes from the story of Dido and Aeneas, while the other includes an elegiac couplet which alludes to the first book of the *Aeneid*.[60]

Other isolated figures from the repertoire of classical mythology are attested in various parts of the province. A fragment from London, probably formerly in the Roach Smith collection, but now lost, showed the head of Mercury;[61] and the same god may have been portrayed in the form of a winged mask on the ceiling of corridor 2 in Verulamium XXI, 2 (see No. 41, D).[62] Cupid was especially popular. He appeared at Southwell, swimming in a marine environment (No. 34, A), and, in an uncertain context, in villas at Droitwich (No. 15, A) and Wigginton

[57]K. Painter, 'The design of the Roman mosaic at Hinton St. Mary', *Antiq. Journ.*, lvi (1976), pp. 49–54. Generally on the relation of floor- and vault-design Smith 1969, p. 104 n. 2.

[58]E.g. Smith 1969, pls. 3.2, 20, 27. Cf. R. Schindler, *Landesmuseum Trier, Führer durch die vorgeschichtliche und römische Abteilung*, 2nd edn. (1972), p. 77, fig. 230 (Trier); Von Gonzenbach, pls. 21, 39, 56 (examples in Switzerland).

[59]Toynbee 1964, pp. 219, 220.

[60]*Ibid.*, pp. 241–6, 263 f., pls. LVIII, LX a.

[61]Smith 1859, p. 62, pl. XIV (3); Liversidge 1968, p. 92, fig. 36 a.

[62]Toynbee 1964, p. 219.

(see No. 46, B) and probably at Boxmoor (see No. 3). He also featured in the mythological scene from Kingscote and probably in that from Winterton (see above). A figure with a *pedum* standing in the lunette of an *aedicula* at Leicester may be either a Cupid or a Psyche (No. 22, B), and a head from Box in Wiltshire could possibly again be a Cupid, though the bulge to the right of the face is probably not part of a wing.[63] A head of Medusa seems to have been shown in a painting at Cirencester, though apparently as a mere decorative motif within a candelabrum (No. 8).

Unidentified divinities or related subjects include the figures in the Deep Room at Lullingstone (No. 26) and the busts from Brantingham (No. 4, A,B). The former are clearly water-nymphs, as the foliage round their heads, the nimbus or diadem and water-pouring breasts of the central figure, and the overturned urn formerly visible beneath the hand of the left figure all indicate; but their precise sphere of competence, and the reason for their portrayal at Lullingstone, are uncertain. They may perhaps be the deities of the local stream.[64] The female figure depicted in the best-preserved of the Brantingham busts (No. 4, A) also wears a nimbus, and so is presumably a deity, a personification, a member of the Imperial house, or something of the sort. But there are no distinguishing attributes. The evidence for identifying the bust from Sparsholt (No. 37, B) is even more exiguous, since even the nimbus is lacking. No guess can be attempted.

An interesting category is constituted by representations which refer to Roman forms of entertainment. The gladiators at Colchester (No. 10, B) are especially interesting since they presuppose a householder with a taste for the amphitheatre and its sports in the last quarter of the first century; he may, of course, have been a legionary veteran or an immigrant official, but he may equally have been a native Briton who had become familiar with these sports in Britain itself. The same subject seems to have been employed now or slightly later in a mosaic at Eccles in Kent; and a familiarity with the amphitheatre is, of course, implicit three centuries later in the mosaic at Bignor which shows Cupids dressed as gladiators.[65] Whether the representations of theatrical masks in the wall-paintings at Leicester (No. 22, A, B) and York (No. 52, A) betoken a comparable interest in the theatre is more questionable, since such masks had become almost a commonplace in architectural wall-decorations since the time of the Second Pompeian Style.[66]

Some figures may well have been culled from real life. It is possible that the men in the murals from the Dorchester mausoleum (No. 13) were civic dignitaries; while the Christian *orantes* in the Lullingstone chapel (No. 27, A) were probably ordinary worshippers, perhaps members of the villa-owner's family. The curtain behind one of the figures suggests that he was dead. The figures shown on the red fields of the wall-decorations in Leicester (No. 22, A-B) and York (No. 52, A) are too fragmentary for identification, but the style of dress in at least three cases suggests priests or magistrates rather than divinities.[67]

Non-figurative subjects merit less attention. The one true still life is the Neronian panel from Verulamium XIX, which again has a classical flavour, depicting objects associated with the god Apollo (No. 40, A). Inanimate objects are also shown, along with growing plants, in front of the main panels in the Painted House at Dover (No. 14); here the reference is Dionysiac (torches, *thyrsi*). A fragment showing a bowl of fruit from the villa at Brading (Isle of Wight) has been classed as a still life, but its role in the decoration is uncertain; it may have formed part of a larger scene or it may have been set freely in an architectural ensemble, like the objects at

[63] Now in Devizes Museum. Liversidge 1969, p. 144, colour pl. 4.4.

[64] Toynbee 1964, p. 221.

[65] Eccles: D.S. Neal, in *Arch. Cant.*, lxxx (1965), p. 90 f. and frontispiece; D.J. Smith, in *Mosaique* ii, p. 271. Bignor: Toynbee 1962, p. 200 (no. 191), pls. 225-6. Gladiators are also shown on a fourth-century mosaic at Brading, Isle of Wight: J.E. Price and F.G. Hilton Price, *A Description of the Remains of Roman Buildings at Morton, near Brading, Isle of Wight* (1881), p. 8 and pl. opposite.

[66] Cf. A. Allroggen-Bedel, *Maskendarstellungen in der römisch-kampanischen Wandmalerei* (1974). Second-Style wall-decorations may, indeed, have drawn many of their ideas from stage-sets: see e.g. Beyen i, pp. 143-208; *idem*, 'The wall-decoration of the cubiculum of the villa of P. Fannius Synistor near Boscoreale in its relation to ancient stage-painting', *Mnemosyne*, ser. 4, x (1957), pp. 147-53.

[67] Cf. the painting of a 'toga-clad figure' found in Bishophill in York in 1973: *Britannia*, v (1974), p. 414.

Dover, or the similar bowls of fruit in Second-Style paintings from Boscoreale and at Oplontis.[68] A different type of representation, the landscape at Fishbourne (No. 18), is so far unique in Britain, although some of the fragments from Lullingstone perhaps derive from a scene with a landscape setting (No. 27, D).

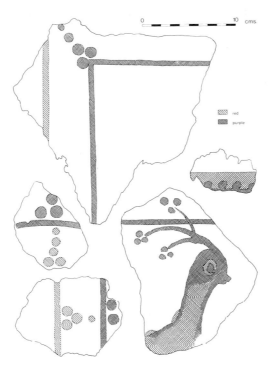

FIG. 1   Fragments of wall-plaster from Acton Scott, Shropshire (after drawings by F. Stackhouse Acton). The purple often shades into brown. Scale, 1:4.

(Drawing by R.J. Ling)

Fauna and flora are ubiquitous. Among the animals preserved on fragments from various sources we may mention a hare from Caerwent; a goat, perhaps one of a balancing pair in a 'peopled' candelabrum, from London; and a dog from Lullingstone (No. 27, D).[69] Birds appeared both perched in candelabra or on plant-tendrils, as at Leicester (No. 22, A, B) and on fragments from London,[70] or as independent decorative motifs, for example in the main wall-fields and in the ceiling-panels of the corridor in Verulamium XXI, 2 (No. 41, B, C, D). A special case is the pair of birds, symbolic of Christian souls, pecking seeds or berries beneath the Chi-Rho monogram at Lullingstone (No. 27, B). Doves seem to be the most popular variety, but at least one of the Leicester birds may have been a peacock, two others look like cockatoos, and a curious blue and red bird on a fragment at Brading was perhaps intended to be an eagle.[71] A crested bird painted on a fragment of plaster found at Acton Scott, Shropshire, is, to judge from a water-colour drawing, too fanciful to justify classification; the crest divides into three branches, each of which ends in a cluster of three spots (FIG. 1).[72] Fish have already been

[68]Hinks, p. 55 (no. 83), fig. 63; Toynbee 1964, p. 217; Liversidge 1969, p. 144, pl. 4.5. The piece has now been returned from the British Museum to the villa at Brading, where it is exhibited in the site museum. Bowls of fruit at Boscoreale and Oplontis: P. Williams Lehmann, *Roman Wall Paintings from Boscoreale in the Metropolitan Museum of Art* (1953), pl. XXIV; Andreae and Kyrieleis, fig. 18.

[69]Caerwent: *Archaeologia*, lx (1906–07), p. 453, pl. XLIII. London: Smith 1859, pl. XIII, 1.

[70]Fragment of a candelabrum formerly in the Roach Smith collection (Smith 1859, pl. XIII, 2) and unpublished fragment of a bird and flowers from Queen Street (from a well filled in the second century), now in the Museum of London (acc. no. 21232). Cf. the birds in the Verulamium peopled scroll (No. 41, A).

[71]Liversidge 1969, p. 144, colour pl. 4.3

[72]The water-colour drawing is in a notebook relating to the excavation of Mrs. F.S. Acton (*Archaeologia*, xxxi (1846), pp. 339–45) now in the Local Studies Library at Shrewsbury (Ms. 6007). Cf. G. Webster, *The Cornovii* (1975), p. 85 f., fig. 34. We have been unable to trace the original fragment.

mentioned as a favourite subject in baths, occurring at Southwell (No. 34) and at least six other sites. Other sea-creatures are a shrimp (?) at Fishbourne (see No. 17), a sea-horse or deer (?) at Southwell (No. 34, A), and an unidentifiable crustacean also at Southwell (No. 34, C: not mentioned).

Floral and foliate motifs are too common to be catalogued and occur mostly in stylised form, for example as framing or filling-elements in ceiling-patterns. More interesting are the delicate spiralling tendrils which climb up an *aedicula* at Leicester (No. 22, A), the naturalistic honeysuckle on a fragment from Winchester (No. 47, C) and the fully plastic garlands shown on fragments from Malton (No. 28), London (the Basilica site), and Leicester (near Bakehouse Lane).[73] Similar, if somewhat harder and less organic, garlands have been restored from pieces found at Sparsholt (No. 37, D, E). As for fruit, the most interesting examples, apart from the Brading bowlful (identified as plums), are the clusters of three yellow berries from Silchester (No. 33), the larger yellow fruits in the Neronian candelabrum at Fishbourne (No. 17), and the succulent orange fruits (oranges? peaches?) in a garland painted in the newly-excavated suburban house at Leicester (No. 24, A), all of which are fully modelled with shadows and highlights.

Among pattern-motifs only one needs comment: the imitation mosaic found at Sparsholt (No. 35), Bignor (Appendix, No. 3, B) and other sites. Here the painter sought not only to reproduce the patterns used by mosaicists but also often indicated individual tesserae with purple, red, yellow, grey or black lines — a curious example of cross-fertilisation between the different media, and one for which there is almost no parallel in the Empire as a whole.[74] Perhaps the pseudo-mosaic was applied to dados, so as to form a visual continuation of a real mosaic pavement.[75] Another motif which may have been inspired by mosaic is the black key-pattern on a white ground found on a fragment at Chedworth (Glos.), although in this no tesserae are indicated (and here there are also painted parallels on the Continent).[76]

Lettering, used presumably, as at Otford (No. 30), to label or comment on painted scenes and the characters within them, has been noted at various sites.[77] In addition to Otford itself, fragments of letters were found at Greetwell (Appendix, No. 8), Godmanchester (Hunts.), Woodchester (Glos.), Northchurch (Herts.) and Wroxeter; while Lethaby quotes a reference to a piece from Tower Hill, London, of 'white wall painting with the letters SVP in reddish colour'.[78] All these examples, too fragmentary to allow interpretation, are in capitals, but an intriguing dipinto in a tiny cursive script, perhaps Greek, has been found at Kingscote, apparently from the same wall as the mythological mural (No. 21). It has not yet been deciphered, so we have no means of knowing whether it is contemporary with, or bears any relation to, the painted scene.

Special mention must be made of the Christian murals from Lullingstone. With their worshipping figures and sacred monograms these are so far unique in Romano-British

---

[73]London Basilica: Liversidge 1958, p. 379, fig. 8; R. Merrifield, *The Roman City of London* (1965), p. 136, pl. 54. Leicester: fragments on display in Jewry Wall Museum (acc. no. 185.1966), found in salvage operations.

[74]A related device is employed on some fragments in France (unpublished).

[75]For a floor-mosaic which actually turns up the lower part of the wall, von Gonzenbach, p. 225 f., pl. 4 (Büelisacker in Switzerland). Cf. some of the examples of wall-mosaic in Britain: Sear, pp. 167-9 (nos. 231, 233, 235), pl. 69, 2.

[76]Fragment on display at Chedworth Roman villa (site museum). A drawing by G.E. Fox is in the Library of the Society of Antiquaries of London (Fox Collection, Box 1). A painted parallel (mid first century) at Kempten in Germany: Parlasca, p. 93, fig. 12 (7, 8), pl. 30 (2).

[77]This was a common practice in Roman Italy: cf. the Odyssey landscapes in the Vatican Museum in Rome (e.g. A. Gallina, *Le pitture con paesaggi dell' Odissea dall' Esquilino* (*Studi miscellanei* vi, 1960-61)), the painted Iliadic friezes in the House of the Cryptoportico and the House of Loreius Tiburtinus at Pompeii (Spinazzola, pp. 905-1008), and the Baths of the Seven Sages at Ostia (e.g. Van Essen, p. 166, fig. 6). For inscriptions on Romano-British mosaics, Smith 1969, p. 94 f. and n. 3.

[78]Godmanchester: *JRS* lviii (1968), p. 211. Woodchester: Lysons 1797, p. 9, pl. XXXI (4-7). Northchurch: Neal 1976, p. 30, fig. XVIII. Wroxeter: fragment found in the Baths Basilica in 1859, now in Rowley's House Museum, Shrewsbury. Tower Hill: Lethaby, p. 172.

painting, although the Chi-Rho at least recurs on the mosaics of Hinton St. Mary and Frampton, on two stone slabs at Chedworth, and on various manufactured objects.[79] They clearly represent a special commission, whereas many, if not most, of the subjects and motifs listed above could presumably have been chosen from the decorators' pattern-books.

The Lullingstone paintings certainly fitted into a decorative programme: whatever the representational scenes depicted on the north and south walls, it is a reasonable assumption that they were Christian in content or in allusion. One would like to know whether any of the other paintings in Britain fitted into religious or thematic programmes like those postulated for Pompeian painting by Karl Schefold and others.[80] On the whole the evidence is too meagre to inform us. It is possible, however, to argue that the decorations in Room 2 of the house at Dover (No. 14) are Dionysiac in flavour: torches and *thyrsi* were both used in Dionysiac worship, the growing plants could refer to the world of natural forces over which Dionysus held sway, and the palm-branches (if such they be) as symbols of victory are often associated with Dionysiac themes or objects, perhaps with reference to the triumphant power of the god,[81] or to the victory which the soul of the initiate would secure over death. On a more mundane level the use of fish and other marine elements in the decoration of plunge-baths (see above) is obviously, in a sense, programmatic.[82] It is rarely possible to compare the themes of wall-paintings and a mosaic pavement in a given room, but the Kingscote painting (No. 21), whatever its interpretation, contained a figure of Cupid and thus presumably showed a love-scene, while the associated mosaic featured a bust of Venus, mother of Cupid and goddess of love. Here at least there is a thematic link, if only at a rudimentary level.

5. SOCIAL IMPLICATIONS AND ORGANISATION OF WORK

Painted wall-plaster is known from almost every part of the province. The map (FIG. A) shows only those sites included in our catalogue or mentioned in the introduction, but a complete distribution map would show a large proportion of all the excavated sites of the Roman period. The greatest concentration of material is in the prosperous lowlands; but fragments have been found as far north as Piercebridge, Binchester and Old Durham (Co. Durham) and Chesters (Northumberland), and as far west as Caernarvon, Llys Brychan (Carmarthenshire), Loughor (Glamorgan), and Camborne (Cornwall).[83]

Painted wall-plaster comes also from every type of site. The majority of examples, as the catalogue shows, belonged to civilian dwellings — town-houses and shops in both large and small towns, and villas. But other civilian buildings also contained painted decorations: basilicas (Caerwent, Silchester), public baths (Wroxeter, No. 51; Verulamium, extra-mural), *mansiones* (Catterick, No. 5; ? Caves Inn, Warwicks.; Godmanchester, Hunts.), market-halls (Leicester, No. 23), tombs (Dorchester, No. 13; Keston and Lullingstone, Kent), and temples (Pagans

[79]Hinton St. Mary: J.M.C. Toynbee, 'A new Roman mosaic pavement found in Dorset', *JRS* liv (1964), pp. 7–14. Frampton: Toynbee 1962, p. 202 f. (no. 199), pl. 234. Chedworth slabs etc.: Toynbee, in *JBAA*, 3rd ser., xvi (1953), pp. 14 ff. Many other objects with the Christian monogram have been discovered since 1953, notably in the Water Newton silver hoard: K.S. Painter, *The Water Newton Early Christian Silver* (1977).

[80]K. Schefold, *Pompejanische Malerei, Sinn und Ideengeschichte* (1952) (now revised and enlarged in a French edn., *La peinture pompéienne* (1972)); M.L. Thompson, 'The monumental and literary evidence for programmatic painting in antiquity', *Marsyas* ix (1960–61), pp. 36–77. Cf. J.M.C. Toynbee in *JRS* xlv (1955), pp. 192–5.

[81]F. Matz, in *Akademie der Wissenschaften und der Literatur* (in Mainz). *Abhandlungen der Geistes- und Sozialwissenschaftlichen Klasse*, 1963, p. 1400; cf. 1398.

[82]Cf. the marine mosaics also found in bath-suites: Smith 1969, p. 86.

[83]Piercebridge and Binchester: information from Mr. R.F.J. Jones; cf. *Britannia*, vi (1975), p. 234. Old Durham: *Archaeologia Aeliana*, 4th ser., xxii (1944), p. 10. Chesters: piece on display in Chesters Museum. Caernarvon: *Y Cymmr.* xxxiii (1923), p. 50. Llys Brychan: *Carmarthen Antiquary*, iv (1962), p. 5, fig. 2. Loughor: R.J. Ling, in *Arch. Camb*, cxxviii, (1979), pp. 35–9, fig. 10. Camborne: *Antiq. Journ.*, xii (1932), p. 71.

Hill, Somerset; Uley, Glos.).[84] Among military sites the most productive are fortresses, where painted plaster occurs in *principia* (York, No. 52), baths, centurions' quarters and other buildings (Chester).[85] In forts there are examples in *principia* (Brecon Gaer; Caerhun, Caernarvonshire), baths (Penydarren, Gelligaer and Loughor, Glamorgan; Chesters; Lancaster), *praetoria* (Binchester, Piercebridge?), and even a gate-house (Brecon Gaer).[86]

Wall-paintings were clearly one of the most characteristic of the amenities of the Roman period. They were apparently, at the same time, a relatively expensive amenity, and one which could be regarded as something of a status-symbol; thus they tend to appear in the centurions' quarters rather than the ordinary *contubernia* of military barrack-blocks, and in the larger and more important rooms of dwelling-houses. In the latter part of the first century, when native farmers were acquiring the trappings of Roman life and building themselves their first rectangular, Roman-style cottages, they might single out one room for special emphasis by giving it a simple painted decoration; this is what seems to have happened in the Flavian timber building at Boxmoor, where only Room *c* has yielded evidence for decoration (No. 2). Even in the fourth century it is possible to find simple rectangular villas or town-houses which evidently had only one painted room: at Iwerne Minster (Appendix, No. 10) it is the westernmost in the series, at Malton (No. 29, A) it is the room at the north-east corner.

In many houses and villas, of course, and especially in the large and well-appointed establishments which developed chiefly in the second century and later, the great majority of rooms would have been painted. At Winterton the main dwelling-house of the villa seems to have had paintings in at least eleven of its sixteen rooms;[87] and at Sparsholt the winged corridor villa and aisled building between them had at least fourteen out of eighteen rooms painted.[88] But, as at Pompeii, the degree of elaboration varied. As a rule the more important rooms, that is those which would be frequently seen by visitors — notably dining-rooms, corridors or peristyles, and bath-suites — were picked out by particularly fine and elaborate decorations, while the minor rooms were more simply treated. At Sparsholt, for example, the large central room in the winged corridor building (Room 7), which was also the only room with a mosaic pavement, received an unusually elaborate decoration which may have included perspectival architecture (No. 36). So too at Bignor the central room in the west wing (Room 28B) was evidently richly painted with imitation marbles (No. 1). At Leicester the wall of the peristyle in the house in insula XVI carried an impressive pseudo-architectural decoration (No. 22), while the plaster from the interior rooms tended to be plainer.[89] It is often true that the rooms with finer wall-decorations were the ones with more elaborate mosaic pavements, or indeed with the only mosaic pavements, in a house.[90] In House 8 at Rudston the perspectival recess and other

---

[84]Caerwent Basilica: unpublished water-colour drawing in Newport Museum. Silchester Basilica: Boon 1957, p. 97. Verulamium, suburban baths (Branch Road): information from Mr. C. Saunders; cf. the possible Neronian bath-building in insula XIX (our No. 40). Caves Inn: *Britannia,* ix (1978), p. 440. Godmanchester: W. Rodwell and T. Rowley, eds., *Small Towns of Roman Britain* (1975), p. 198. Keston: *Archaeologia* xxii (1829), pp. 345 (note y), 349; *Arch. Cant.,* lxix (1955), p. 98 f. Lullingstone mausoleum: Meates 1962, p. 21; Toynbee 1964, p. 219; Meates 1979, p. 131. Pagans Hill: *Proceedings of the Somersetshire Archaeological and Natural History Society,* xcvi (1951), pp. 116 f., 126. Uley: *Britannia,* ix (1978), p. 457.

[85]Chester baths: unpublished fragments (1964 excavations) in the Grosvenor Museum (we are grateful to Dr. G. Lloyd-Morgan for showing us these). Centurions' quarters: see No. 7 and the material cited in n. 37 above. Theatre-like buildings NW of *principia: Journal of the Chester Archaeological Society,* xxxiv (1939), p. 37. Extra-mural building: *ibid.,* lii (1965), pp. 5, 8. Further evidence from York: *Britannia* viii (1977), p. 383. The fortress at Caerleon has also yielded painted plaster (information from Mr. G.C. Boon).

[86]Brecon Gaer *principia: Y Cymmr.* xxxvi (1926), p. 44. Caerhun: see n. 37 above. Penydarren: V.E. Nash-Williams, *The Roman Frontier in Wales* (1954), p. 72. Gelligaer: *Cardiff Naturalists' Society's Transactions,* xlii (1909), pp. 40, 49 f., 57; Nash-Williams, *op. cit.,* pl. XXIX B. Loughor, Chesters: above, n. 83. Lancaster: *Britannia* v (1974), p. 418; cf. n. 14 above. Binchester, Piercebridge: above, n. 83; the Piercebridge building, originally thought to be a barrack-block, now seems to be something more elaborate. Brecon Gaer gate: *Y Cymmr.* xxxvi (1926), p. 19.

[87]Liversidge 1976, pp. 281-7.

[88]We are grateful to Mr. D.E. Johnston for sending us information.

[89]Wacher, p. 348.

[90]On the social aspects of mosaic pavements, Smith 1969, pp. 71-4.

painted motifs (No. 31) come from the room of the charioteer mosaic; at Brantingham the painted busts and 'wheel'-motifs (No. 4) were found in the room with the Tyche mosaic; and in the 'Town House' at Malton the only room to have yielded wall-paintings (No. 29, A) is that of the Seasons mosaic. There is a similar correlation between elaborate wall-decorations and underfloor heating in living-rooms (as opposed to bath-chambers). The Brantingham and Malton rooms just mentioned had hypocaust systems, as did the painted rooms in the house at Dover (No. 14).

At the other end of the spectrum the service-rooms in a house, such as cellars and kitchens, naturally had very simple decorations or lacked painted plaster altogether. In the cellar of Verulamium XXI, 1 the decoration consisted merely of purplish-red bands on a yellow ground; in that of XXII, 1 of little more than red bands on a white ground. In the winged corridor building at Winterton, Room 3, which contained three ovens and was thus clearly a kitchen, was one of the few rooms which yielded no wall-plaster. In the similar building at Sparsholt, Room 10, which contained a hearth, and Room 9a, part of which served as a fuel-store and stoke-hole for a hypocaust, were probably the only two rooms with bare walls.[91]

There can be no doubt, then, that wall-paintings were socially desirable, and, at least in their richer and more elaborate forms, marked a certain degree of affluence on the part of the patrons. Some of the patrons were also people of culture, or pretensions to culture, as the Virgilian scenes from Otford (No. 30) demonstrate.[92] But painting was still evidently a cheaper form of decoration than some others. Patterned and figured mosaic pavements, for example, however crude their quality, seem to have been used far more rarely than painted wall-decorations. The fact that the daily wages laid down for painters in Diocletian's Edict of 301 are higher than those for mosaicists[93] does not affect the relative cost of the work, since laying a mosaic pavement would certainly have taken much longer than carrying out a set of wall-paintings. Even more expensive were wall-mosaics and marble veneers. Wall-mosaics are known from only four villas and from the large public baths at Wroxeter and Silchester.[94] Veneering in marble and other stones, if one leaves aside the exceptional Flavian palace at Fishbourne and another grandiose rural dwelling, the villa at Woodchester, was used mainly in public buildings such as the fora at Colchester and Leicester, the Basilica and temples at Silchester, and a building close to the Forum and Basilica in London.[95] A similar situation applied in Roman Italy, where marble inlay and wall- or vault-mosaics are rarely found in private houses, except for limited applications such as *nymphaea* or fountain-niches.[96] That painting was to some extent a cheap substitute for these more durable decorative forms is suggested by the imitation mosaic at Sparsholt (see above) and by the great popularity of painted marbling, not only in the dado but also in the main zone of wall-decorations (e.g. Catterick, No. 6).

We can fairly say that the demand for painted plaster of the sort that we find in Britain came, above all, from the Romanised middle and upper middle classes. How was the craft organised to meet this demand?

[91]Verulamium: *Antiq. Journ.*, xxxvi (1956), pp. 2, 4; xxxvii (1957), p. 12 (we are grateful to Prof. S.S. Frere for supplementary information). Winterton: I.M. Stead, *Excavations at Winterton Roman Villa* (1976), pp. 58-60, 281. Sparsholt: information from D.E. Johnston.

[92]Cf. the evidence which (fourth-century) villa mosaics shed on literary culture in Britain: Smith 1969, pp. 94,|116 f.; A.A. Barratt, *Britannia* ix (1978), 307-13.

[93]Ed. Diocl. vii, 6-9 (for the text, T. Frank, *An Economic Survey of Ancient Rome*, v, 1940, pp. 305-421; S. Lauffer, *Diokletians Preisedikt*, 1971).

[94]Sear, pp. 167-9, pls. 69, 2; 70, 1. Wall- and vault-mosaics were especially favoured in public bath-buildings in the Roman world, partly because of their durability in a humid environment, and partly, no doubt, because of the dazzling effect produced by glass tesserae when reflecting, or reflected in, water.

[95]Fishbourne: Cunliffe, ii, pp. 24 ff. Woodchester: Lysons 1797, p. 9, pl. XXX. Colchester: M.R. Hull, *Roman Colchester* (1958), p. 173 f. Leicester: *Britannia*, iv (1973), p. 49, pl. IV. Silchester: Boon 1957, pp. 97, 120; 1974, pp. 115, 156, 213. London: Lethaby, p. 175.

[96]Two well-known exceptions are, of course, the veneered walls in the House of the Relief of Telephus at Herculaneum and the House of Cupid and Psyche at Ostia.

Early work, since there was no native tradition of wall-painting, must have been carried out by immigrant decorators. This is corroborated by the closeness of figures and other representational painting in the Neronian and Flavian periods to work on the Continent: the Verulamium still life (No. 40), the Fishbourne fruits (No. 17), the Colchester gladiator (No. 10, B), and the Fishbourne landscape (No. 18) are all fully in the classical tradition of Mediterranean painting, even if Professor Cunliffe's attempt to identify the actual artist of the last-named is a little too bold (see p. 116, n. 1). Similarly the favourite scheme of red fields and black intervals which first came to prevail in Flavian times was certainly brought by painters from the other north-western provinces, where it was well established at this period.[97] The movement of decorators is well attested in the Roman world. A mosaic pavement from Lillebonne in northern France was signed by a mosaicist from Puteoli (Pozzuoli) in Italy and by his apprentice, perhaps a Carthaginian; an epitaph from Perinthus in Thrace names an artist who is represented as saying that he had laid mosaics in many cities; and an early Christian epitaph from Szombathely in Hungary commemorates a pair of travelling painters ('pictores pelegrini').[98]

But the immigrant painters must soon have set up schools in Britain and trained natives to carry on their tradition; so we can expect to find specifically British tendencies or motifs appearing. This certainly happens. British versions of the red and black candelabrum schemes, for example, seem on present evidence to have been simpler than the Continental versions, in that they lacked an animal or bird frieze in the predella and had, instead, simply a high marbled dado. There is no evidence, either, that the red fields were ever framed by columns and entablatures, as happened at Cologne and Mercin-et-Vaux.[99] Several motifs found in Britain are, to our knowledge, unique: the free-floating columns in the marbled decoration in Verulamium XXVIII, 3 (No. 44, A), the calyx-ornaments in the forks of the scroll in Verulamium XXI, 2 (No. 41, A), the water-pouring breasts of the central nymph at Lullingstone (No. 26: but see the literary reference cited in p. 138, n. 1), and the disintegrated leaf-capital in the decoration at York (No. 52, A). So too the idea of a Cupid swimming with his cloak fluttering from his shoulders (Southwell, No. 34, A) is evidently unparalleled, and suggests a provincial decorator muddling, or taking liberties with, his inherited figure-types.

And yet paintings in Britain remain stylistically close to Roman-Italian work: the Southwell Cupid, whatever the anomalies of his posture and dress, is painted in a fully classical style. There was no real Romano-Celtic synthesis, as there was in sculpture. The present writers can think of only one painted figure, apart possibly from the Christian *orantes* from Lullingstone (No. 27, A), which displays a certain provincial naïveté: the unpublished Cupid from the villa in Bays Meadow, Droitwich (No. 15, A). Here in the third century the clumsy outlines and misplaced right wing betoken a painter who had no capacity for, or interest in, working in the metropolitan tradition.[100]

To judge from the quantity of decorations which must have been required, there would have been at least one, and probably more than one, *atelier* in every major town, not to mention the minor towns. Can we recognise any local idiosyncracies which distinguish these *ateliers*? Everything is against it — the very number of the workshops and the inevitable complexity of their inter-relationships; the flexibility of the medium and the great variety of subjects and motifs employed; and the woeful inadequacy and imbalance of the surviving evidence. The

[97]The earliest example in the north-western provinces, that from Kempten, dates to the middle of the first century: Parlasca, p. 101 f., pls. 32, 33. Cf. the table of dates in Barbet 1975, p. 112.

[98]Lillebonne: *Inv. mos.*, i. G. Lafaye and A. Blanchet, *Gaule* (1909), ii, *Lugdunaise, Belgique et Germanie*, p. 80 (no. 1051) and pls. Perinthus: *CIG*, 2025; cf. 2024. Cf. J.M.C. Toynbee, *Some Notes on Artists in the Roman World* (1951), pp. 43-50. Szombathely: *CIL* iii, 4222.

[99]Cologne: Linfert 1973; cf. Linfert 1975, pp. 20 ff., pls. 14, 16, 18, 20-22, 26, 27. Mercin-et-Vaux: Barbet 1974 b, pp. 108 ff.

[100]Cf. p. 36 and n. 44 above. This figure is the painted counterpart of mosaics like the Rudston Venus and the Sherborne Apollo and Marsyas, which are again, in their own medium, exceptions to the classical norm: Smith 1969, p. 118 f.

situation is totally different from that which applies to mosaic, a much more specialised craft, one which had a more limited repertoire of patterns and motifs, and one of which the remains are much better preserved. In mosaic it is possible, in the fourth century, to recognise at least four regional 'schools';[101] in painting it is possible to recognise none. The hopelessness of the task is pointed by the fact that even in Pompeii, Rome and Ostia, with their wealth of surviving

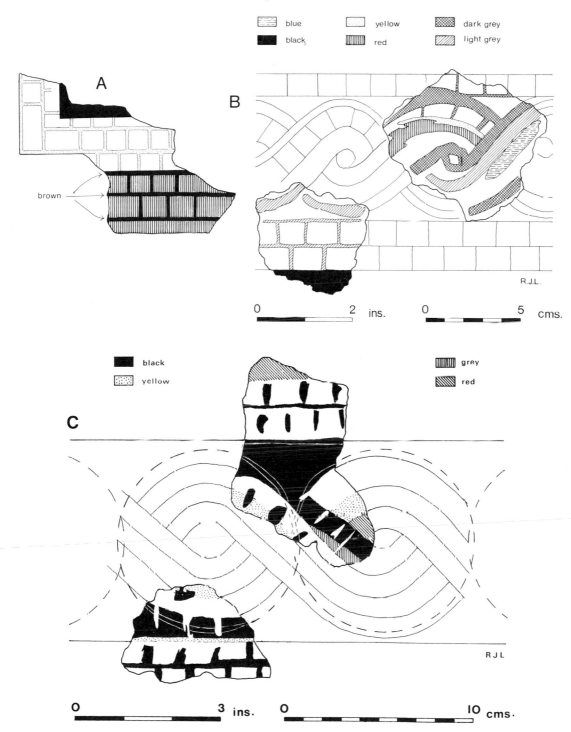

FIG. 2   Painted imitations of mosaic. (A)   Compton Abdale (after J. Christiansen: no scale). (B)   Bignor (after Lysons). Scale, 1:2.   (C)   Lufton: circular guide-lines indicated by broken lines. Scale, 1:2.
(Drawings by R.J. Ling)

[101]Smith 1969, pp. 95-113; cf. D.J. Smith, 'Three fourth-century schools of mosaic in Roman Britain', in *Mosaïque* i, pp. 95-116. A fifth school has been suggested by D.E. Johnston: 'The central southern group of Romano-British mosaics', in Munby and Henig, pp. 195-215.

paintings, it is not yet possible to distinguish clearly between the different workshops or to isolate the broad regional trends.[102]

Nonetheless we can tentatively point to certain motifs which are on present evidence confined to, or most commonly found in, particular regions, and which may possibly therefore betray the presence of a regional style. Some of these are discussed in the catalogue. For instance imitation mosaic has so far been found only at sites in the south and west — Sparsholt (No. 35), Bignor (Appendix, No. 3, B: FIG. 2 (B)), Compton Abdale (Glos.: FIG. 2 (A)) and Lufton (Somerset) FIG. 2 (C)).[103] Frames incorporating a light-coloured stripe on which dark

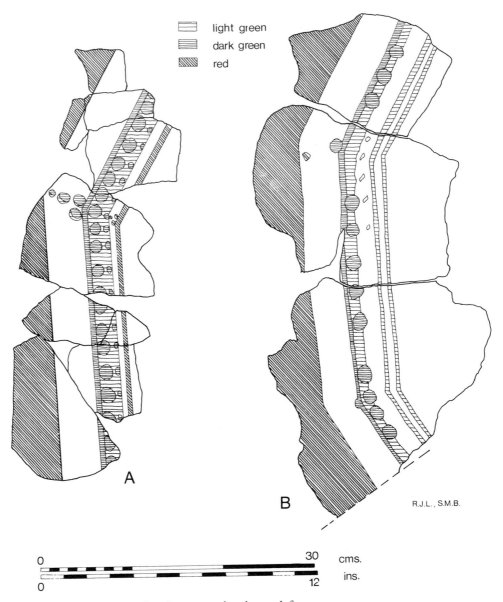

FIG. 3   Fragments of wall-plaster showing spotted polygonal frames.
(A)   Frocester Court (after E.G. Price). (B)   Caerwent (after water-colour in Newport). Scale, 1:4.
(Drawing by R.J. Ling and Tina Baddeley)

[102]Attempts at Pompeii have produced conflicting results: e.g. H.G. Beyen, 'The workshops of the Fourth Style at Pompeii and in its neighbourhood', *Mnemosyne*, ser. 4, iv (1951), pp. 235-57 (= *Studia archaeologica Gerardo van Hoorn oblata* (1951), pp. 43-65); L. Richardson, in *MAAR* xxiii (1955), pp. 111-60 (with a survey of previous work in the field, pp. 113-16); cf. Peters. Dr. Agnes Allroggen-Bedel is currently working on the local stylistic features of wall-painting at Herculaneum.

[103]Liversidge 1969, p. 134, fig. 4.1 *b, c, d.* The Lufton fragments are in Yeovil Museum; we are grateful to L.C. Hayward for letting us see them; cf. *Proc. Somerset Archaeological and N.H. Soc.* cxvi (1972), pp. 65 f.

spots are superimposed are found in paintings from sites spaced, broadly speaking, along the Severn valley: Wroxeter (No. 51), Droitwich (No. 15, D), Caerwent (Monmouthshire), and Frocester Court (Glos.) (FIG. 3; cf. p. 201 and n. 3). More locally a distinctive pyramidal grouping of spots, dark and on a white ground, links the Wroxeter Baths ceiling (No. 51) with fragments from a nearby villa at Acton Scott (FIG. 1; cf. p. 201 and n. 2). Imitation marbling in which lozenges in one colour are set inside rectangular panels in another seems, apart from an example in the Deep Room of the Lullingstone villa,[104] to have been concentrated in Yorkshire and North Lincolnshire, occurring in the late first and second centuries at Malton (No. 28), Catterick (No. 5, C) and Aldborough (Appendix, No. 1), in the early fourth century at York (No. 52, A), and probably again in the fourth century at Winterton, Lincs.[105] 'Wheel'-like ornaments (concentric bands of colour set within a concave-sided octagon and divided into sectors by radial 'spokes') come from two sites in the East Riding of Yorkshire: Brantingham (No. 4, C) and Harpham (No. 20). Another site in the area, North Newbald, produced a 'flower or "wheel" of light red with "spokes" of dark red on dark red ground'.[106]

A slightly more complex situation is revealed by the intersecting green and yellow garlands of the ceiling-pattern from Witcombe (No. 50). This is very reminiscent of fragments across the Severn at Caerwent, where in Room 8 of House VII N there was evidently a pattern or patterns based on similar garlands, either green or half-red and half-yellow; sometimes these intersected at right angles, as at Witcombe, sometimes they formed obtuse angles, indicating a polygonal framework (PLS. I, II).[107] Another version of the Witcombe pattern, albeit on a much smaller scale, is attested by fragments from Dyer Court in Cirencester, in which blue and green garlands enclosed red circles much as the Witcombe garlands enclosed purple and green circles.[108] But that this was not a pattern confined to the south-west is shown by its recurrence, again on a much smaller scale, and here with pink or blue circles, on fragments from the villa at Winterton. We are obviously dealing in this case with a rather wider interchange and circulation of ideas.[109]

But it must be stressed that, even when motifs are confined to one region, no great theories can be constructed on the fact. It may yet turn out, when more material is available, that the motifs were used more widely than at present appears. In any case very few of the fragments which have been mentioned can be accurately dated. If the linking motifs belong, say, to the same half century, they may have some validity in establishing a regional trend; but, if they occur over a period of two or three centuries, like the marbled lozenges in Yorkshire, it is more difficult to believe that there is any genuine continuity of workshop tradition. As for identifying individual workshops, this will only be possible when we can point to groups of decorations with a number of common motifs used in a comparable way.

6. TECHNIQUES OF PLASTERERS AND PAINTERS

Before considering the methods used in the recovery and restoration of Romano-British painted plaster, it is worthwhile to summarise the materials and techniques used by the plasterers and painters of Roman times.[110] Evidence will be drawn not only from Britain but also, where necessary, from elsewhere.

---

[104]Meates 1955, pp. 72, 99, fig. 11.

[105]Liversidge 1976, p. 282 f., fig. 143, pl. XXXIV, c, d.

[106]P. Corder in Proceedings of the Leeds Philosophical Society (Literary and Historical Section) v (1941), p. 238.

[107]Unpublished drawings in Newport Museum (Caerwent drawings 37, 38, 39).

[108]Liversidge 1962, p. 48, fig. 7.3, 4.

[109]Liversidge 1976, p. 281 f., pl. XXXI, d, e. Cf. the candelabra and foliate rods painted on red fields in decorations at Leicester (No. 22, A-B), Verulamium (No. 41, A-C), Winchester (No. 47), Scampton (No. 32), and Colchester: see p. 130, 175, 196.

[110]See generally for this section N. Davey, A History of Building Materials (1961), pp. 97-119; Frizot 1975; R.J. Ling, 'Stuccowork', and P. Pratt, 'Wall painting', in Strong and Brown, pp. 208-29. On plastering in Greek times: R. Martin, Manuel d'architecture grecque, i. Matériaux et techniques (1965), pp. 422-41; A. Orlandos, Les matériaux de construction et la technique architecturale des anciens Grecs, i (1966), pp. 135-53.

The basic materials used in the production of plaster in Roman Britain were, as in most of the Roman world, lime and a fine aggregate, usually some form of sand.

Lime

Lime is obtained by burning a calcareous material, generally limestone, dolomite, marble, or chalk. When heated to a temperature of about 900°C (1652°F), these rocks, which are basically forms of calcium carbonate, lose half their weight through the expulsion of carbon dioxide, being converted into quicklime (calcium oxide). This quicklime is unstable in moist air, and if treated with water crumbles to a white powder (slaked lime or hydrate of lime: calcium hydroxide), at the same time giving off much heat. For building-purposes it is slaked with sufficient water to create a slurry, or suspension of the powder in water, and run into a putty which is then mixed with sand and/or other fillers to produce a suitable plaster or mortar. The lime sets by taking back carbon dioxide from the air and reverting to calcium carbonate.

Britain contains a wide range of readily-accessible limestones and chalk deposits which could have been (and some of which certainly were) burnt in the Roman period. The purest lime can be made from the mountain limestone of the Carboniferous beds at Buxton, in the Forest of Dean, in the Mendips, and in North and South Wales; from the white chalk of the Upper Cretaceous beds (Upper Chalk) of East Anglia, Southeast England, the Thames Basin and Yorkshire; and from the oolitic limestone in the Bath and Portland areas. Sometimes the limestone may be contaminated with other materials in varying quantity and form, chiefly clay (silica and alumina). The lime produced from this type of limestone will contain, when hydrated, compounds of cementicious value such as calcium silicates and calcium aluminates. This type of lime is termed 'semi-hydraulic': that is, it has the partial ability to set under water or in damp conditions and is not wholly dependent on atmospheric carbon dioxide.

It seems quite likely that the Romans used lime from any, or all, of these sources depending on proximity and availability. As an example, lime from a Roman slaking-pit excavated at Park Street, near St. Albans (Verulamium) by Helen O'Neil was shown on analysis at the Building Research Station, Watford, to contain lime of the semi-hydraulic type, similar in composition to the local greystone cretaceous limes of the Luton-Dunstable area, possibly the most easily accessible source for the people of Verulamium.[111]

Further research would be needed to determine whether the Romans prepared an eminently hydraulic type of lime from the Lias Limestones of Warwickshire, Somerset and South Wales; the Magnesian and Dolomitic Limestones of the Nottingham, South Shields and Hartlepool areas; and semi-hydraulic lime from the Carboniferous Limestone stretching from the Peak District southwards to the Forest of Dean and the Mendip Hills.

Burning of the limestone was evidently done normally in a simple type of kiln known in later times as the Periodic or 'flare' type. It was cylindrical in form, narrower at the top, and towards the bottom had a circumferential ledge (fortax) upon which a rough arch or dome of limestone lumps was formed on a wooden framework, so that it could support further limestone to fill the kiln completely. A fire was lit either beneath this dome or in the mouth of a draw-tunnel (or 'throat') leading to the kiln-chamber. This fire was kept stoked with wood over several days, until burning of the limestone was completed. This method of burning limestone had been used in the ancient world long before the Roman occupation of Britain: Cato, writing in the second century B.C., describes the process in some detail.[112] Actual examples of kilns of Imperial date, somewhat squatter in proportion than those described by Cato, have been excavated in North Africa, Germany, France and Britain, and successful experiments in firing one have been conducted in the Rhineland.[113] The slaking of the lime had to be very

[111]Davey 1945, p. 103; *Chemistry and Industry*, 1950, p. 46 f., fig. 9.

[112]Cato, *de Agricultura* 38.

[113]W. Sölter, *Römische Kalkbrenner im Rheinland* (1970); D.A. Jackson, L. Biek and B.F. Dix, 'A Roman lime kiln at Weekley. Northants', *Britannia*, iv (1973), pp. 128–40; cf. now B.F. Dix, 'Roman lime-buring', *Britannia* x (1979), p. 261 f. A different type of kiln (the Running kiln), in which alternate layers of limestone and fuel were piled within the chamber, has been identified on a villa-site at Chew Valley in Somerset: P.A. Rahtz and E. Greenfield, *Excavations at Chew Valley Lake* (1977), pp. 46–9, 349 f., fig. 33. Cf. *Arch. Camb.* cxxii (1973), p. 110 f.

thorough, since any particles of quicklime remaining unslaked could cause subsequent 'pitting' or 'popping' of the mortar or plaster, due to delayed hydration of the particles. The ancient writers such as Vitruvius and Pliny the Elder laid great emphasis on the necessity to slake the lime thoroughly and to store the resulting slurry for a long time before use.[114] In fact the longer it was kept — for several months, or even years — the more complete would be the maturing. To test that it was properly matured Vitruvius recommended chopping it with an *ascia* (adze or mattock); if it stuck to the tool like glue, it was ready for use. This procedure of thorough slaking must have been closely followed in Roman Britain, since of all the many samples of painted renderings so far handled by the writers none has shown any significant sign of 'pitting' or 'popping'.

The Romans were fully aware that the pure or non-hydraulic limes could be converted into hydraulic or partially hydraulic ones by adding suitable materials. Such materials were pounded tiles, bricks and pottery, burnt clay, various slags, pumice and earths and clays of volcanic origin, such as trass from the Rhine district and Bavaria, santorin earth from the island of Santorini (Thera) in the southern Aegean, pozzolana from Italy, kieselguhr (diatomaceous earth), and zeolitic clays. In Britain where, possible importation from the Continent apart, suitable materials of volcanic origin were not used, artificial ones were produced either by crushing bricks and the like or by burning clay and grinding it to a powder. The temperature to which clay had to be heated to produce the best results varied with the type of clay, but usually it was about 850°C.

The Romans used hydraulic mortars or plasters produced in this way very extensively in damp positions where it was important to prevent the penetration of moisture, for example for rendering basement and retaining walls.[115] They were also used for lining the inner surfaces of channels, drains, baths, tanks and aqueducts, for bonding masonry in waterlogged ground, and for torching roofing-tiles to prevent the penetration of driving rain. Many examples of wall-renderings or plaster containing brick- or pottery-dust have been found in Romano-British excavations, especially in bath-houses; and the well-known type of flooring known as 'opus signinum' is made in the same way.[116]

Aggregate

Considerable care was taken in the choice of aggregate used in preparing lime mortars for rendering walls and ceilings. For example, of 58 samples of wall-renderings from Roman buildings throughout Britain examined by one of the writers (N.D.), over 50 contained particles which passed through a screen with slots 0.48 in. (1.22 cm) wide, and of these the coarser ones occurred almost entirely in the mortar used for the backing-coats, often due to the re-use of material from earlier buildings. The finer grades were used for the finishing-coats. Similar observations have been made by M. Frizot on plasterwork in France.[117] Vitruvius, while recommending quarry-sand for the mortar used in structural work, prefers river-sand for plaster surfacing: 'fresh quarry-sands . . . are useless for plasterwork because they are too thick-textured, and the lime, when mixed with straw, cannot because of its violent action dry without cracks.' He also points out the disadvantages of sea-sand, which on account of its salt content causes efflorescence and breaks up the plaster.[118]

In Britain sand was no doubt obtained from the nearest convenient source.[119] There have been various scientific examinations aimed at determining the precise source in given samples,

[114]Vitruvius vii, 2; Pliny, *NH* xxxvi, 176.

[115]Cf. Vitruvius vii, 4, 1-3; Pliny, *loc. cit.*

[116]Pliny, *NH* xxxv, 165; cf. M.E. Blake, *Ancient Roman Construction in Italy from the Prehistoric Period to Augustus* (1947), p. 322 f.

[117]Frizot 1975, pp. 246, 270-1; cf. Frizot 1977, pp. 38-40 (plasterwork in relief). On measuring the grains of the aggregate generally see Frizot 1975, pp. 62-5, 69 f., 73-6.

[118]Vitruvius ii, 4.

[119]This is certainly true of Gallo-Roman mortars and plasters: Frizot 1975, *passim*, esp. pp. 300 f.

but this is often difficult. In some cases, however, it is possible to recognise a sand at a glance; for example, a plaster from Chester clearly incorporates the local red sand (see Catalogue, No. 7).

Another type of aggregate used in the finishing-coat or coats of the best-quality work in Roman Italy is marble-flour or other forms of crystalline calcite (or even, in at least one case, alabaster-dust).[120] Marble-flour has been identified in the surface-plaster of a painted wall in Cologne and in samples studied by Frizot in France,[121] and one may assume that it was also present in some good-quality work in Britain; but again scientific examination has not been carried out.

Another ingredient, added for a different purpose, was hay or straw. This was used, much as plasterers in subsequent periods have used hair, as a means of binding and strengthening the mixture, especially in the thick undercoats. Vitruvius refers to it in the passage quoted above, and plaster found in Britain regularly contains the imprints left by rotted bits of hay.

Mixing and application

The proportion of lime slurry to the aggregate was carefully controlled, and the resulting mortar or plaster was generally uniform and free from contamination. A mixing-trough *(mortarium)* was used. One such is depicted on Trajan's Column in Rome, and another in a wall-painting in the tomb of Trebius Justus on the Via Latina (first quarter of the fourth century); in each case a labourer is working the mixture with a long-handled tool (on Trajan's Column apparently an *ascia*, in the tomb of Justus a shovel or *rutrum*).[122] An actual trough was discovered by Major J.G.S. Brinson during excavations in 1947 on a Roman site in Chelmsford, Essex, and it throws light on the method of construction. A hole was first excavated in the ground then lined with boards at the ends and sides and on the bottom to avoid contamination of the mix. The side-boards were retained in position by means of vertical uprights. A nearby pit, lined with tile-chippings, was also apparently used for mixing mortar; it contained a residue of mortar which preserved the imprint of a pointed stake used to stir the mixture.[123] Simpler mixing-pits have been found at various sites.

In wall-plasters the proportion of lime and sand varies according to the layers, the inner containing a higher proportion of sand than the outer. In examples analysed by one of the writers (N.D.) the ratio in the undercoat or coats appeared to vary between 1 part by volume of lime to 2 to 3 parts of sand; in the finishing-coat the ratio varied between 1 part by volume of lime to 1 to 2 parts of sand.[124] Similar results have been obtained by Rebecca Wetzel with fragments of plaster from York.[125] She has established that the surface-plaster consisted of 1 part by volume of lime to 1.1 to 1.9 of filler (an average of 1:2.6 by weight). No specific proportions for wall-renderings are laid down by the ancient writers, but the proportions specified for mortar used in structural work (one part of lime to three of quarry-sand, or one of lime to two of river- or sea-sand)[126] compare closely with those found in the underlying render-coats.

The number of layers found in British work also varies but is normally two or three at the

[120]The evidence and bibliography are conveniently summarised in table-form in Barbet and Allag, opp. p. 1070. Cf. Vitruvius vii, 3, 6; Pliny, *NH* xxxvi, 176.

[121]Cologne: Noll *et al.* 1973, p. 79; 1975, p. 58 f. France: Frizot 1975, pp. 191 f., 195 f., 227-9, 290-2; cf. Frizot 1977, p. 42 (stucco relief).

[122]Trajan's column: C. Cichorius, *Die Reliefs der Trajanssäule* (1896-1900), pl. LXXI (255) and iii, pp. 126, 129. Tomb of Justus: *Nuovo Bullettino di Archaeologia Cristiana,* xvii (1911), pl. XI, fig. 5; *Cahiers archéologiques* xii (1962), p. 57, fig. 4. The figure on Trajan's column, since he has an *ascia* rather than a *rutrum*, may be testing lime during the slaking process rather than mixing mortar: on the two tools see below, n. 134.

[123]J.G.S. Brinson, in VCH *Essex* iii (1963), p. 67, pl. XI A.

[124]Davey 1945, p. 104 f. For the undercoats at least, similar proportions have been obtained in analyses of the French material: Frizot 1975, *passim* (cf. p. 303 f.: bonding mortars); Frizot 1977, pp. 41-3.

[125]We are deeply indebted to Miss Wetzel for giving us information on her results, obtained in the course of research for an M.A. dissertation at the University of Bradford.

[126]Vitruvius ii, 5, 1; Pliny, *NH* xxxvi, 175. Later writers suggest a higher proportion of lime (Faventinus 9; Palladius i, 10, 3).

most. Practically all the examples examined by N.D. were applied in two coats: a thick under-coat or levelling-coat, and a finer surface-layer. Sometimes the undercoat was applied in two layers; sometimes, in the coarser work, the finishing-coat was reduced to a mere skim of whitewash. All this is a far cry from the standards laid down by Vitruvius, who recommends an initial rendering-coat and six further layers (three of sand-mortar and three of marble-stucco); only for ceilings is a lesser standard permissible (one rendering-coat, one coat of sand-mortar, and a final surface of stucco containing chalk (?) or marble-dust).[127] One or two better-quality decorations of the first century B.C. in Rome and Pompeii actually attain, or nearly attain, the Vitruvian ideal;[128] but Augusti's observations at Pompeii show that the majority are very similar to work in Britain, with either a first layer 3 to 5 cm thick and a finishing-coat 0.75 mm to 1.3 cm thick, or two undercoats respectively 2 to 4 cm and 5 mm to 1 cm thick and a finishing-coat 2-5 mm thick.[129]

When renderings were applied to a masonry wall, the necessary adhesion was sometimes obtained by 'pecking' the surface with a pick or pointed hammer, thus giving a mechanical key.[130] If the rendering was applied to a clay or *pisé* wall, as for example in Building XXI, 2 at Verulamium, a key was obtained by impressing or incising the clay in 'herringbone' fashion; the pattern could be achieved with stamps or rollers or could be carefully cut with a trowel.[131] When bundles of reeds or straw were used in timber framework or for ceilings, a technique mentioned by Vitruvius and found not only in Britain (for example in the ceiling from Collingham: No. 12, A) but also in other provinces,[132] the bond would have been more than adequate.

Once the first render-coat was applied, there was no further need for keys. Vitruvius advises that each layer should be spread when its predecessor was not quite dry, presumably so that the 'suction' of the drier surface would make the new work adhere to it, thus helping to bond the layers into one homogeneous mass. This is why the first layer would normally be the thickest: to prevent the porosity of the wall-fabric, especially in masonry walls, from drying the mortar too rapidly. One imagines that only if a layer of mortar had become too dry would 'pecking' be resorted to. The moisture from the setting layers would of course initially be drawn inwards by capillary action; but eventually, when the plastering was completed, it would be drawn back to the surface, thus providing the ideal conditions for fresco painting.[133]

In addition to the mixing-tools already mentioned, the *ascia* and the *rutrum*,[134] ancient plasterers used two main implements very similar to those used by their modern counterparts: a mason's trowel *(trulla)* and a float *(liaculum)*.[135] Many examples of iron trowel-blades, rhomboidal or leaf-shaped with an offset tang for insertion in a wooden handle, have been found in the Roman world; British examples come, for instance, from Silchester and Caerleon.[136] The tool is also represented on funerary reliefs in France and Germany, along with other masons' tools.[137] Floats were depicted on a Pompeian painting, now lost, and on a Gallo-Roman relief which showed decorators at work, while an actual wooden example was

[127]Vitruvius vii, 3, 3-6 (he himself implies that this standard was not always attained: vii, 3, 8). Later writers relax the standard for wall-plaster to three layers of sand-mortar, two of marble-stucco: Pliny, *NH* xxxvi, 176; Faventinus 22; Palladius i, 15.

[128]The House of Livia and Farnesina house in Rome: see e.g. Cagiano de Azevedo 1958, p. 101. Decorations at Pompeii: Klinkert, pp. 127-9, figs. 1-3. Cf. Barbet and Allag, pp. 963-7, and table opp. p. 1070.

[129]Augusti, pp. 331-5.

[130]Cf. Barbet and Allag, pp. 960-2. Generally on methods of attachment *ibid.*, pp. 939-63; Frizot 1975, pp. 295 ff.

[131]Verulamium: *Antiq. Journ.* xxxvii (1957), p. 13, pl. II *b*; Frere, pp. 160 ff. Lullingstone: Meates 1955, p. 100 f. Colchester: P. Crummy in *Britannia* viii (1977), p. 80 f., fig. 10. Cf. Barbet and Allag, pp. 950-4.

[132]Barbet and Allag, pp. 939-46. Cf. *Liverpool AAA* xxiii (1936), p. 40, pl. XX, 2*a* (Chester).

[133]Generally on layers of plaster and their application Klinkert, pp. 120-9.

[134]K.D. White, *Agricultural Implements of the Roman World* (1967), pp. 28 ff., 67 f.

[135]*Trulla*: Palladius i, 15. *Liaculum*: Vitruvius ii, 4, 3; vii, 3, 7 ('liaculorum' needlessly corrected to 'baculorum' by various commentators).

[136]Silchester: two examples on display in Reading Museum; cf. *Archaeologia* lv (1896-97), p. 252. Caerleon: *Arch. Camb.* xcv (1940), p. 136, no. 42, pl. VIII.

[137]E.g. Espérandieu, iii (1910), p. 82, no. 1881; cf. p. 83 f., no. 1884; vi (1915), p. 408, no. 5226.

recovered from a well at the Saalburg Roman fort in Germany.[138] The only securely identified float from Britain, found in a cellar at Verulamium, is of iron and has a blade 53 cm long, so that it might have been rather heavy for use on a wall and may have been employed rather for compacting mortar floors.[139] Other, less important tools were of course the plumb-bobs, rules and squares with which the plasterer ensured that his surfaces were true, as prescribed by Vitruvius. One relief in Trier shows an almost complete set of implements required in plastering: a trowel, a plumb-level, an *ascia*, and a broad brush such as would have been used to apply coats of whitewash.[140]

One last aspect of the application of plaster is re-decoration. Here, like mosaicists, wall-plasterers and painters did not normally bother to remove the previous decoration but merely applied another surface over it, whether in the form of a skim of whitewash, or a new layer of plaster. In the second case the old decoration was normally 'pecked' to provide a key; this procedure was rather more successful than the application of whitewash, which often flaked away. Re-decorations could be frequent, as already mentioned (p. 29). An interesting example is provided by the *mansio* at Catterick (No. 5), where a normal three-layer plaster decoration was covered by two successive surfaces, each of which received new paintings. The complete sequence can be summarised:

Phase I.   (a)   Levelling-coat composed of a mixture of coarse sand and lime with the addition of chaff.

              (b)   A rendering of finer mortar about 8 mm thick.

              (c)   A coat of lime-plaster about 2 mm thick, heavily worked and smoothed to a fine surface, on which the decoration was applied.

Phase II.   A lime slurry coat with a brush finish.

Phase III.   A coat of plaster about 2 cm thick, applied after the previous surface had been 'pecked'; the decoration was applied while the coat was still moist.

Application of the paintings

There has been much controversy over the years whether Roman wall-painters worked in the fresco technique, or in tempera, or in a combination of the two.[141] A fresco technique, in which pigments are applied while the plaster is still damp, so that lime-water coming to the surface forms a translucent layer of calcium carbonate over the colours and fixes them, is clearly what Vitruvius describes: 'when the colours are carefully laid upon the wet plaster, they do not fail but are permanently durable, because the lime has its moisture removed in the kilns and becoming loose-textured and feeble is compelled by its dryness to seize upon whatever happens to present itself . . .'[142] With only one pigment does he tell us that it is necessary to use a tempera technique, i.e. to apply it with an organic binding-medium: black, obtained by burning resin, pine-chips or wine-dregs, must be mixed with size (*glutinum*) before being applied to walls.[143]

[138]Pompeian painting: *Bullettino dell' Instituto di Corrispondenza Archeologica,* 1879, p. 134, no. 8; *Annali dell' Instituto di Corrispondenza Archeologica,* 1881, p. 107 f., pl. H. Sens relief: Espérandieu, p. 10 f., no. 2767; A.M. Uffler, 'Fresquistes gallo-romains, le bas-relief du Musée de Sens', *Revue archéologique de l'Est et du Centre-Est,* xxii (1971), pp. 393–401. Saalburg float: L. Jacobi, *Das Römerkastell Saalburg* (1897), pp. 163, 218 (fig. 32, nos. 18, 18a), 227.

[139]Frere, p. 168, no. 18, fig. 62, pl. L *b.*

[140]F. Hettner, *Die römischen Steindenkmäler des Provinzialmuseums zu Trier* (1893), p. 91 f., no. 194 (= Espérandieu, vi (1915), p. 408, no. 5226).

[141]The bibliography is voluminous. Among the recent contributions see especially Augusti; Klinkert; Cagiano de Azevedo 1958; idem, 'Tecniche della pittura parietale antica', *Boll. ICR,* xxxiii (1958), pp. 9–16; Mora. Schiavi's theory that Roman wall-painters used an encaustic technique (E. Schiavi, *Il sale della terra* (1961), pp. 150–3) is expressly excluded by the Roman writers: see esp. Pliny, *NH* xxxv, 49.

[142]Vitruvius vii, 3, 7.

[143]Vitruvius vii, 10, 2–4. We also hear that purple was mixed with honey (Vitruvius vii, 13, 3) or egg (Pliny, *NH* xxxv, 45), and that another purple could be obtained from mixing whortleberries with milk (Vitruvius vii, 14, 2); but the role of these additives was to prepare or preserve pigments or to produce a special glowing effect, not to bind them to plaster.

The researches of the Istituto Centrale del Restauro in Rome have confirmed that fresco was used at least for the main elements in Roman wall-paintings. Examination of the murals in one of the rooms of the so-called House of Livia on the Palatine has revealed the 'giornate di lavoro', the areas of fresh plaster which were laid for each session of painting; and elsewhere it is possible to detect the seams, generally corresponding to divisions in the decorative scheme, which mark the transition from one day's plaster to the next.[144] In a room in the House of the Lararium at Pompeii the upper zone of a wall has been plastered and painted while the lower two thirds have never received the final coat of plaster; the decorator was apparently trimming the lower edge of the completed zone when he was rudely interrupted by the first outburst from Vesuvius.[145] It seems too that the central panel-pictures within decorative schemes in Roman Italy were often painted on fresh plaster inserted into the existing surface after the rest of the work was finished; sometimes they were painted in the workshop and transported to the site in wooden frames.[146]

All this does not exclude the possibility that colours were sometimes applied in tempera. This technique is quite likely for those ornaments which were applied over a coloured background, and which have a matt finish or are even in slight relief, while the background has the typical Pompeian sheen (although here there are also other possibilities: notably the use of 'fresco secco', in which pigments arc applied to a dry ground but are first mixed with lime-water so as to reproduce the fixing reaction of true fresco). Scientific analysis has yielded conflicting results. While P. Mora has found no trace of organic media,[147] Selim Augusti believes that Pompeian paintings were regularly carried out in tempera, the pigments being mixed with a saponified solution of lime, to which hot wax was added. He also claims that a similar mixture, containing chalk in suspension, was applied to the plaster as a priming for the paint.[148] At Cologne chromatographic analyses of paintings from the Roman buildings beneath the cathedral have revealed a weak presence of amino-acid, which would be explained if the pigments had been mixed with animal-size.[149] This tallies with a passage of Pliny, who writes that 'the finest size is made from the ears and genitals of bulls' and that the most reliable variety 'comes from Rhodes and is used by painters and physicians.'[150]

In Britain it is often clear at a glance that paintings have been executed in fresco, especially where the surface was prepared with a rough brush-coat of lime slurry, as at Kingscote (No. 21), and the painted motifs have smoothed out the serrations left by the brush (PL. III). At Leicester a recently excavated decoration (No. 24, B) shows the seams between 'giornate di lavoro' (areas of fresh plaster), carefully placed so as to coincide with divisions in the painted scheme. Scientific examination has in some cases confirmed the use of a fresco technique, for example at Downton (Wilts.), where no medium could be detected. One sample from Verulamium, analysed in the National Gallery Laboratory in London, gave a positive test for protein, but the pigment in question was bone-black, so the trace of protein may have been due to incompletely combusted animal-matter. Two samples from Stanton Low (Bucks.), however, both of a thick purple-red paint, contained a small amount of extractable, glue-like protein, and the pigment was probably here applied in the tempera technique.[151] We may suspect that fresco

---

[144]Cagiano de Azevedo 1949, p. 148f., figs 5, 9 (House of Livia 'tablinum'); *Boll. ICR*, vii–viii (1951), p. 34 (Farnesina paintings); *Boll. ICR*, xxv–xxvi (1956), p. 36 (House of Livia, upstairs bedroom); *Boll. ICR*, 1967, p. 36, fig. 28 (Aula Isiaca). Cf. Mora, p. 68.

[145]Spinazzola, fig. 515.

[146]Barbet and Allag, pp. 980–3.

[147]Mora, p. 63.

[148]Augusti; cf. *idem*, 'Restauro e conservazione della pittura pompeiana', in *Atti del Settimo Congresso Internazionale di Archeologia Classica* (1961), i, pp. 159–62. Cagiano de Azevedo too accepts that colours were mixed with a soapy substance: 1958, p. 102.

[149]Noll *et al.*, 1973, p. 86; 1975, p. 56 f.

[150]Pliny, *NH* xxviii, 236.

[151]Downton, Verulamium, Stanton Low: J. Plesters, 'Examination of Roman Painted wall-plaster', *WAM* lviii (1961–63), pp. 337–41.

was the normal technique, but that pigments were sometimes mixed with an organic medium, particularly if the surface was dry or if refined detail was being applied over a background colour.

III Detail of painting at Kingscote, showing evidence of fresco technique.
Photo: N. Davey

Another controversy surrounds the sheen which characterises the better-quality murals of Pompeii, and of Britain too (Leicester, No. 22). Augusti attributes it to the wax in his medium,[152] but it seems likely that wax would produce a dull gloss, whereas the Pompeian examples have a brilliant lustre. Mora believes that *boli*, or argillaceous earths like kaolin, were added to the pigments so as to make them susceptible of receiving a polish; but this theory rests partly on a mistranslation of Vitruvius, and in Cologne at least no kaolin could be detected in analyses.[153] Klinkert suggests that a mixture of size-water and marble-dust was rubbed over the paintings.[154] What is clear is that the surface was burnished with floats or similar implements after the ground-colours had been applied: the relevant sentence of Vitruvius is best translated, 'But when the plaster has been rendered solid by working over with floats and smoothed till it has the firm whiteness of marble the walls will have a brilliant lustre when the colours are laid on and polished *(cum politionibus)*.'[155] Microscopical examination of the paintings from the House of Livia revealed that the alabaster grains in the surface-plaster were rounded by friction, and Roman paintings frequently show tiny parallel scratches identical to those left on fresh plaster by the passage of a hard stone or metal object.[156] An object found at Silchester actually seems to have been used for the burnishing: it is described as a 'marble rubber *c*. 15 × 10 cm with an iron strap-handle at the back and traces of red, yellow, blue and green paint upon the

[152] Augusti, pp. 330 f., 354.
[153] Mora, *passim* (esp. p. 72); but *politiones*, as a verbal noun, can mean 'polishings' or possibly the 'surfaces polished' (i.e. the surface-plaster) but not 'substances used to achieve a polish'. Cologne: Noll *et al.* 1973, p. 87; 1975, p. 59.
[154] Klinkert, pp. 141–4.
[155] Or possibly 'with the surface-layers' (see above n. 153): Vitruvius vii, 3, 7.
[156] Cagiano de Azevedo 1949, p. 148. Cf. Mora, p. 63.

surface.'[157] It seems that a stucco containing powdered marble or other varieties of calcite will take a polish from simple burnishing. Alternatively some marble-dust could have been added to the pigments. Analysts at Cologne found that the red paint in their samples was permeated with calcite crystals, which they concluded had been deliberately mixed with the pigment to produce a glinting effect; working of the plaster by the craftsman would force the tiny mirror-like faces of the crystal-fragments to align themselves parallel to the surface and thus reflect the light.[158]

FIG. 4   Drawing of Leicester ceiling (catalogue No. 23), showing guide-lines (dotted). Scale, 1:12.
(Drawing by N. Davey)

Before actually painting a decorative scheme, the craftsman would mark it out carefully on the surface. This was done sometimes by 'line-slapping', that is holding a cord against the damp plaster, then drawing it back and letting it rebound so as to leave an imprint (the only British examples known to the writers are at Boxmoor (No. 3) and from a late third-century bath-house at Lancaster).[159] But normally guide-lines would be scored with a pointed instrument. There are many examples of such scored lines in Britain, especially in repeating patterns where it was important to achieve a regular spacing and constant size of the elements. In the painted ceiling from the market-hall at Leicester, for instance (No. 23), the pattern was constructed by first drawing a grid of intersecting lines parallel to the axes of the surface, then superimposing a second grid on the diagonals of the first, and finally inscribing compass-drawn circles round the points of intersection (cf. FIG. 4). These lines then formed the basis for the decoration of roundels and foliate forms applied by the painter. Other uses for guide-lines were to mark the upper edge of the dado (Beadlam, Yorks.: unpublished),[160] to provide a reference-point for motifs within the dado (Leicester, No. 22, A), to mark the spine of a garland (Leicester,

[157] Boon 1974, p. 211 and n.3. A similar object has now been found at Caerleon.

[158] Noll *et al.* 1973, p. 80 f.; 1975, p. 51 f.

[159] R.J. Ling in G.D.B. Jones and D.C.A. Shotter (eds.), *Roman Lancaster*, forthcoming. The technique occurs in Italy (Barbet and Allag, pp. 985, 993, 1014), North Africa (Aurigemma, p. 42) and Gaul (*Gallia*, xxvi (1968), p. 172; Barbet 1974 a, pp. 34, 215 f., fig. 188; Barbet and Allag, pp. 1052-4, fig. 59).

[160] Information from D.S. Neal; excavations by A.L. Pacitto and I.M. Stead (cf. *YAJ* xliii, 1971, pp. 178-86).

No. 24, A) or the stem of a candelabrum (Winchester, No. 47), and to indicate the curvature of the volutes in a continuous scroll (Verulamium, No. 44, A, ii). There is no evidence of preliminary sketches for figures, such as exist in paintings in Roman Italy;[161] the only guide-lines within a representational scene are the compass-drawn grooves for the nimbi of the female personages at Kingscote (No. 21). Nor is there any evidence for designs in red ochre (the *sinopia* of Renaissance frescoes), although these occur frequently at Pompeii.[162]

It is probable that schemes were measured out in multiples or simple denominators of the Roman foot; but it is hardly ever possible to establish precise units of measurement in a British decoration, since the material is almost invariably fragmentary, and one can never be sure which standard was being used (the Roman foot varies from 28.2 to 33.2 cm). One exception is the dado of an early second-century decoration at Cirencester (No. 9), where there is a battlement-meander whose sides are carefully and consistently set out 37.5 cm long: surely 1¼ feet. It would be interesting to see whether measurements based on a foot of 30 cm can be identified in building-plots, mosaic pavements or other measurable elements at Cirencester.[163]

For both schemes and figure-motifs the painter presumably used pattern-books. There is no direct evidence for these in Britain, but it is difficult to explain the recurrence of similar motifs in different parts of the province, or the incidence of ideas which are also found on the Continent, in any other terms. In France the Gallo-Roman relief already mentioned (p. 55) seems to show the master-artist or patron consulting a pattern-book while the decorators are actually at work. In addition to patterns we can postulate trial-pieces, like the Cupid painted on a sherd of samian found in Cologne;[164] but again the evidence is lacking in Britain.

The main tool used by wall-painters was, of course, a brush *(penicillus)*. Pliny reveals that plasterers' brushes were made of pigs' bristles, and the same probably applied to most paint-brushes, although finer hair may have been used for finer work (in late medieval times, in addition to pigs' bristles, there are records of brushes made of squirrels' tails and badgers' hair).[165] No doubt the brushes came in different sizes; a broad one would be used for large, coloured surfaces, and narrower ones for more detailed work: coloured stripes of different thickness may often betray the width of the brush with which they were painted. No brushes complete with bristles have survived, for obvious reasons; but brush-handles of bone have been recognised, for instance, in the effects of a Roman tomb at St. Médard-des-Prés in western France. The same tomb, while containing implements which were obviously used by a painter of wooden panels rather than of walls, gives a glimpse of the remaining apparatus which a wall-painter would need: bottles containing pigments, palettes, a mortar and pestle for grinding the colours, etc.[166] Another occasional implement would be a stamp, no doubt of wood, for reproducing mechanical detail, such as the plant-motifs and V-shaped elements in the paintings from Collingham (No. 12: cf. PL. IV).

In Britain there have been a few discoveries of containers with pigments and improvised palettes, but nothing more spectacular. At Witcombe parts of two pots had pink and yellow paint adhering to them; at Silchester there was a pot of red ochre, and a Purbeck marble *mortarium* with traces of the same pigment; at Lullingstone there was a pink *mortarium* containing 'a mass of blue, gritty material . . . which on analysis proved to be paint'; and at Cow Roast near Northchurch (Herts.) finds from a well-shaft included 'a colour-coated beaker con-

[161]Barbet and Allag, pp. 1025–44.

[162]*Ibid., passim* (esp. pp. 985 f., 1016–22, 1051 f.).

[163]For modules in Roman painting cf. Barbet 1973, p. 76; and, for modules in building-plots in Britain, C.V. Walthew, 'Property boundaries and building plots', *Britannia* ix (1978), pp. 335–50. Generally on Roman feet A. Grenier, *Manuel d'archéologie gallo-romaine* iii, 1 (1958), pp. 35–40.

[164]A. Linfert, 'Römische Vasenmalerei?', *Kölner Jarhbuch für Vor- und Frühgeschichte* xiv (1974), p. 99 f., pl. 7 (3).

[165]Pliny, *NH* xxviii, 235. For medieval times L.F. Salzman, *Building in England down to 1540* (1952), p. 172; cf. Cennino Cennini, *Il libro dell' arte*, 64, 65, 67.

[166]B. Fillon, *Description de la villa et du tombeau d'une femme artiste gallo-romaine, découvertes à Saint-Médard-des-Prés (Vendée)* (1849), pp. 26–61; Borda, p. 383 f. Another recently excavated tomb with paint-pots: H.G. Bachmann and W. Czysz, 'Das Grab eines römischen Malers aus Nida-Heddernheim', *Germania* lv (1977), pp. 85–107.

taining a mixture of haematite and chalk, perhaps intended as a pigment for wall painting'.[167] Finds from Water Newton include a series of pot-bases containing deposits of various pigments, amongst them white, red, pale red, and yellow-green (unpublished). A potsherd from Woodeaton (Oxon) contained Egyptian blue and has been identified as a palette, although it too could equally well have formed part of a container.[168] Certainly a palette, however, was the oyster-shell containing red paint found with the paint-pots at Witcombe.[169] Similar discoveries have been made in medieval contexts, for example at Glastonbury Abbey and at Hardham church in Sussex (c. 1100).[170] A full list of paint-containers and palettes from Roman sites in Britain is included in Table I (p. 221).

IV   Fragments of plaster from Collingham, showing use of stamped motifs (with modern copies). Scale, 3:8. *Photo: N. Davey.*

Pigments

The pigments used in the ancient world are described by Vitruvius and Pliny and have been discussed at length by Augusti in his study of pigments from Pompeii.[171] We shall confine ourselves to listing those which have been identified by analysis in Britain. The evidence is provided by samples from three sites in York examined by Rebecca Wetzel (to whom we are deeply indebted for information), samples from Downton (Wilts.), Stanton Low (Bucks.) and

---

[167]Witcombe: *TBGAS* lxxiii (1954), p. 17. Silchester: Boon 1974, p. 211. Lullingstone: Meates 1955, p. 154. Cow Roast: *Britannia* vi (1975), p. 257.

[168]E.M. Jope and G. Huse, in *Nature* cxlvi (1940), p. 26.

[169]See above, n. 167.

[170]We are grateful to Mr. W.D. Park for information on this material. He points out, however, that the shells may have been used by illuminators rather than wall-painters: cf. Theophilus, *De Diversis Artibus*, i, 28, 33; iii, 54.

[171]S. Augusti, *I colori pompeiani* (1967): he does not, however, distinguish between pigments used by wall-painters and those used by other craftsmen. Cf. Vitruvius vii, 7-14; Pliny, *NH* xxxv, 30-50.

Verulamium examined by Joyce Plesters at the National Gallery Laboratory, and samples from Witcombe analysed at the British Museum. Colouring-matters have also been identified at Hucclecote (Glos.). Comparative data will be cited from Cologne.[172] See also Tables I and II, compiled by L. Biek (pp. 220-222).

WHITE. Calcium carbonate, probably obtained chiefly from chalk. At Cologne a white pigment is said to consist of dolomite, aragonite and calcite, and so could have been derived from a mixture of chalk and dolomitic limestone.

BLACK. Carbon: from soot or charcoal (splinter-like fragments were visible in the Downton material, but there were no traces of organic matter at Cologne). Despite Vitruvius, no binding-medium could be detected at Downton. At York the necessary tests were not carried out, and at Cologne testing was prevented by practical difficulties.

BLUE. Blue frit, or Egyptian blue, an artificially produced glassy pigment containing copper calcium silicate ($CuO.CaO.4SiO_2$). The pigment is coarse-grained (excessive grinding would weaken or destroy the colour) and is sometimes mixed with or applied over white, perhaps to ensure its adherence. Blue frit, which is often easily recognised by eye, is used not infrequently in Britain (in addition to Downton and York, the writers have observed it on paintings from Leicester, No. 24, B, and Wigginton, No. 46, B; cf. examples at Northchurch and Sparsholt).[173] Balls of the crude material, about ½ in. (1.27 cm) in diameter, have been found in many places, such as Silchester and Woodeaton (cf. Table I).[174]

YELLOW. Hydrated ferric oxide, found in nature in crystalline form (goethite) and in earthy form (yellow ochre). Yellow plaster exposed to heat will turn red through dehydration (anhydrous ferric oxide: see below), as has frequently happened at Pompeii.

GREEN. Green earth *(terre verte)*, a naturally-occurring pigment containing potassium, aluminium, iron and magnesium hydrosilicates in the form of the minerals glauconite or celadonite. In medieval times it was obtained in Cornwall.

RED. (1) Anhydrous ferric oxide, found in nature in crystalline form (haematite) and also in earthy form (red ochre).

(2) Cinnabar or vermilion (mercuric sulphide). An expensive and rarely-used pigment, so far identified in Britain only in York, where it was applied over a thin layer of yellow. Both Vitruvius and Pliny warn that exposure to excessive light will blacken the colour, and they recommend a coating of hot wax and oil on walls painted with vermilion; but wipings taken from the fragments at York yielded no trace of wax.

Other colours could, of course, have been achieved by mixing these pigments. Blue and yellow produced green; red and blue purple; red, yellow and black brown; and so forth.

One last colouring-agent may be mentioned: the gold leaf found on a fragment of wall-plaster at Colchester.[175] Unfortunately this fragment has apparently not been submitted to scientific scrutiny. The use of gold leaf on wall-paintings is extremely rare, but is attested in the paintings of the Aula Isiaca in Rome (*c.* 25-20 B.C.) and in those of the Golden House of Nero (again identified purely with the naked eye).[176]

[172]York: see n. 125. Downton, Stanton Low, Verulamium: see n. 151. Witcombe: *TBGAS* lxxiii (1954), p. 60. Hucclecote: *TBGAS* lv (1933), p. 348. Cologne: Noll *et al.* 1973, pp. 79-86; 1975, pp. 50-6.

[173]Northchurch: Neal 1976, p. 30. Sparsholt: information from D.E. Johnston.

[174]Jope and Huse, *loc. cit.* (note 168). At Verulamium two balls 3 cm in diameter were found: Frere, p. 55.

[175]M.R. Hull, *Roman Colchester* (1958), p. 31.

[176]Aula Isiaca: *Boll. ICR* 1967, pp. 38, 55, figs. 51, 52. Golden House: Hinks, p. 31 f. (no. 55 *b, c*). Cf. Barbet 1978, p. 109.

7. TECHNIQUES OF RECOVERY AND RESTORATION

The work of conservation of Romano-British painted plaster to be described has been carried out under the auspices of the Department of the Environment, first at the Building Research Station at Watford and subsequently at the Department's centre for the conservation of Roman plaster at Lacock and then at Potterne, near Devizes in Wiltshire.

Although for very many years hundreds of fragments of painted plaster have been recovered from Roman buildings excavated in Britain, and are preserved in museums, only recently have serious attempts been made during excavation to collect the pieces and endeavour to reassemble them to reveal the design.[177] Buildings situated north of the Alps, or north of the frostline, as in Britain and other parts of Northern Europe, suffered from frost damage, and it is not surprising that they soon decayed when occupation ceased. Some buildings were also deliberately dismantled for their valuable materials, particularly roofing-tiles. Rain then penetrated the dilapidated buildings and during successive winters frost caused any plaster remaining on the walls and ceilings to fall and break into a multitude of fragments. Occasionally portions of the painted plaster on the lower parts of walls remained in position to a height of several feet, and were protected by an accumulation of debris piled against them. This relatively small amount of plaster was thus preserved. As far back as the late eighteenth century some plaster so preserved was excavated at the Roman villa at Comb End, Gloucestershire, on a wall about 20 feet long. An illustration of the plaster was given by Lysons (see Appendix, No. 7). This seems to be the earliest example recorded. The design shows the dado and part of the panels above it, displaying the feet and pieces of the draperies of several human figures. In more recent times excavations have revealed a few instances of decorated walls of the Roman period standing to a height of about 5 feet or so above floor-level. These finds have usually been made in basement rooms and cellars which must have been filled quite quickly with earth and debris, sometimes deliberately, or in the lower rooms of buildings on downward slopes which could have been more readily buried than the upper rooms. Such instances were revealed during excavations at Lullingstone in 1949 (the Deep Room: see Catalogue, No. 26) and at Dover in 1971 (here sealed by the rampart of the Saxon Shore fort: No. 14). At both these sites many fragments of plaster were also recovered from the infilling, those at Lullingstone including material from an upper storey.

Fragments of plaster are usually found distributed in a variety of ways on the floors of an excavated building. First, the fragments may lie scattered widely apart, having fallen from the ceiling or walls during the general decay of the building, or as a result of its deliberate demolition. Plaster from four walls, and maybe a ceiling, may thus be found intermixed. Secondly, when deserted buildings were exposed to climatic changes, for example humid conditions followed by frost, the bond of the plaster to the wall or ceiling was broken, and the plaster fell in sheets, some lying face down on the floor, or, as is more usual, lying in concertina-fashion at the foot of the wall, in layers alternately face up and face down. Thirdly, and more rarely, a decorated partition-wall may have fallen flat on to a floor, in which case the plaster, although badly fractured, lies almost in its entirety with the fragments correctly disposed in relation to each other, in spite of the fact that they may have spread apart somewhat at the moment of impact.

It is worth stressing the enormous difficulties posed by fragmentary material. When faced with many hundreds of fragments from a site, it is a highly tedious undertaking to restore the pattern. When the designs are essentially geometric or architectural, the identification and the reconstruction is generally fairly straightforward. The few figured scenes, on the other hand, are relatively more difficult to interpret and reconstruct; and when as so often happens over half the material may be missing, the correct juxtaposing of the various areas that have been put together may clearly be in doubt, as for example at Kingscote (No. 21) and York (No. 52).

---

[177]Of the conservators working abroad special reference should be made to A. Barbet. Cf. A. Barbet, 'La restauration des peintures murales d'époque romaine', *Gallia* xxvii (1969), pp. 71-92; Barbet 1973.

In such cases attempts at interpretation must be made with caution, for the decorations can be unpredictable. Some seem almost to have been improvised, while others are quite serious attempts to reproduce, perhaps from memory, some mythological, allegorical or historical subject. It would be unwise to be too pedantic in trying to interpret what in fact the painter had in mind and was trying to represent.

Recovery of fallen plaster

Clearly the task of reconstruction is facilitated greatly if the plaster fragments can be lifted carefully and methodically in small areas as was done at Verulamium and Leicester, the position of each area being recorded on a plan of the room. Where fragments lie scattered and inter-mixed, they have to be picked up piece by piece and placed in boxes or trays. Here again it is helpful if the area from which each tray of pieces was collected is noted. When the plaster lies in layers at the foot of the wall, it may be possible to lift it in layers, thereby keeping the pieces in their correct relative position. This procedure can also be followed where, as in the third case mentioned above, the plaster lies spread uniformly across the floor. It is unwise to treat the plaster fragments in the field with polyvinyl acetate or other impregnating materials as this may seal in the dirt and render it difficult to remove.

The writer's attention was first drawn to the problems of lifting fallen plaster when in 1955 and 1956 excavation carried out by Professor Sheppard Frere at Verulamium uncovered much material (see above, pp. 27 f.). Simple procedures had to be adopted for lifting it, and for subsequently reconstructing it. These have already been described in *Britannia* iii (1972);[178] but for completeness the methods devised are summarized here.

To find Roman wall-plaster still in position adhering to a wall for any appreciable height above floor-level is a rare occurrence. Its preservation *in situ* is difficult. The paintings when exposed are liable to deteriorate from moisture rising up the interior of the wall from the foundation, or from soil which may be banked up at the rear of the wall, as might be the case with basement walls, or walls that have been buried. If therefore the wall-paintings are to be preserved *in situ* all practical measures must be taken to reduce the access of moisture. Moisture evaporating from the painted surface may cause efflorescence and discoloration, and any salts that may be contained in the water may crystallize out near the surface and cause spalling. Attempts to preserve the wall-paintings by applying preservatives which, if used to excess, may form an impervious skin should be avoided. Also, attempts to reduce the moisture, for example, by inserting porous tubes embedded in the body of the wall, or by the installation of electrical devices to draw the moisture away are usually not very effective.

The best solution, therefore, has been to strip the decorated plaster from the wall and remount it for display in more suitable and drier surroundings.

The work of reconstruction of painted plaster has been rendered difficult by the dispersal of fragments from an excavation. In one instance, plaster had been dispersed to four places, and the task of bringing the pieces together for treatment was tedious and took many months. Occasionally well-intentioned investigators have removed important pieces of decorated plaster from an excavation-site for study and have failed to return the material to the main bulk. On another occasion important plaster was stolen when put on display to visitors at an excavation-site. Care must therefore be taken to ensure that *all* the plaster fragments are kept together and carefully stored until required for examination and reassembly.

As an example of the often difficult problems encountered during the recovery of fallen plaster the experience at Southwell is chosen. Part of a villa of considerable size was excavated by C.M. Daniels to the east of Southwell Minster in 1959.[179] The site from which the decorated plaster was recovered was small and congested. Medieval robbing had removed about one third of the Roman bath, and workmen had removed a considerable amount of the plaster before

---

[178]Davey 1972.
[179]C.M. Daniels, 'Excavations on the site of the Roman villa at Southwell, 1959', *Trans. Thoroton Soc.* lxx (1966), pp. 13-54.

they were stopped. The bulk of the decorated plaster lay directly on the floor of the bath, but many fragments also occurred in the demolition-rubble covering the area. Later drains and ducts crossing the site added to the difficulty of excavation. After an initial rushed 'dig', the site was left, partially excavated, for many months before the building-contractor moved in. Some flooding occurred, but the waterlogged rubble was carefully removed to reveal the fallen plaster lying on the floor. This was then lifted in numbered areas and conveyed to the studio at Lacock.

At some date after the foundation of the villa, a cold bath had been added to its eastern wing. This was almost completely demolished later on, and replaced by a new bath 25 by 25 feet in size. It was from this later bath that the fragments of elaborately-decorated plaster were recovered. Some time in the early third century this second bath was demolished and a considerable amount of its wall-plaster was sealed beneath a new floor, laid over the remains of the bath. When we consider that the painted plaster decorated a structure which was itself a rebuilding of an addition to the original east wing of the building, and that the earliest pottery from this area of the excavation was of the second half of the second century, it is unlikely that the paintings date much before, if at all, the last quarter of the century. They appear to have been demolished in the early third century. Two large and four small areas of plaster have been restored (No. 34). Plate LXIX shows the large piece with a Cupid in course of reconstruction, and Plate V shows some examples of marine life.

V   Southwell, plaster with marine subjects in course of conservation.
Photo: Department of the Environment: Crown Copyright reserved.

The excavations carried out at Verulamium by Professor Frere yielded much decorated plaster which it was possible to reconstruct. The first plaster recovered in 1955 was found lying with the decorated face downwards in Building XXII, 1 (No. 42). It had come from a timber-framed clay wall. Some simple technique had to be devised for lifting it. The method used is illustrated in *Britannia* iii (1972), pl XVI. It was lifted in convenient areas. Having cleared one of these areas of loose earth, the back of the wall-plaster was covered evenly with a layer of plaster of Paris (dental grade). This was reinforced with strips of plasterer's scrim. Care was taken to work the plaster of Paris and the scrim so as to embrace the edges of the wall-plaster, thus gripping it and enabling the area to be lifted easily. This particular wall-plaster was subsequently restored at Lacock and is now in the Verulamium Museum.

In 1956 three more areas of fallen plaster, of considerable extent, were found in a late second-century building (XXI, 2: Catalogue, No. 41, A, B, D). Two of the murals were found in a corridor. They had fallen face downwards, one on top of the other. The first one to fall, evidently from a ceiling, had a purple-red ground with yellow barley-stalks enclosing panels with doves and feline heads (No. 41, D). This plaster was subsequently restored and is exhibited in Verulamium Museum.

The plaster lying above it had a red ground and bore very slender candelabra, from which floral swags in yellow or blue depended (No. 41, B). It had fallen with a clay *pisé* wall, the surface of which had been impressed in herringbone fashion, while the *pisé* was still soft, to provide a key for the plaster undercoat (see above, p. 55). The undercoat with the damp clay behind it must have required a considerable time to dry out sufficiently before the application of the second coat. During this period its surface had been splashed with white and purple colour-wash, probably quite accidentally while the purple ceiling above was being painted. After restoration this plaster was initially exhibited at the British Museum, but has now been transferred to Verulamium.

VI   Verulamium, plaster fragments of dado (Catalogue No. 43) found in remains of an Antonine house
beneath a later house in Insula XXVIII, numbered in readiness for lifting.
Photo: M. B. Cookson

The third area of plaster belonged to a frieze which had fallen from the north-west wall of the courtyard; presumably when it was in position on the wall it had been protected by a verandah. The ground is bright yellow and has an 'inhabited scroll' painted upon it in green and containing panthers' heads and pheasants (No. 41, A). The scale of the scroll, the long area of plaster recovered, and its fine state of preservation made this discovery unique in Britain. The plaster is now displayed in the British Museum, along with a restoration of the panel-decoration below it.

Some more plaster fragments were recovered by Frere in the remains of a burnt Antonine house beneath Room 6 of a large house in insula XXVIII (No. 43). They probably formed part of a dado. Plate VI shows the fragments as uncovered, and Plate XCI as reconstructed.

Reassembly of fallen plaster

Apart from the obvious reason for attempting to reassemble the many hundreds of plaster fragments recovered from an excavation, which is to discover the *décor* of the rooms from which it came, it has also been possible to determine the height of rooms, the position of doorways and windows and other architectural details (e.g. at Boxmoor: Nos. 2, 3). It may take some months of often tedious and laborious sorting of the many fragments to achieve this, but the end-result justifies the effort. The sort of decorative schemes which have emerged are discussed above, pp. 31 ff.

The earliest work of reassembly was carried out on plaster recovered at Verulamium in 1956 at the Building Research Station, Watford, where in the temperature- and humidity-controlled rooms there was no difficulty in conditioning the plaster fragments and impregnating them using organic solvents. The procedure adopted was briefly described in 1960.[180] The decorated surface of the areas of wall-plaster, raised in the manner already described, was washed carefully with water. When dry, the surface was treated with five per cent polyvinyl acetate in toluene to fix any fugitive pigment. Japanese tissue was then pasted over the surface with Polycell — a cellulose adhesive — as shown in Plate VII to retain the fragments in their correct position in

VII Verulamium, paper tissue being applied to decorated fragments to hold them correctly in position. *Photo: Building Research Station, Watford: Crown Copyright reserved*

relation to each other. The plaster was then reversed — decorated surface downward — on to plate glass as shown in Plate VIII. The mortar which had formed the undercoat was removed by means of spatulas, leaving only the rendering coat. Any dirt that had accumulated in the joints between the fragments was removed, and the fragments were then closed up. A mirror below the plate glass helped in this process. Impregnation of the mortar was carried out slowly, over a

[180]N. Davey, 'Notes on remounting decorated wall-plaster from Verulamium', *Archaeological Newsletter* vi, 12 (1960), pp. 282-3.

VIII   Verulamium, wall-plaster reversed on to plate glass and the back surface prepared for impregnation.
Photo: Building Research Station, Watford: Crown Copyright reserved

IX   Verulamium, reinforcing frame of expanded aluminium in position.
Photo: Building Research Station, Watford: Crown Copyright reserved

period of three or four days, care being taken to prevent as far as possible the penetration of the solution to the decorated surface. Gaps between the mortar fragments were filled with dry sand to prevent the seepage of the solution to the glass plate. A mixture of clean washed sand and the impregnating solution was then applied, and reinforced with expanded aluminium mesh, mounted on aluminium frames as shown in Plate IX. When the sand mix had hardened, the mortar slabs were reversed and the Japanese tissue removed by applying moisture. The dry sand in the gaps between the plaster fragments was then removed, and the gaps filled with a mixture of fine sand and the same impregnating material. The slabs were then mounted on a rigid framework of duralumin by angle cleats (PL. X), in such a manner that the complete assemblage could be dismantled for transportation and re-erection in various places for display.

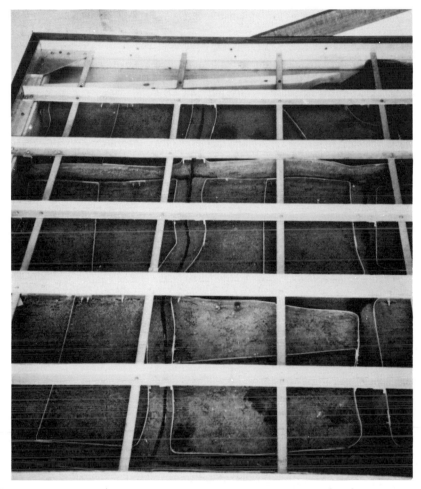

X   Verulamium, showing the method used for mounting the restored sections of plaster to a duralumin framework.
Photo: Department of the Environment: Crown Copyright reserved

Before the restored plaster was exhibited at the British Museum and Verulamium Museum, it was put on temporary display at the Society of Antiquaries in Burlington House and at Goldsmiths Hall.

In the frieze (No. 41, D) there were sixteen slabs of plaster prepared as described, but the impregnating material was varied as an experiment. For the slabs numbered 1, 8, 9, 11 and 12 (Pl. XI) nitrocellulose ('Durofix'), supplied by Messrs. Rawlplug Company, and a solvent consisting of 70 per cent acetone and 30 per cent amyl acetate were used. For the slabs numbered 2, 3, 4 and 10 polystyrene ('Trolitul'), made by Dynamit Actien Gesellschaft (British Agents, B.J. Hamlin and Co., London), and a solvent of benzene were used. For slabs 6, 7 and 16 polystyrene ('Lustrex G.P.'), supplied by Monsanto Plastics Ltd., and a solvent of benzene were used, while for slabs 5, 13, 14 and 15 acrylic resin ('Bedacryl 122 X'), supplied by Imperial Chemical Industries, and a solvent of toluene were used.

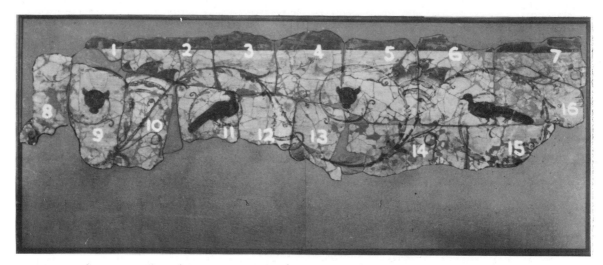

XI   Verulamium, decorated frieze from the courtyard of Insula XXI, 2 (Catalogue No. 41, A), showing the
     numbered slabs of the reconstruction.
Photo: Department of the Environment: Crown Copyright reserved

When the work of conservation was continued later in the less-closely controlled conditions
of the laboratory set up by the Ancient Monuments Division of the Department of the
Environment at the Old Tannery, Lacock, Wilts., the interior of which is shown in Plates XII
and XIII, the procedure described above was modified and simplified for a variety of reasons. In
the temperature- and humidity-controlled laboratory at the Building Research Station there had
been no difficulty in drying the decorated plaster fragments, a procedure so necessary when
using organic solvents. If the plaster is damp, clouding of the impregnating material with
organic solvents may result and this defect can be difficult to rectify. When such solvents as

XII   Lacock, part of the laboratory.
Photo: Department of the Environment: Crown Copyright reserved

XIII   Lacock, storage accommodation.
Photo: Department of the Environment: Crown Copyright reserved

XIV   Studio erected at Potterne in 1970.
Photo: Department of the Environment: Crown Copyright reserved

XV   Potterne, part of the studio, showing fragments of plaster being sorted by N. Davey.
Photo: Wiltshire Newspapers

benzene and toluene are used in large quantities, not only are they inflammable but the vapours given off can be objectionable. Careful attention must be given to the adequate ventilation of the working area if such solvents are used. It was decided, therefore, to use water emulsions for impregnation, thus avoiding the use of organic solvents. This also eliminated the necessity for complete drying of the plaster fragments. The plaster fragments could be washed with water,

XVI Preliminary washing by N. Davey of the fragments as received from the excavation.
Photo: Department of the Environment: Crown Copyright reserved

and while still damp could be impregnated with polyvinyl acetate emulsion, which is based on polyvinyl alcohol with a small percentage of dibutyl phthalate.

In 1970 the Department of the Environment erected a studio at Potterne near Devizes, Wilts., where the work of restoration has since continued (Plates XIV, XV).

The procedures adopted at Lacock and Potterne may now be described in full. It should be stressed again that much of the plaster received has been very fragmentary and/or was not carefully raised and recorded at the time of excavation, so that reassembly has often posed considerable problems.

The plaster fragments are first reduced to a uniform thickness by keeping only the finishing-coat, which usually varies in thickness from 6 to 16 mm. The painted surface is then carefully cleaned by swabbing with water (PL. XVI). The fragments are next immersed in a solution composed of one part of 'Unibond' to six to eight parts of water depending on the porosity of the plaster. After drying, the fragments are laid out on non-absorbent tables for sorting and identifying the pattern.

When small areas of pieces have been assembled, paper tissue is pasted on the surface using 'Polycell' cellulose adhesive diluted with water (Pl. XVII). The pieces of plaster are thus held correctly in place, and when the whole area is reversed it can be reinforced by applying plasterer's scrim glued in position with 'Unibond' (PL. XVIII). When this has hardened, the area of plaster is ready for mounting for display on suitable frames. These usually consist of sheets of expanded aluminium mesh on wooden frames or fixed to multi-ply wood or blockboard. 'Polyfilla', which is a finely ground gypsum plaster with a cellulose filler, has proved to be very suitable for fixing the fragments in position on the frameworks (Pl. XIX) and for filling in missing areas (see below). The paper tissue is quite easily removed from the decorated surface of the plaster by applying moisture.

XVII   Applying paper tissue to the painted plaster.
Photo: Department of the Environment: Crown Copyright reserved

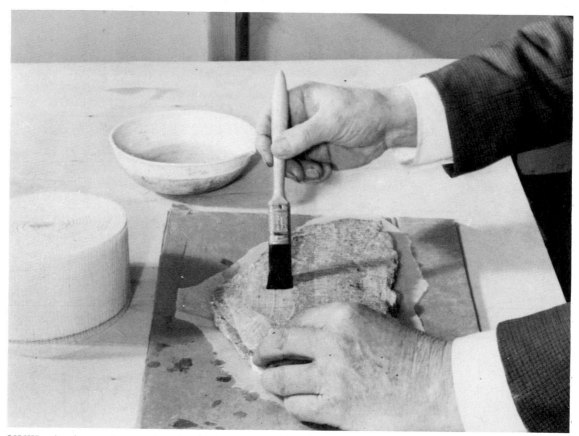

XVIII   Applying plasterers' scrim to the reverse side of the painted plaster.
Photo: Department of the Environment: Crown Copyright reserved

The experience gained at Verulamium in 1956–57 proved invaluable when dealing with the decorated plaster from the house in Blue Boar Lane, Leicester (No. 22). This was found very jumbled and in completely random distribution. It was picked up carefully in areas, by the methods adopted at Verulamium, tissue being gummed to the plaster surface to ensure that any loose pieces of plaster were secured in their proper position. This tissue is seen in Plate XX being removed from one of the pieces in the studio at Lacock. That the method of lifting was satisfactory is illustrated by Plate XXI, showing a group of pieces reversed after lifting, and with tissue removed to reveal some of the decoration, which included a mask. Another group of pieces revealed a second mask, and Plate XXII shows this partially restored. The photograph in

XIX   Applying 'Polyfilla' to the plaster for transferring to the frames.
Photo: Department of the Environment: Crown Copyright reserved

XX   Leicester, N. Davey removing the tissue from an area of plaster after lifting.
Photo: Department of the Environment: Crown Copyright reserved

XXI   Leicester, joining fragments of wall-plaster after reversal.
Photo: Oxford University Institute of Archaeology

XXII   Leicester, one of the painted masks after restoration.
Photo: Department of the Environment: Crown Copyright reserved

Plate XXIII was taken during the process of mounting the treated plaster on frames, which were eventually transported to the Jewry Wall Museum at Leicester.

The treatment of decorated plaster recovered at Catterick (No. 5) presented some unusual problems. There were many boxes of loose fragments, but these were treated, sorted and arranged to reveal the overall pattern. Inspection of the fragments showed that there had been an earlier painted surface which was visible in the cross-section. Each fragment was therefore

XXIII Leicester, showing how the areas of reconstructed plaster are mounted on expanded aluminium fixed to
     timber frames.
Photo: Department of the Environment: Crown Copyright reserved

split at this interface by the careful use of fine chisels, to reveal the earlier decoration. But under
this earlier decoration was an even earlier one. Only part of this, however, was revealed by
removal of some of the paint layer. Reconstruction of the two later decorations was carried out
by making up the plaster in sections as shown in Plates XXIV and XXV, where they are seen
lying in position on the floor of the laboratory at Lacock, awaiting transportation to York
where they were mounted for display by screwing them to multi-ply boards fixed to the wall of
the Museum.

XXIV   Catterick, the second scheme of decoration, assembled in sections. See Catalogue No. 5.
Photo: Department of the Environment: Crown Copyright reserved

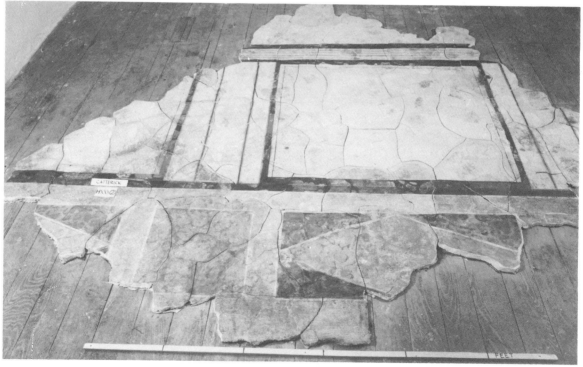

XXV   Catterick, the third and final scheme of decoration, assembled in sections. See Catalogue No. 5.
Photo: Department of the Environment: Crown Copyright reserved

Infilling and presentation

It was possible to reconstruct quite large areas of wall plaster from the material recovered at Verulamium and Leicester as comparatively little plaster was missing. The amount of infilling required was in consequence quite small. In many other instances more than half the material has been missing and this has rendered the precise design difficult to interpret, the more so when it is of a pictorial nature as at Lullingstone and Kingscote, restored respectively in 1973 and 1976 (Nos. 27, A; 21).

Where completion of a design is desirable, the spaces which would have been occupied by the missing fragments are filled with Polyfilla, and this is painted with water-colours to tone in with the original plaster. The difference between the original plaster and the infilling must always be apparent on close inspection. When viewed from 3 or 4 feet away the difference may not be so obvious.

Plaster from vaults

With plasterwork from vaults or the soffits of arches, reassembly of the fragments of plaster has been carried out on frameworks curved to the proper radius, determined from the precise measurements of fragments. Curvature varies from the small-scale vault of the cold plunge-bath at Sparsholt (No. 37, C) to the vast span of the *caldarium* at Wroxeter (No. 51). Another example from Sparsholt is part of the decorated soffit of an arched doorway in the bath-building (No. 37, A). In each case expanded aluminium was bent to the correct curvature and fixed to a temporary wooden framework to hold it conveniently in position while the plaster fragments were being positioned and mounted.

POSTSCRIPT

After the text of this book was completed, R.L. was invited to give a paper on Romano-British wall-painting at the German Archaeological Institute in Berlin, where he benefited greatly from the comments of various colleagues, notably Prof. V.M. Strocka and Dr. H. Mielsch. Some of their views on the dating and interpretation of British paintings differ from those expressed in these pages. For example both Prof. Strocka and Dr. Mielsch felt that the figure-painting from Kingscote (No. 21) and Tarrant Hinton (No. 38) must, on stylistic grounds, be earlier than the late third or fourth century; Prof. Strocka proposed a date round 200 or even earlier. For the Dover paintings (No. 14) Dr. Mielsch suggested the date which we have now tentatively adopted: namely the first half or middle of the third century. His view was that the closest Roman parallel was not, as we originally argued, the decoration of the Via Merulana house, but that of the Paedagogium on the Palatine (which he dates round the middle of the third century). On the interpretation of the Kingscote mural Mielsch believes that the seated figure with the shield cannot be Achilles at the court of King Lycomedes, because the seat is too low to have been a chair or throne appropriate to a courtly context. Dr. W. Trillmich suggested that the figure might be Aphrodite/Venus posing with the shield of Ares/Mars.

Thanks are also due to Dr. Michael Donderer, of the University of Erlangen-Nürnberg, for discussing the sections of the Introduction relating to mosaics and for making a number of valuable comments.

Since 1979 the location of some of the material in the Catalogue has changed. It has not proved practicable to check every item, but the most important changes known to us are: Nos. 10, 11 (Colchester) now in Colchester and Essex Museum (in storage); No. 21 (Kingscote) now in the Corinium Museum, Cirencester.

Since it was not possible to publish more than a few of the plates in colour, a microfiche of 60 coloured frames has been included in a pocket at the back of the book to show the colours of as many of the other panels as was practicable. For the list see p. 231.

CATALOGUE

The criteria which have governed the choice of items in the catalogue have already been detailed (p. 28). Surviving material appears in the main part of the catalogue; a few decorations known primarily from old drawings and photographs are grouped in an appendix.

The restorations, unless otherwise stated and/or marked with an asterisk (*), are the work of Norman Davey, following the methods described in the Introduction. Attention will be drawn where necessary to particular problems involved in the restoration; but it is not always practicable to distinguish between what is original and what is restored, especially where this would necessitate a great deal of detailed discussion. Often, therefore, we have been content to describe the 'finished product' without stating in detail the deductions by which it was reached.[1] Wherever possible, photographs of the restored pieces are accompanied by diagrams illustrating the relationship of the original fragments to the reconstructed motif or design. But again this has not always proved practicable, especially with the very large pieces.

Nor has it proved practicable to use a colour-chart to describe the colours. While this might have been desirable in many instances, there are just as many where the original tones cannot be identified with certainty and any claims to precision would be misleading.

The measurements are given in centimetres, the width first and the height second (except, of course, for ceiling-plaster, where the order is immaterial). Unless otherwise stated, the figure given is the maximum dimension of the restored surface. Items marked † are those which have not been seen by one of the writers (R.L.) and for which accurate measurements are lacking. The location of sites is given according to the old counties, in the belief that these will be more familiar to the reader than the new. Dates are always A.D.

As regards terminology, few observations need be made. Generally speaking a 'band' is from 2 to 20 cm wide, a 'stripe' from 5 mm to 2 cm, a 'line' is anything narrower than a 'stripe'. A 'zone' is anything wider than a 'band'. Terms which may not be familiar to the general reader are listed in a brief glossary (pp. 19-21).

---

[1] The second writer has not necessarily found himself in agreement with all aspects of some of the restorations.

No. 1. BIGNOR, Sussex.   Villa, Room 28B. Late third or early fourth century. Now in site museum. PL. XXVI.

Part of wall-decoration restored from fragments found in 1961. 1.04 m × 1.56 m. Imitation marble veneering.

Details of the restoration are problematic, but included are (1) a roundel painted pinkish-yellow with darker pink and purple veins, (2) samples of various other coloured marbles: dark green with white grains; yellow with dark red veins; dark brownish-red; black with white veins; pink with purple and pinkish-yellow mottling and dark purple veins. Some of the panels were recessed or had frames in relief.

The panels with a yellow or pinkish-yellow basis are presumably intended to represent giallo antico; the dark green is presumably serpentine. The standard of painting is somewhat crude but still compares not unfavourably with that of imitation marbling in other parts of the Empire in the third and fourth centuries; the motif in general enjoyed increasing popularity from the late third century onwards, especially for the decoration of dados, but also for the panels of the main zone.[1] Particularly popular was the use of a tondo as the focal point of a panel, often, as in the Constantinian paintings of Rooms o" and n' in the house under Ss. Giovanni e Paolo in Rome, set within a lozenge or interlocking squares.[2] For a tondo with a decorated frame, as in the Bignor decoration, one can compare remains of decorations in the Sede degli Augustali at Ostia and in the hypogeum of Via Livenza in Rome.[3] Nearer to Britain, the motif occurs in a third- or fourth-century tomb near Trier.[4]

Various other painted fragments were found in the Bignor villa in the excavations of the early 1960s, including pieces of a column with scale-decoration and a simple volute-capital reminiscent of those in the mid fourth-century Christian paintings from Lullingstone (No. 27, A, B). For nineteenth-century finds at Bignor see Appendix, No. 3.

References: *JRS* lii (1962), p. 189; *Britannia* xiii (1982), forthcoming. Excavator: S.S. Frere.

[1]Borda, pp. 135–142; Mielsch 1978, pp. 164, 201 ff. (with bibl.).
[2]*Ibid.*, pp. 163 f., pls. 82 (4), 83 (3).
[3]Ostia: Van Essen, pp. 179 f.; pp. 164 (n. 54), 203. Via Livenza: L. Usai, in *Dialoghi di Archeologia*, vi (1972), pp. 397 f., figs. 3, 4.
[4]F. Drexel, in *Germania romana*, 2nd edn., ii (1924), p. 31, pl. XXXV, 2; P. Steiner, in *Trierer Zeitschrift*, ii (1927), pp. 64–66, figs. 18, 19. The nearest British parallels are at Aldborough and Cirencester (Appendix, Nos. 1, 6).

No. 2. BOXMOOR, Herts.   Villa, Period 1 timber building. Late first century (Flavian period). Now in Hemel Hempstead, Dacorum Civic Centre. FIG. 5.

Two areas of painted plaster found (1966) lying in Room *a*, where they had fallen from the west wall of Room *c*. Measurements of the restored slabs:

(A) Part of dado and lower edge of main zone. 1.51 m wide × 88.5 cm high.

(B) Area from upper part of main zone. 88 cm wide × 89.5 cm high.

The two pieces give a clear idea of the decorative scheme.[1] A dado of pink panels divided by black stripes and spotted with black, white and purple was crowned by an orange zone bisected by a horizontal red stripe. Above this came a pair of red panels with pale green borders separated by a black vertical fascia containing a candelabrum. The candelabrum, which had a stem composed of three stripes, purple, white and orange, was decorated with at least two horizontal discs: one at the top coloured pale green, pink and cream, with little yellow-white trefoils hanging from either end, and the second about 30 cm lower, coloured pale green, cream and yellow. The red panels had inner borders consisting of yellow lines with beaded ⊥ formations set diagonally at the corners.

Part of a frieze survives: a white band bisected by two horizontal grey lines and sandwiched between orange and purple stripes, the whole surmounted by a grey or black zone.

The decoration abutted on to a door-reveal at the left, as the bevel in the plaster shows.

The scheme of decoration, with its red panels and black dividing strips, is a favourite in Britain and the other north-western provinces, being especially closely paralleled, for the main

Photo: M. B. Cookson.

XXVI No. 1 Bignor. Restored piece of wall-decoration.

zone at least, by Flavian decorations in Temple II at Elst (Holland) and in a house under the Imperial Baths at Trier. Both have the same pale green borders set between white lines and the same candelabra with vertical stems interrupted at intervals by discs.[2] A close British parallel, lacking only the candelabra, is provided by a Flavian scheme at Cirencester (No. 8), which, like the Boxmoor decoration (and unlike the continental examples, where the dados are more ornate), has a pink, speckled dado.

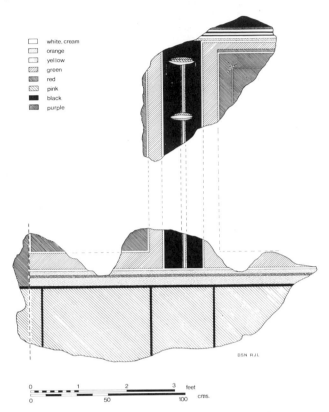

FIG. 5   No. 2: Boxmoor, areas of wall-plaster from Period 1 timber building. Scale, 1:25.
(Drawing by D.S. Neal, adapted by R.J. Ling)

Reference: Neal 1976, pp. 58, 88, pl. 26 and frontispiece.
Excavator: D.S. Neal, Hemel Hempstead Excavation Society.

[1]The description is aided by photographs and drawings made at the time of the excavation.
[2]Barbet 1974 b, figs. 18, 19. The Elst example has yellow inner border-lines like ours; the Trier example has, instead, embroidery motifs of the type familiar in the Pompeian Fourth Style (*c.* 50–79).

No. 3 BOXMOOR, Herts.   Villa, Period 3. Second half of second century or early third century. Now (1979) in London, Fortress House (in storage). FIG. 6.

Area of plaster collapsed face down from south wall of Room 11, apparently next to doorway into Room 9. 1970 excavations.

84 cm wide × 1.50 m high. The curving door-reveal at the left is pale blue, and next to it is a column painted with yellow and white fluting and a red tendril spiralling anti-clockwise up it. Near the top of the surviving fragment a yellow, red-rimmed collar circles the column; at the bottom there are traces of another. The fluting grades in width to suggest shading at the edges and a highlight at the middle. An interesting technical detail is the presence of cord-imprints used in marking out the edges of the column before painting (cf. Introduction, p. 59).

The column was presumably the right-hand one of a symmetrical pair framing the doorway,[1] so that the tendrils would have spiralled upwards and outwards from the opening (compare the rule which governs spirally-fluted columns in Pompeian paintings).[2]

Other fragments of wall-plaster from this phase, dumped on the north side of the north corridor, included the head and shoulders of a Cupid (?) almost half lifesize and fragments of a body or bodies, all on a pale blue background.

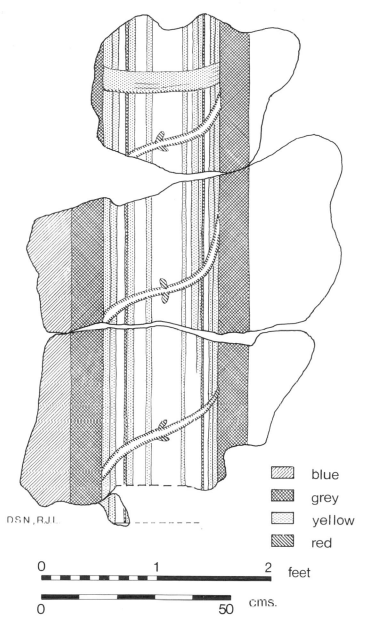

blue

grey

yellow

red

0   1   2   feet

0   50   cms.

D.S.N., R.J.L.

FIG. 6 No. 3: Boxmoor, area of wall-plaster from door-jamb in Period 3 building. Scale, 1:10.
(Drawing by D.S. Neal, adapted by R.J. Ling)

Reference: Neal 1976, pp. 64, 88–91, figs. LI, LII (F) and frontispiece.
Excavator: D.S. Neal, Hemel Hempstead Excavation Society.

[1] Cf. Neal 1976, fig. LII (F).
[2] Barbet 1977, p. 114.

No. 4. BRANTINGHAM, Yorks. Villa. Middle or second half of fourth century. Now in Hull, Transport and Archaeology Museum. PLS. XXVII–XXX. FIGS. 7–10.

Two large pieces and two groups of smaller pieces reconstructed from scattered fragments found in Room 1 (1962 excavations).

(A) 75.5 cm wide × 67 cm high. A nimbed bust set within a roundel. The face is reddish with some white overpainting and with shading in purple and dark brown; the hair is picked out in purple, with red and orange highlights. Round the neck the drapery describes regular arcs with equidistant folds, coloured orange with brown shadows and white highlights. The nimbus is white and the background black, while the frame, traces of guide-lines for which are visible at the right, is painted white with orange lines, evidently in imitation of a moulded stucco frame.

XXVII   No. 4 (A)   Brantingham, restored bust within roundel.

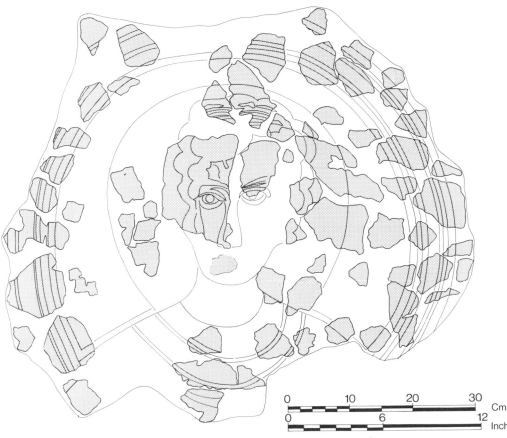

FIG. 7   No. 4 (A): Brantingham, restored bust within roundel. Diagram showing position of original fragments. Scale, 1:6.

(Drawing by J. Thorn)

The somewhat simplified style of the head, executed with strong, dark outlines and little modelling, presages that of the late fourth-century figures from Lullingstone (No. 27, A). Characteristic of both sets of paintings are the large, staring eyes, a feature common in Roman art of the Tetrarchic period and later.[1]

The practice of setting busts in medallions is a favourite one in the Roman arts, being used in paintings, mosaics and relief sculpture from at least the first century A.D., and perhaps going back ultimately to the *imagines clipeatae* of triumphal and sepulchral art.[2] There is no restriction to the types of figure portrayed in this way, which range from real people to satyrs and maenads, personifications and divinities. Here there are no distinguishing attributes, but the presence of the nimbus indicates either an allegorical subject or a goddess or perhaps a member of the Imperial family.[3] The dark background is perhaps more typical of the late Roman period than of the early Empire and finds an interesting echo in the mosaic pavement of the same room in the Brantingham villa, where nimbed busts, both male and female but equally unidentifiable, are set in arcuate panels with a red background.[4] It is possible, though not certain, that our roundel may have come from the ceiling, in which case the ceiling-decoration to some extent reflected that of the floor below.[5] For another, earlier medallion-bust see No. 37, B.

Not too much attention can be paid to the distinctive round-necked drapery, since the restoration is partly hypothetical. It is at least possible that the curves of the neckline formed part of a cloak fastened over the right shoulder, like those worn by the porphyry figures of the Tetrarchs now at St. Mark's in Venice.[6]

XXVIII   No. 4 (B) Brantingham, part of face within rectangular panel.

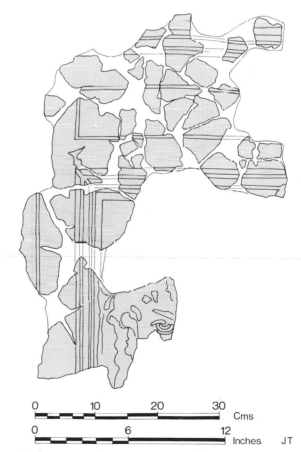

FIG. 8   No. 4 (B): Brantingham, area of plaster with part of face in rectangular panel. Diagram showing position of original fragments. Scale, 1:6.   *(Drawing by J. Thorn)*

(B) 44 cm wide × 63 cm high. Part of the right side of a human face, probably again female, set within a rectangular panel. The eyes are blue and again large and staring in the fourth-century manner; the hair is reddish-brown with purple shading. The background this time is blue, but the frame of the panel is virtually identical to that of the roundel (A), a white band

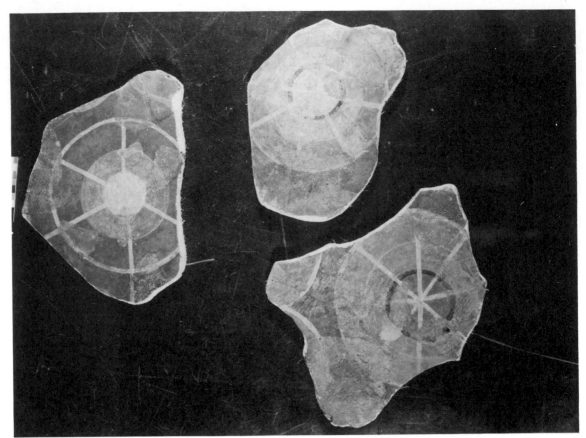

XXIX   No. 4 (C)   Brantingham, wheel-like motifs.

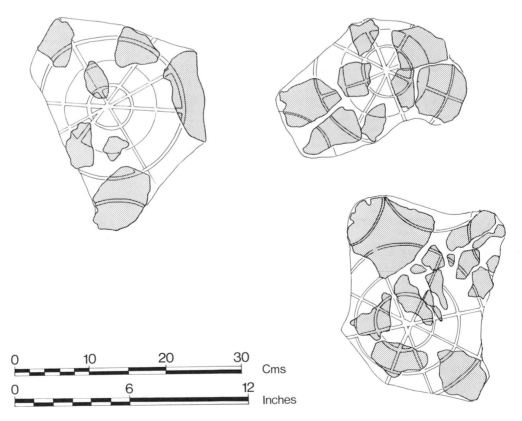

FIG. 9   No. 4 (C): Brantingham, wheel-like motifs. Diagram showing position of original fragments. Scale, 1:5.
(Drawing by J. Thorn)

with orange lines running within it. Part of a similar frame is visible above, separated from the first panel by a red zone in which is set a pale blue oblong. At the left the surface rises in relief, perhaps forming a moulding against a door-jamb.

Several other pieces of framing-elements incorporating the same red zones and imitation stucco mouldings have also been reconstructed. One piece shows a projecting moulding.

Photo: Department of the Environment: Crown Copyright reserved

XXX No 4 (D) Brantingham, restored fragments of curving lines.

(C) (i) 19 cm × 24 cm. (ii) 29.5 cm × 22 cm. (iii) 31 cm × 24 cm. Three reconstructed fragments showing wheel-like elements. Concentric circles in different colours (pink, pale blue and yellow in varying order) are divided into six or eight sectors by radial yellow white lines and set within concave-sided octagons. Repeated curvilinear elements like this are most likely to have come from a ceiling, since they suggest an all-over pattern of the type most frequently found in ceiling-decorations (see Introduction, pp. 37-9). For a possible reconstruction of the Brantingham pattern see FIG. 10. Fragments of plaster from another East Yorkshire villa, at Harpham, show various curvilinear motifs including a wheel-like design very similar to ours (No. 20).

(D) (i) 25 cm × 44 cm. (ii) 47 cm × 32 cm. Two reconstructed fragments with brown and white curving lines on an orange-yellow ground, perhaps derived from drapery like that of the bust (A), perhaps derived from curvilinear panel-frames (some of the arcs have been marked out with grooves). Other smaller fragments from similar elements.

References: J. Liversidge, in *Britannia* iv (1973), pp. 99-103, pls. XV, XVI; Liversidge 1977, pp. 90-5, figs. 5.6, 5.7.
Excavator: I.M. Stead, Department of the Environment.

[1]Cf. the portraits of the period: e.g. R. Calza, *Iconografia romana imperiale da Carausio a Giuliano (287-363 d.C.)* (1972), plates *(passim)*.

[2]Innumerable examples can be added to those cited by Winkes, p. 99, nn. 198-201. E.g., in painting, Schefold, pp. 136-38, pls. 179, 180 (Pompeii, middle and third quarter of first century); Mielsch 1978, p. 171, pl. 90 (1-4) (Rome, Via Genova, early fourth century); Y. Tsafrir, in *Israel Exploration Journal* xviii (1968), pp. 176-80, pls. 14-17 (fourth century). In Britain, as well as the painted bust from Sparsholt (No. 37, B), there are mosaic busts of Seasons at

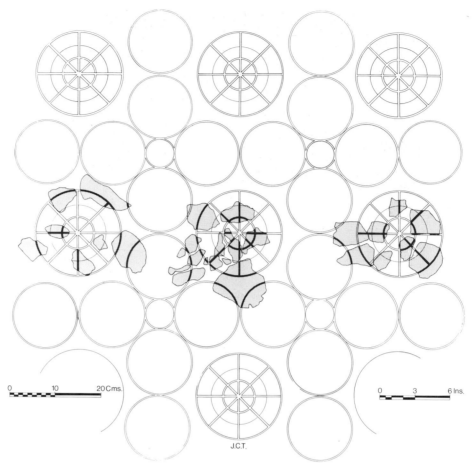

FIG. 10   No. 4 (C): Brantingham, a possible reconstruction of the ceiling-pattern (by J. Thorn). Scale 1:8.
(Drawing by J. Thorn)

Cirencester (second century?) and Lullingstone (fourth century) (Toynbee 1962, pls. 210-12, 228; cf. Bignor, pl. 218). For a dark background cf. glass medallions: H. von Heintze, 'Das Goldglasmedaillon in Brescia', in *Festschrift Eugen von Mercklin* (1964), pp. 41-52, pls. 23, 26-8 (third and early fourth centuries). *Imagines clipeatae*: Pliny, *NH* xxxv, 12-13; Winkes.

[3]Cf. Levi, p. 289.

[4]*Britannia* iv (1973), pls. V, VI B, IX A, XIII, XIV.

[5]Such direct reflections are rarer than is usually thought: the best examples are provided by marine fauna in the mosaic pavements and painted vaults of bath-buildings, e.g. at Münsingen in Switzerland: Kapossy, pp. 9-26.

[6]R. Delbrück, *Antike Porphyrwerke* (1932), pp. 84-91, pls. 31-4; cf. A. Ragona, *I tetrarchi dei gruppi porfirei di San Marco in Venezia* (1963).

No. 5.   CATTERICK, Yorks.   Building III, 4 (probably a *mansio*). Second century (the life of the building seems to have extended from mid Hadrianic to late Antonine times; it was certainly destroyed by the early third century). Now in York, Yorkshire Museum. PLS. XXIV-XXV, XXXI-XXXII. FIGS. 11-12.

Part of wall-decoration, restored from fragments found (1959) in disorder. Three successive phases of decoration, the first two pecked to give a purchase to the new layer of plaster. The third-phase plaster has been separated from the earlier layers.

(A) First phase. A small patch exposed at the top left reveals a horizontal red border and a green plant above it, both on a white ground. The border is 6.5 cm wide and has black lines running parallel to it, two below and one above; the plant stands on the upper line and has a stock formed by an inverted cone, from which sprouts a pair of leafy branches, the leaves growing on long stems from either side of each branch.

XXXI   No. 5 (A)   Catterick, detail of first-phase plaster, restored.

(B) Second phase. 3.25 m wide × 2.51 m high. Above a pink dado at least 31 cm high comes a decoration formed by coloured bands 5.5 to 7.0 cm wide on a white ground. The main zone, delimited by red bands above and below, is slightly under 1.50 m high and contains rectangular panels framed by similar red bands, with inner borders formed by single black lines. A pair of black lines runs between the panels and the upper edge of the main zone, and from the top corners of the panels run three lines of black spots forming a diagonal ⊥-formation. Between the two surviving panels is a crudely-painted red chalice from which grows a plant consisting of balancing sprigs (yellow stems and greenish-blue leaves) growing on either side of a vertical axis; evanescent red brush-marks a part of the way up may be the remains of birds or flowers. A yellow border 7 cm wide divides the main zone from the upper zone, on which no decoration can be seen.

(C) Third phase. 3.34 m wide × 2.80 m high. The dado, 75 cm high, consists of panels of imitation marble veneering set in a surround of white speckled green. The panels are alternately squares and horizontal oblongs, the oblongs containing inset lozenges. The squares and lozenges are painted with yellow and white mottling on a pink ground (intended to reproduce giallo antico ?); the triangles round the lozenges with green and white mottling on a yellow ground (serpentine ?). The main zone, with a white ground and delimited above and below by bands of dark reddish purple 4.0 to 4.5 cm wide, is divided into alternate rectangular panels and vertical fasciae, their rhythm corresponding to the alternation of oblongs and squares in the

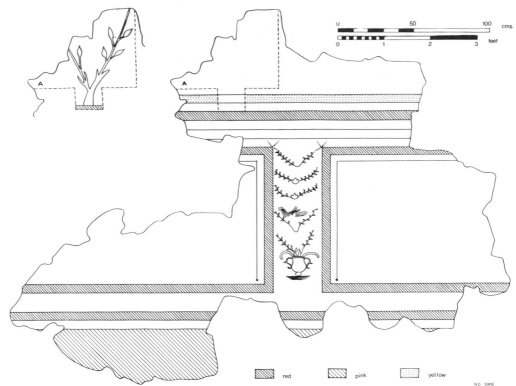

FIG. 11 No. 5 (B): Catterick, restoration of second-phase plaster. The first-phase plant (top left) is green; and the vase and plant between the panels are red and greenish-blue. Scale, 1:25.

(Drawing by N. Davey and Tina Baddeley)

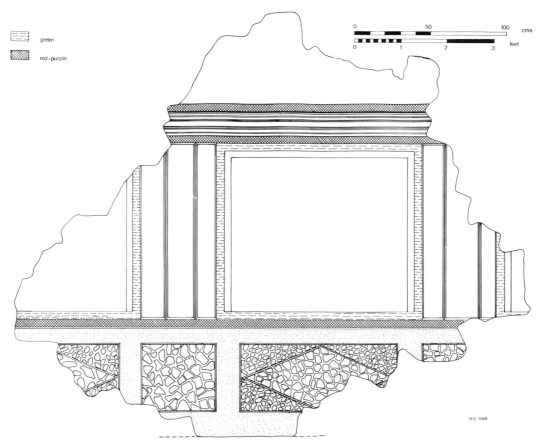

FIG. 12 No. 5 (C): Catterick, restoration of third-phase plaster. The dado is painted in imitation of variously coloured marbles. Scale, 1:25.

(Drawing by N. Davey and Tina Baddeley)

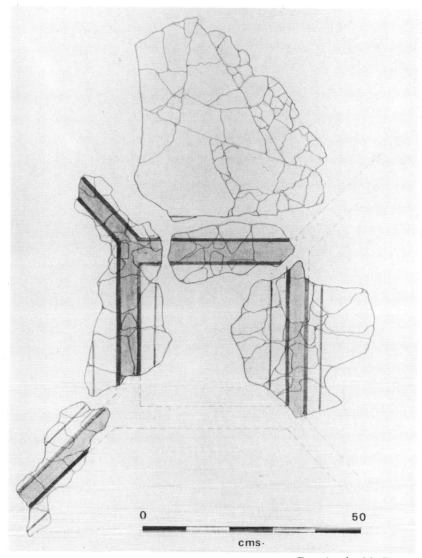

Drawing by N. Davey.

XXXII No. 5 (D) Catterick, restored fragments of ceiling-decoration.

dado below. The panels, 1.10 m high, are framed by a green band 3.0 to 4.0 cm wide with an inner border formed by a single black line along the top and at the sides. The vertical fasciae are divided into three parts by two vertical stripes, each purple edged with yellow. At the top of the main zone is a white frieze divided by horizontal yellow and watery grey lines to give the impression of plaster mouldings. A further purple band separates the frieze from the upper zone, which is again undecorated.

The motif of lozenges set within horizontal oblongs seems to have been especially favoured for dados in the Yorkshire area: see parallels at Aldborough (Appendix No. 1), Malton (No. 28), York (No. 52), and, in north Lincolnshire, at Winterton.[1]

(D) Further fragments recently restored: (1) part of a door-jamb (Phases II and III); (2) parts (PL.XXXII) of what may be the ceiling of Phase III (bands of yellow ochre from 3 to 5 cm wide between brown-purple stripes, all on a white ground; a junction of three bands suggests an octagonal system); (3) part of the angle of wall and ceiling, masked by a red-purple band (Phase III).

Reference: Davey 1972, pp. 260–1, figs. 6–7, pls. XVIII, XIXA.
Excavator: J.S. Wacher, Department of the Environment.

[1]Liversidge 1976, pp. 282 f., fig. 143, pl. XXXIV, *c, d.*

No. 6. CATTERICK, Yorks. Insula VII, shop. Third or fourth century. Now in York, Yorkshire Museum. PL. XXXIII. FIG. 13.

Part of wall-decoration restored from fragments which had slid to the bottom of the wall. Excavated in 1959.

1.17 m wide × 1.40 m high. Imitation marble panelling. The dado, rather faded but apparently painted purple up to a certain height and orange above, is surmounted by a sequence of black, white and purple bands, respectively 2.0, 3.0 and 2.5 cm wide. Surviving from the main zone are parts of two panels separated by a vertical fascia which consists of three bands, the

0   10   20   30   40   50   0   6   12
Cms   Inches

FIG. 13   No. 6: Catterick, restoration of part of wall-decoration from shop in insula VII. Diagram showing position of original fragments. Scale, 1:8.

(Drawing by David Honour)

XXXIII No. 6 Catterick, restored piece of wall-decoration from shop.

outer ones coloured red and pale green respectively, and the middle one white with a vertical green line along its axis. The left panel is white with green veins, mainly in the form of circular lines, each containing a couple of vertical strokes. The right panel is white with orange veins forming both small circles or ovals and large 'fried eggs' (the 'yolk' of which is a red blob inside an orange blob which is set in turn inside a yellow area).

Reference: Davey 1972, p. 261, pl. XIX B.
Excavator: J.S. Wacher, Department of the Environment.

NO. 7. CHESTER. Fortress, centurion's quarters west of *principia*. Late first century (Flavian period). Now in Chester, Grosvenor Museum. PL. XXXIV.

Wall-decoration of a timber-framed room found in excavations in Crook Street (1974). Most of the plaster was present, apparently trampled and buried in the course of demolition (probably in the early second century); a sample was retained for reconstruction.

A dado of creamy white (41 cm high) resting on a narrow band of pink (9 cm) was decorated with large clumps of reeds coloured red and black. The main zone apparently consisted of large fields of red separated by black intervals, and above this there was a frieze in which yellow played a part. This is the scheme suggested by statistical analysis of the colours present in the part of the room exposed (totals in square inches): pink (baseboard) 219 (4.26%); white (dado and vegetation) 1226 (23.84%); red 2682 (52.15%); black 642 (12.48%); yellow 374 (7.27%). Reconstruction of small areas has confirmed the lower part:

(A) 75 cm × 61 cm. Baseboard, dado containing clump of reeds, lower part of red field.

(B) 55 cm × 53.5 cm. Upper part of dado, corners of contiguous red field and black interval.

(C) 36.5 cm × 36 cm. Part of red field containing horizontal yellow stripe.

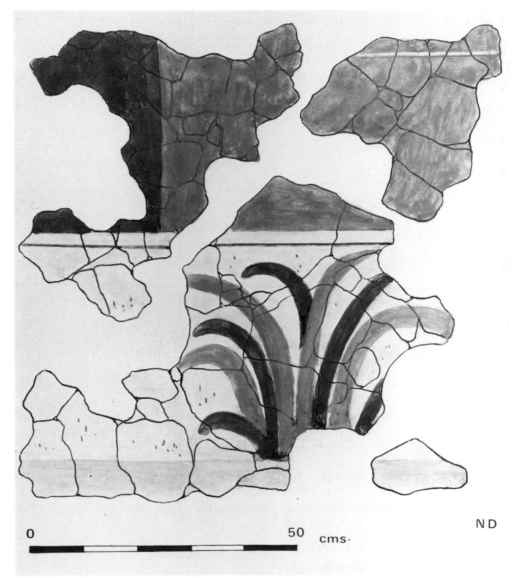

XXXIV   No. 7   Chester, restored piece of wall-decoration from Crook Street.

The plaster is very coarse and contains a high proportion of the local red sand; the painting is simple in form and crude in execution.

The inclusion in the dado of clumps of reeds or similar plants is a favourite motif in wall-paintings of the Flavian and immediately successive periods, both in Italy and in the other north-western provinces.[1] There, however, the plants are generally combined with figures and other motifs, especially wading birds, and are invariably set on a black ground; here, in what is a relatively crude and simple decoration, they seem to have been unaccompanied, and are set against a light-coloured ground. A possible parallel on a black ground was found in the Neronian proto-palace at Fishbourne,[2] and one on a maroon ground occurs on an unpublished fragment found in excavations at Gloucester on the site of the *colonia* east gate (dated on pottery evidence to the late first or early second century).[3] For a much later example see No. 13, A (Dorchester).

Reference: *Britannia* vi (1975), p. 240.
Excavator: T.J. Strickland, Grosvenor Museum.

[1]E.g. Pompeii: Schefold, pls. 98, 100, 112, 127, 131, 136, 137, 148 (3), 151 (2) (all dated by Schefold to the time of Vespasian); cf. Peters, pls. 60, 78 (fig. 36), 79, 86-88. Gallo-Roman parallels at Mercin-et-Vaux (interrupted by plinths supporting columns in the main zone), Trier and elsewhere: Barbet 1974 b, pp. 108 f., 114 f., 129 ff., figs. 1, 5, 19, 21; 1975, pp. 96, 107-10, figs. 1, 9-10 (all perhaps late first or early second century). Swiss parallel in Room E of a bath-suite outside the east defences of the fortress at Vindonissa (red and green leaves or green and yellow leaves alternately): *Gesellschaft pro Vindonissa, Jahresbericht 1969/70* (1970), p. 67 and fig. 6 (date uncertain). Pannonian examples in the villa of Nemesvámos-Balácapuszta: E.B. Thomas, *Römische Villen in Pannonien* (1964), pls. XXIX, XLVIII, L, LII, LV (last third of first century).
[2]B.W. Cunliffe, *Excavations at Fishbourne* ii (1971), pl. XIII a top left (upside down).
[3]We are grateful to Carolyn Heighway for allowing us to study this material.

No. 8. CIRENCESTER, Glos. Insula V, timber-framed shop. Late first century (Flavian period). Now in Cirencester, Corinium Museum. PL. CXXII.

Wall-decoration reconstructed from fragments excavated in 1961. The work was carried out under Dr. Davey's supervision by an assistant, Susan Wormwell, who worked with the help of a grant from the Gulbenkian Foundation.

3.47 m wide × 2.11 m high. The dado, at least 68.5 cm high, is pink with black, white, red and pale blue splashes. The main zone, restored as 1.31 m high, consists of three large red panels, the central one bordered by a yellow band. The intervening spaces are black. Set within each panel are yellow border-lines, punctuated at intervals by discs with white bobbles round them, and decorated at the corners with diagonal lines of spots in a ⊥ -formation.

A small part of the upper decoration has been reconstructed, showing a white band, a black stripe, and the start of a dark red zone at least 6 cm high.

The scheme of decoration is very close to that from the contemporary timber building at Boxmoor (No. 2), the main difference being the absence here of any candelabrum in the black spaces between the panels. There are also fragments of a similar decoration from another site in Cirencester (Dyer Court, 1957 excavations).[1]

Numerous fragments from the 1961 excavations in Insula V are still in storage. Most come from beneath the south-east end of the masonry shop V 4 and one of the rooms of its neighbour V 3.[2] They show elements which clearly belong to the decoration reconstructed or to another very like it, as well as other elements which, while using a similar range of colours, seem to belong to different decorative schemes. Some pieces with curving yellow, red and green frames may derive from a ceiling. One fragment shows a head (a *gorgoneion?*) on a horizontal disc, perhaps part of a candelabrum.[3]

References: J.S. Wacher, *Antiq. Journ.* xlii (1962), p. 9; Davey 1972, p. 259 f., fig. 5; Liversidge 1977, p. 75 f., fig. 5.1a.
Excavator: J.S. Wacher, Cirencester Excavation Committee.

[1]Liversidge 1962, p. 41, fig. 1, pl. IV a.
[2]See plan in Wacher, fig. 69.
[3]Toynbee 1964, p. 219.

No. 9. ★**CIRENCESTER**, Glos. Building XXIII, 1. Early second century. Now in Cirencester, Corinium Museum. PL. XXXV. FIG. 14.

Part of wall-decoration removed from a wall where the plaster survived intact to at least half-height. Excavated in 1962.

Photo: J.S. Wacher

XXXV No. 9 Cirencester, dado of wall-decoration in Building XXIII, 1, photographed before lifting.

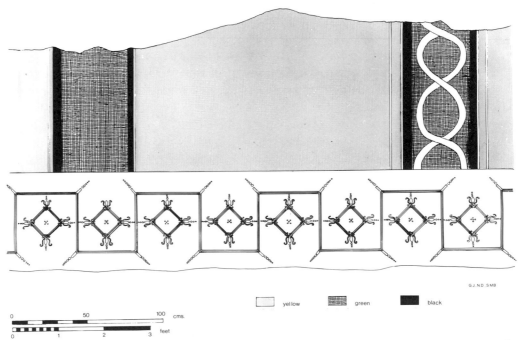

FIG. 14 No. 9: Cirencester, Building XXIII, 1: part of painted wall-plaster found *in situ*. Scale, 1:25.
(Drawings by N. Davey and G. Jones, adapted by Tina Baddeley)

3.06 m long x 1.50 m high. Above a black dado 56 cm high, a system of orange-yellow panels divided by dark green vertical fasciae. The dado is decorated with a battlement meander delicately and carefully painted in contiguous lines of white and purple.[1] In each bay of the meander, whose sides consistently measure 37.5 cm (1¼ Roman feet?), is set a diamond framed by the same white and purple lines and decorated at each angle with a white lyre-shaped ornament, above which float a couple of spots. At the centre of the diamond is a rosette of five white spots, the central one marked by a small hole (created by a compass-point ?).

In the main zone the only dark green fascia preserved has traces of a pair of interweaving white ribbons. It is separated from the neighbouring panels by a black band between white lines; and a further white line is set a short distance within the edge of the left panel. The colours are much faded: the orange of the panels has largely worn away, revealing a pink undercoat.

References: J.S. Wacher, *Antiq. Journ.* xliii (1963), p. 19, pl. XI; *JRS* liii (1963), p. 143, pl. XIII; Davey 1972, p. 258 f.
Excavator: J.S. Wacher, Cirencester Excavation Committee.

[1]For a similar meander, this time yellow, on a black dado cf. a decoration in the baths at Virunum, probably also second-century in date: Praschniker and Kenner, pp. 33, 183, 218, 228, figs. 15, 163.

No. 10. *COLCHESTER, Essex.   Timber-framed house outside west gate. Last quarter of first, or early second century. Now with the Colchester Archaeological Trust, East Hill House (in storage). PL. CXIV. FIG. 15.

Fragments of wall-plaster found in confusion in one of the rooms south of corridor, Balkerne Lane excavations 1976.

(A) Fragments reconstructed to form part of a vertical fascia between two rectangular fields. The fascia carries a voluminous vegetal candelabrum in white on a pinkish-red ground framed by a white stripe. The fields to left and right were again pinkish-red and had broad black borders, marked off by another white stripe. Along the bottom edge of this scheme ran a continuous yellow band 6.5 cm wide separated by another white stripe from a pink dado with black splashes.

(B) Fragments of a small panel with a gladiatorial scene on a pale green ground. The largest piece (17 cm wide × 24 cm high) comes from the right-hand end of the panel and shows a gladiator with a crested helmet, perhaps of the class of the *hoplomachi*.[1] Defeated, he has dropped his shield and moves to our right, raising his left hand in a one-finger gesture to petition for his life. His right arm hangs by his side, still clutching a narrow-bladed sword. The figure-type is a familiar one in gladiatorial representations and recurs in more or less identical form in a stucco relief at Pompeii (lowered hand empty, raised hand with all fingers extended),[2] in a mosaic from Zliten in Tripolitania,[3] and in a terracotta relief perhaps from Cuma, now in Brussels (the lowered hand behind the back);[4] in each scene, as here, the discarded shield lies at the gladiator's feet. In addition to his helmet, the Colchester figure wears a short loin-cloth (*subligaculum*) belted at the waist; whether he also has a breastplate and greaves (*ocreae*) is uncertain, and there is no trace of the normal arm-guard (*manica*) on the right arm. The shield, lying in the bottom right corner of the panel, is of a large semi-cylindrical type and is painted white on the exterior, presumably to simulate silver; it carries a pink emblem of uncertain form, set within a red and yellow rectangular frame. Fragments of another gladiator, perhaps the victorious opponent, including his belt and shield, have survived, but there is too little to shed light on his pose and class.

The figures are finely painted in pink with over-painting in yellow and white. The skill and delicacy of the work is fully consistent with a date in the last decades of the first century and has much in common with some painted details from the Neronian phase at Fishbourne, namely the fragments of a candelabrum containing fruits resting on a disc and a tiny piece which carries part of a shrimp (?) (No. 17). These objects, like the Colchester gladiators, are shown against a green background, a rare feature in Roman painting.[5]

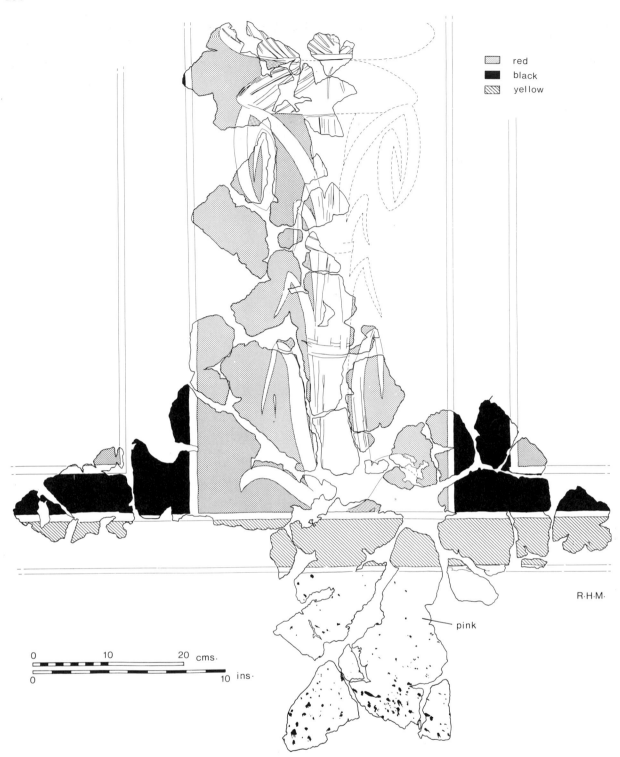

red
black
yellow

R·H·M·

pink

0   10   20 cms.

0   10 ins·

FIG. 15   No. 10 (A): Colchester, reconstructed fragments of wall-decoration from house in Balkerne Lane. The candelabrum is carried out in white, cream and pink. Scale 1:5.
(Drawing by R.H. Moyes)

The frame of our scene is carried out in stripes of purple, yellow, white, red and orange. At the bottom is an extended area of pinkish red, and it is tempting to conjecture that the panel was set in the middle of one of the fields whose lower corners survive in (A); this would accord with a regular practice in the Pompeian Fourth Style of wall-decoration (flourishing at the time of Pompeii's destruction in 79).

Reference: *Catalogue* (Newsletter of the Colchester Archaeological Trust), i (Summer, 1977), pp. 5–6.

Excavator: P. Crummy, Colchester Archaeological Trust.

[1]On the classes of armour and gladiators see G. Lafaye, in Dar.-Sag. ii (1892), pp. 1583-90; *EAA* iii (1960), pp. 937-47.

[2]F. Mazois, *Les ruines de Pompéi*, i (1824), pl. XXXII (fig. I, extreme right); cf. J. Overbeck and A. Mau, *Pompeji in seinen Gebüden, Alterhümern und Kunstwerken* (1884), p. 189 f., fig. 108. A more sedate version of the type occurs in the same frieze (Mazois, *loc. cit.* (fig. III, second gladiator from left); Overbeck-Mau, *op. cit.*, fig. 109) and in the relief at Chieti (*Studi Miscellanei*, x (1963-64), pl. XXXVII, fig. 89).

[3]S. Aurigemma, *I mosaici di Zliten* (1926), p. 159. fig. 94. On the dating, G. Ville, 'Essai de datation de la mosaique des gladiateurs de Zliten', *Mosaique* i, pp. 147 ff.

[4]D. Faccenna, in *Bullettino del Museo della Civiltà Romana*, xix (*Bull. Comm.*, lxxvi, 1956-58), p. 41 (n. 7),pl. VIII, 2. Cf. also a samian figure-type: F. Oswald, *Index of Figure Types on Terra Sigillata* (1936-37), pl. XLIX, no. 1047. A similar pose could be used also for a victorious gladiator: cf. Faccenna, *art. cit.*, p. 74 and fig. 15; *Germania* lv (1977), p. 119 and pl. 24.

[5]The shrimp (?), however, has a more turquoise ground and may derive from a marine decoration like those from Southwell and Sparsholt (Nos. 34; 37, C).

No. 11 *COLCHESTER, Essex.   Courtyard house outside north gate. Second quarter of second century. Now (1979) with the Colchester Archaeological Trust, East Hill House (in storage). FIG. 16.

Remains of panel-decoration from west wall of room in north wing (Middleborough site, excavated 1978). The reconstruction is based on fragments *in situ* at the base of the wall and in the adjacent demolition debris.

Above a pink baseboard there was a dado consisting of yellow rectangular panels, sometimes framed by white lines, on a grey ground. This was crowned by a continuous pale green border, 4.5 cm wide, edged by white lines. In the main zone the whole surface appears to have been pinkish red apart from further pale green borders, again edged by white lines, but here rather narrower (2.5 cm), which formed large rectangular fields. These were separated, according to the normal fashion, by narrow intervals. Further fragments suggest that this scheme was surmounted by a white zone shaded with stripes of green to suggest a stucco cornice.

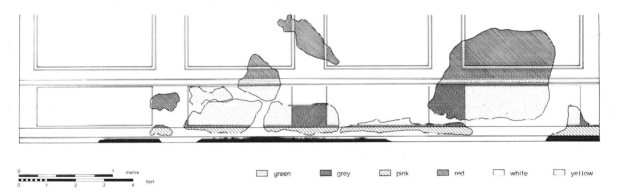

green   grey   pink   red   white   yellow

FIG. 16 No. 11: Colchester, Middleborough site: reconstruction of wall-decoration. Scale, 1:40.
(Drawing by P. Crummy and B. Stannard, adapted by R.J. Ling)

The closest parallels for the scheme of the main zone, painted entirely in one colour apart from framing bands, are two decorations in House XXI, 2 at Verulamium (No. 41, E, F). Here one room had green walls with panels formed by red bands, another red walls with panels formed by yellow and purple (?) bands; in each example, as at Colchester, the coloured bands were edged with white lines.

Unpublished.

Excavators: H. Brooks and P. Crummy, Colchester Archaeological Trust.

No. 12. COLLINGHAM (Dalton Parlours), Yorks. Villa, bath-building. Third or fourth century (the building was destroyed after *c.* 360). Now in Leeds, City Museum (on loan). PLS. XXXVI-XXXVIII. FIGS. 17-20.

A corner of a ceiling-decoration and three pieces of wall-decoration, restored from fragments found in the north-east corner of the hypocaust of the western room (1977 excavations).

(A) Ceiling-decoration (1.62 m × 1.59 m). On a white ground, an all-over pattern of contiguous octagons (43.5 to 45.5 cm across) with small square panels in the interstices and triangles along the edges. The main frames are painted, presumably in imitation of stucco or stone relief, in three grades of watery greyish yellow, darker along the edges and lighter towards the centre, where they give way to a plain white strip suggesting a highlight. The octagons and interstitial fields have single inner border-lines with beaded corners, some painted purple and others grey-yellow. Within the octagons there are roundels with green, purple, or orange frames; again the colours are graded in three ever-lightening shades to a white central stripe, and inside and outside runs a single line of greyish-yellow.

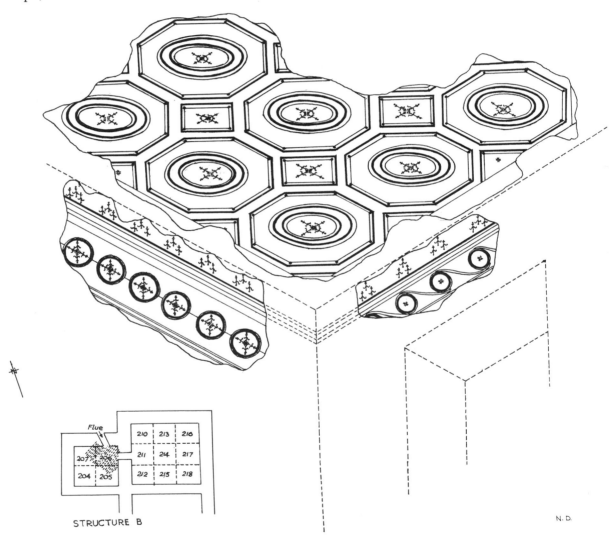

FIG. 17   No. 12: Collingham (Dalton Parlours), conjectural arrangement of restored ceiling- and wall-plaster.
(Drawing by N. Davey)

Within each roundel and each of the little square fields is an identical ornament executed in red and consisting of four V-shaped elements set together, point inwards, with stylised plant-motifs growing out from them. The plant-motifs have two pairs of curling offshoots, the outer pair smaller than the inner, and they end at both base and tip with a tiny knob. The triangles along the edge contain just the cluster of V-elements, here set close to the hypotenuse. The ceiling is framed by broad bands of colour, purple on one side, yellow on the adjacent side.

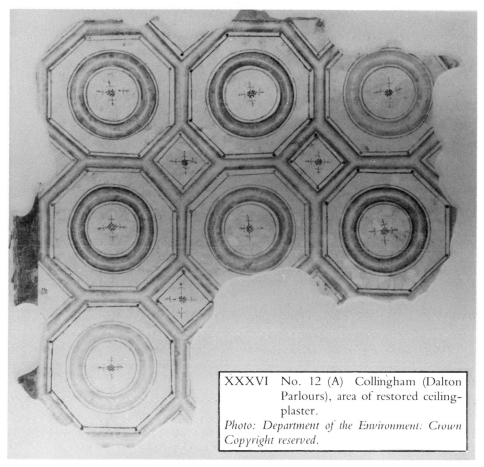

XXXVI No. 12 (A) Collingham (Dalton Parlours), area of restored ceiling-plaster.
Photo: Department of the Environment: Crown Copyright reserved.

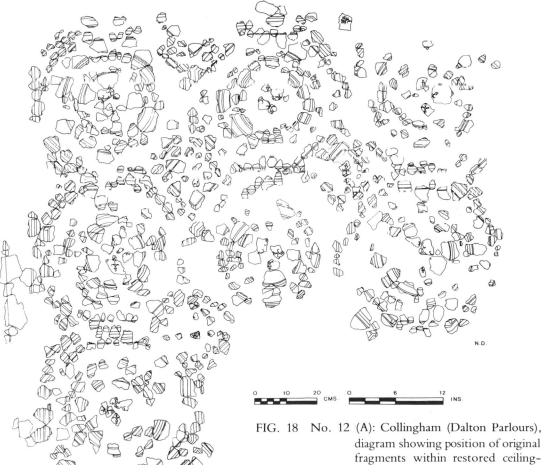

N.D.

0 10 20 CMS.   0   6   12 INS.

FIG. 18 No. 12 (A): Collingham (Dalton Parlours), diagram showing position of original fragments within restored ceiling-decoration. Scale, 1:12.
(Drawing by N. Davey)

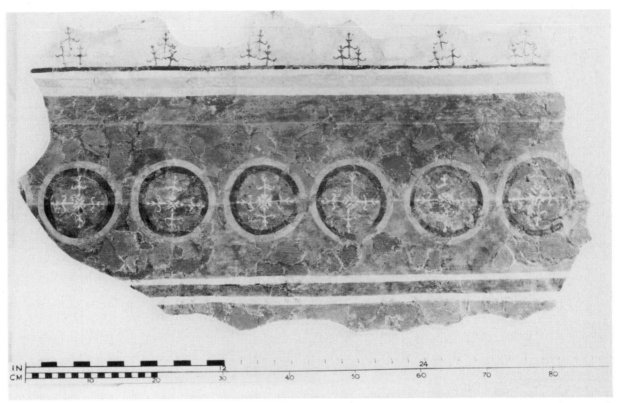

XXXVII   No. 12 (B)   Collingham (Dalton Parlours), restored frieze of roundels.

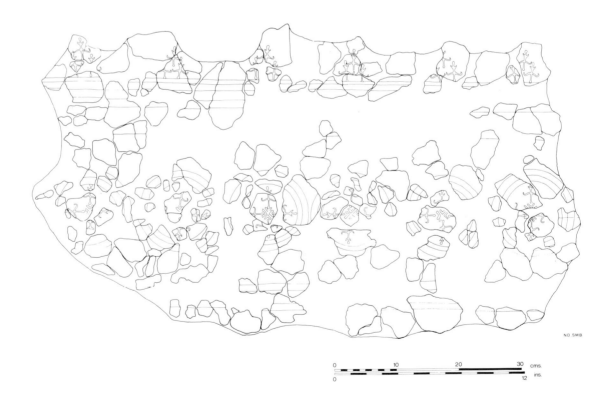

FIG. 19   No. 12 (B): Collingham (Dalton Parlours), restoration of part of painted frieze from bath-building. Diagram showing position of original fragments. Scale, 1:6.

(Drawing by N. Davey and Tina Baddeley)

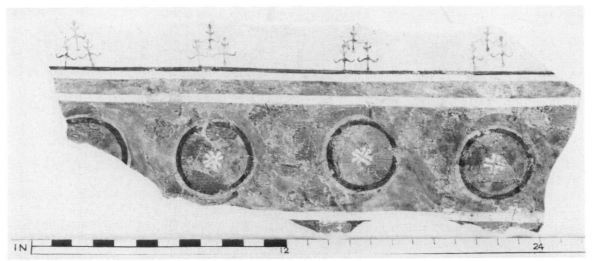

XXXVIII No. 12 (C) Collingham (Dalton Parlours), restored frieze with cable pattern.

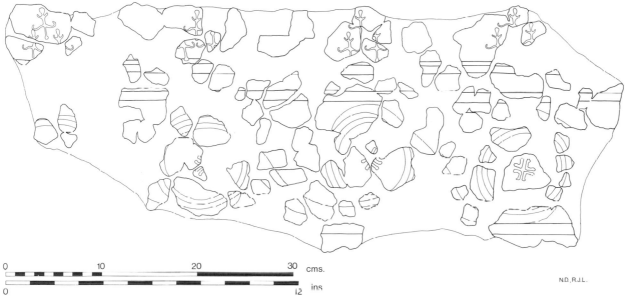

FIG. 20 No. 12 (C)· Collingham (Dalton Parlours), restoration of part of painted frieze from bath-building. Diagram showing position of original fragments. Scale, 1·4

(*Drawing by N. Davey and R.J. Ling*)

(B) 88 cm × 51 cm. A series of roundels (outer diameter 13.0 cm), framed by contiguous bands of yellow (outside) and purple (inside), sits astride the division between a red and a yellowish-green band, so that the enclosed area is half red, half green. Each roundel contains a white motif identical to the ornaments in the roundels of the ceiling. Beyond the red and green bands, which are each 11.5 to 12.0 cm wide, are different sequences of colour. The green band is followed by a purple stripe between two white stripes, and, beyond this, the edge of a red zone or panel; the red band by a narrower green band, a yellow stripe on a white ground, and a narrow purple stripe. From the latter grows a series of ornaments based on the plant-motifs which form the arms of the ornaments in the ceiling-medallions, here painted olive-green and arranged in sets of three, the middle one higher than the other two.

(C) 65 cm × 26 cm. A kind of cable-pattern set in a green band 13 cm wide and consisting of small roundels (outer diameter 9.5 cm) framed by contiguous lime-green (outside) and black (inside) bands and linked by red S-curved ribbons which run from the top of each roundel to the bottom of the next. Within the roundels are white ornaments compounded of four V-elements arranged with points inwards. Outside the green band come different sequences: on one side a white stripe and part of a purple stripe, on the other a red stripe on a white ground, followed by the same narrow purple stripe and olive-green ornaments as in (B) above.

(D) 32 cm × 21 cm. The corner of a white panel with purple and yellow inner border-lines. The main border is formed by a pinkish-orange stripe and a red band. Beyond this, on one side, is a white band between olive-green stripes and part of a purple zone.

A striking feature of the three pieces of wall-decoration is the bright colouring, with red, olive-green, purple and white dominant. Pieces (B) and (C) are best interpreted as horizontal friezes above the panels of the main zone, perhaps therefore set slightly lower than in the perspective drawing (FIG 17). Piece (D) is probably the corner of one of the panels of the main zone.

An interesting technical feature is that the V-elements and plant motifs of (A), (B) and (C) seem to have been printed with stamps rather than painted freehand. Further fragments of plaster not incorporated in the reconstructions show the same stamped elements in different colours and combinations: most strikingly, sets of V's arranged in alternating series to form a reticulate pattern, white or orange on a black ground. The only possible parallel known to the writers for this use of stamps is from another Yorkshire site, the fort at Malton (No. 28).

The design of the ceiling belongs to a favourite Roman type. Octagonal patterns are found all over the Empire, both in painting and in stucco relief, the first examples occurring in the mid first century A.D. Our precise pattern, with rows of octagons contiguous along one side containing roundels, can be paralleled in the stuccoed vault of a stairway in Nero's Domus Transitoria in Rome (here with the interstitial squares set parallel with rather than diagonally to the axes of the vault) and in painted ceilings from Gaul (Paris, Strasbourg, Pierrebuffière), Germany (Berchtesgaden) and Libya (Sabratha).[1] For a British parallel at Wroxeter, probably Antonine or later, see No. 51. The idea of imitating stone or stuccowork by purely pictorial means is also fairly common in interior decoration, for instance for ovolos and other enrichments (York, No. 52, A, and the ceiling-coffers of the Constantinian palace beneath the cathedral at Trier)[2] or figures (painted frieze of centaurs in the House of the Menander at Pompeii).[3] Another British ceiling-decoration inspired by the same idea has been identified at Gadebridge, Herts. (No. 19).

Further fragments of wall-painting were found in the larger, eastern room of the Dalton Parlours bath-house. In these there are two layers of decoration, the later of which seems to correspond in its somewhat coarse technique to the plaster from the western room, while the earlier has a well-burnished surface and a predominant use of yellow, both suggestive of a date in the second century or earlier.

Unpublished.

Excavator: P. Mayes, West Yorkshire Metropolitan County Council.

[1]Domus Transitoria: G. Carettoni, in *Not. Scav.* 1949, p. 54, fig. 5. Paris, Rue de l'Abbé d'Epée: *Gallia* xxxv (1977), p. 323 and fig. 5; H. Eristov, in *Cahiers de la Rotonde* ii (1979), pp. 15–21, figs. 1–6, 13 (first half of second century?). Strasbourg: F. Petry and E. Kern, in *Cahiers alsaciens d'archéologie, d'art et d'histoire* xviii (1974), pp. 70–72, fig. 7; cf. *Gallia* xxxii (1974), pp. 382–3 (second or third century). Pierrebuffière: F. Delage, in *Gallia* x (1952), p. 16 (no. 23) and fig. 14 (dating uncertain). Marzoll, near Berchtesgaden: R. Christlein, in *Bayerische Vorgeschichtsblätter* xxviii (1963), p. 44, pl. I (2) (second half of second century). Sabratha: Aurigemma, pl. 124 (top right).
[2]Reusch, pp. 236–46.
[3]A. Maiuri, *La Casa del Menandro* (1933), pp. 64–74, figs. 25–33, pl. VIII.

No. 13. DORCHESTER, Dorset. Poundbury cemetery, Mausoleum R 8. Mid fourth century. Now in Dorchester, Dorset County Museum. PLS. XXXIX–XLII, CX. FIGS. 21, 22.

Two areas of wall- and vault-decoration reconstructed from fragments fallen in southern part of mausoleum. Excavations 1969–70.

(A) Lower part of wall (84 cm wide × 63 cm high). The restoration shows a black dado carrying remains of two plants, one with thick green leaves, the other a clump of reeds coloured green with white highlights. Above this come broad red and blue bands and a narrow

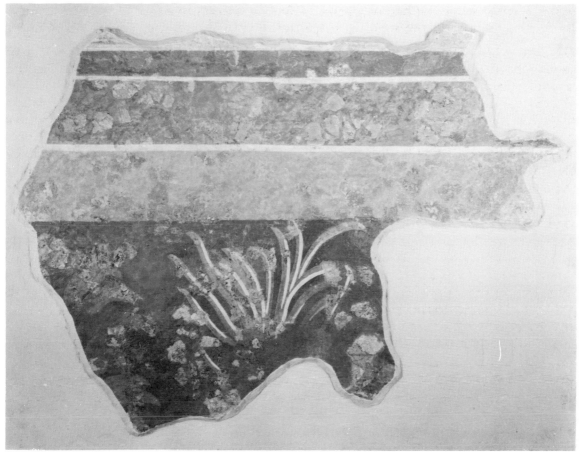

XXXIX No. 13 (A) Dorchester (Poundbury), restored piece of dado in Mausoleum R 8.

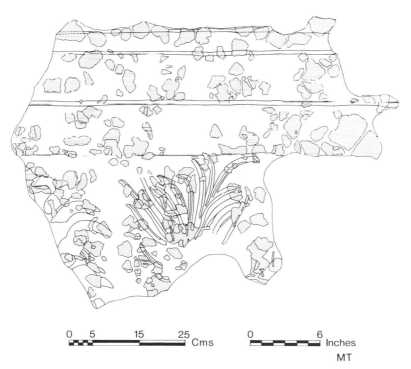

FIG. 21 No. 13 (A): Dorchester (Poundbury), restoration of dado with plants from
Mausoleum R 8. Diagram showing position of original fragments. Scale, 1:8.
(Drawing by Margaret Tremayne)

purple one, each band separated from the next by a white stripe. For an earlier example of clumps of reeds in the dado see No. 7 (Chester).

(B) Upper part of wall and spring of vault (87 cm wide × 1.275 m high). On the wall are the heads and shoulders of four standing male figures, two-thirds lifesize, part of a continuous series on a pale blue ground. The figures are represented at two levels, those in the background higher than those in front, in accordance with the familiar convention of vertical perspective adopted increasingly in Roman art from the second century onwards to express background scenes and figures. In the back row, at the left, is a man with black hair and beard, who stands frontally but turns his head to look to his right. He wears a light purple cloak, its folds picked out by light blue and dark purple lines, fastened at the right shoulder; in front of the same shoulder, leaning slightly to the left, passes a staff, indicated in black with a continuous white highlight along the left edge. The face of the second figure in the back row has worn away, but

FIG. 22   No. 13 (B): Dorchester (Poundbury), restoration of figure-frieze and part of ceiling
from Mausoleum R 8. Diagram showing position of original fragments. Scale, 1:8.
(Drawing by Magaret Tremayne)

traces remain of pale green drapery with a black band on his left shoulder. Beside the head is another staff, here preserved to its tip, which is decorated with a round knob. Overlapping this second figure at the right is a beardless man wearing dark purple drapery with folds indicated by light purple and grey lines. His head, too, is turned to his right but is, in addition, slightly lowered; a staff again passes in front of the right shoulder.

In the foreground in front of the middle figure, his head at a very similar angle to the last described, stands an elderly man whose ruddy face contrasts sharply with his hair, which is yellow with white highlights. He wears a white tunic or dalmatic with black neckline and *clavi*. Traces of a further foreground figure with a brownish-red skin-colouring survive at the left.

From elsewhere along the south wall came fragments of other draped figures, including parts of two clean-shaven faces, one of which wore a 'close-fitting white hat and red garments over the shoulder'. One fragment showed the lower end of a staff with a knobbed (probably double-knobbed) terminal and part of a hand holding it. Another piece bore traces of a small Chi-Rho in white against a blue background.

Photo: Dorchester Excavation Committee.

XL No. 13 (B) Dorchester (Poundbury), fragments of figure-frieze from Mausoleum R 8, before restoration. See also PL. CX in colour.

It is difficult, given the state of the original fragments, to make judgements on the style, but one well-preserved head restored from fragments found at the west end of the south wall shows a combination of a strong, dark outline and an impressionistic treatment of the features, which are rendered in quick strokes of flesh-pink, peach, pale purple, white and lemon-yellow (PL. XLII). A striking feature of the series of figures is the extent to which variety has been pursued. The size and angle of the heads, the colouring of hair and faces, the presence or absence of beards, the colouring of the drapery — all are details in which the changes are rung from figure to figure. Yet the heads preserved, which come from the west half of the south wall, are all more or less turned to look right (that is to the east).

Above the heads of the figures traces of horizontal bands of colour have been restored, curving over into the vault. The sequence runs: black, white, pale blue, white, purple, red, white (white and purple stripes between the last two). The width of the bands is not always certain. In the last zone the white has a pinkish tinge grading to greenish. The section restored gives no idea how the central part of the ceiling was decorated; but fragments of further figures

XLI   No. 13 (B)   Dorchester (Poundbury), restored section of figure-frieze from Mausoleum R 8.

and drapery in green, white and crimson have been ascribed to the ceiling on the basis of the deep level at which they were found and of the impressions of reed bundles on the reverse.

The interpretation of the paintings remains a matter for speculation. The south wall included at least nine figures, and assuming that the series was continuous for the whole length of eighteen feet (approximately 5.50 m) there would have been thirty-one or two in all. Whether they were all looking east, like those on the right half of the wall, or whether the missing figures of the other half of the wall were looking west, creating a focal point at the centre of the series, is entirely uncertain. Nor can we identify the figures with any confidence. The fact that they lack nimbi, the characteristic attribute of divinities and allegorical figures in the fourth century, suggests that they are human; and it is possible that the staffs with knobbed terminals are the insignia of some civil office. It is interesting to note that, if the series of figures was carried all the way round the interior of the mausoleum, there could have been a total of about one hundred figures, the number of the local *ordo* of decurions. Perhaps the mausoleum, one of the only two painted monuments in the parts of the Poundbury cemetery so far excavated (about two acres), belonged to one of their number. But this is, of course, little better than guesswork. Another theory, suggested by Professor J.M.C. Toynbee, namely that the persons portrayed are perhaps relations or ancestors of the deceased gathered for the ceremony of interment or the annual commemoration of the dead, though more probable, is equally difficult to substantiate.

References: C.J.S. Green, in *PDNHAS*, xci (1969), p. 184; xcii (1970), p. 138; idem, *The Funerary Wall Paintings and Cemetery at Poundbury, Dorchester, Dorset* (B.A. dissertation, London, 1971); Wacher, p. 326, pl. 62; Liversidge 1977, p. 99 f., fig. 5.9.
Excavator: C.J.S. Green, Dorchester Excavation Committee.

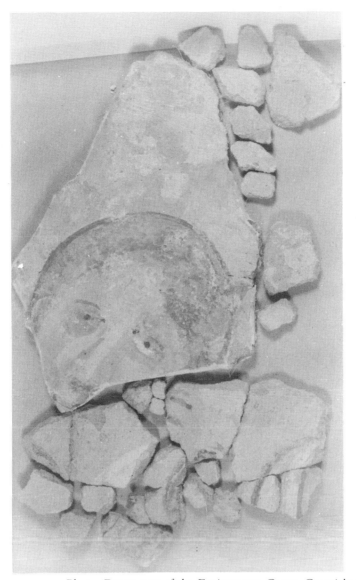

XLII   No. 13 (B)   Dorchester (Poundbury), further fragments from figure-frieze.

No. 14. ★DOVER, Kent.   House.   Second half of second or early third century (the painted rooms were largely destroyed and buried by the construction of the wall of the Saxon Shore Fort about 270). *In situ.* FIG. 23.

Painted wall-plaster with illusionistic architectural schemes (discovered in 1971) is preserved on the walls of Rooms 2, 3 and 4 to a maximum height of nearly two metres. In each room the scheme was more or less identical: a projecting podium, viewed from above, surmounted by a series of panels separated by pilasters. The pilasters carried semi-columns on their front faces and rested on a low plinth which was also carried along the foot of the intervening panels; these panels had broad borders of different colours framing a white field, and in front of each, shown as if resting on the podium, was a different object (torches, plant-sprays, etc.).

The decoration is best preserved in Room 2. Here the front face of the podium, about 50 cm high, is formed by greenish-black panels speckled yellow and divided by white lines running along purple stripes; there is an alternation of broad and narrow panels corresponding to the articulation of the main zone above. The upper surface is brownish-yellow. The plinth beneath the pilasters and in front of the intervening panels is coloured in shades of pink, light for the horizontal surfaces, darker for the vertical, so as to give the impression of light falling from above. At the same time this light-source must be at the central point of the wall, since it glances off the visible sides of the projecting plinths, which are shown perspectivally receding towards a central vanishing axis. The shading of the semi-columns, too, denotes a central light-source. These semi-columns are yellow with brown shading, and the pilasters behind them brownish-pink; both have Attic Ionic base-mouldings.

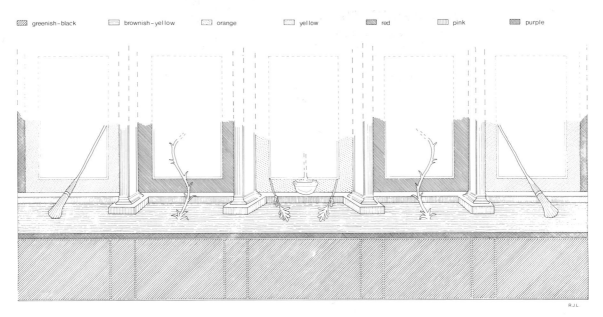

FIG. 23   No. 14: Dover, 'Painted House': partial reconstruction of south wall in Room 2 (not to scale). The torch is brown and yellow, the plant-forms yellowish-green, and the pilasters and semi-columns again shades of brown and yellow.

(Drawing by R.J. Ling)

Of the panels in the main zone the lower parts of seven survive: three in the right half of the west wall, one at the left end of the north wall, and three in the left half of the south wall. There were evidently five along the north and south walls, and three to north of the doorways in the east and west walls; what happened on the spur-walls to the south of these two doorways is unclear. The colours of the panel-frames, like the lighting and the perspective, were symmetrical round the central point: from outside in, yellow, red, and orange. In the one surviving corner (north-west) there was a broad purple band in lieu of a pilaster. The objects represented in front of the panels were as follows. North wall (left to right): (1) an inverted torch leaning with its handle to the right, (2–5) lost. South wall (left to right): (1) a torch as on the north wall, (2) a plant tendril, apparently growing from the top of the podium, winding up the centre of the panel, (3) two inverted leafy (palm?) branches leaning at either side and, in the middle resting on the plinth, a bowl from which grows a vertical stem, (4) lost, (5) the bottom of another inverted torch. West wall (right to left): (1) a stem with a fillet tied to it, perhaps the lower part of a *thyrsus*, (2) an inverted leafy (palm?) branch leaning to the right, a fillet tied to the stem, (3) a bowl. All these objects cast shadows, again broadly according with a central light-source. East wall: (1–3) lost.

In Room 3, where the plaster is preserved to the foot of the panels on the east wall, the main differences are that the front face of the podium is coloured reddish-purple instead of greenish-black and that the sequence of colours in the panel-frames is varied (from the left: red, yellow, orange).

In Room 4, where the plaster again survives on the east wall, the front face of the podium is once more greenish-black. There was room here for only three panels (still shown with central-ised perspective). Traces remain of objects resting on the podium.

The only other painted plaster preserved *in situ* belongs to a simple decoration of white panels with red border-lines in the corridor which runs along the north side of the house. But large quantities of fragments from the ceilings and/or upper parts of the walls of the main painted rooms were also recovered and are currently being reconstructed; it is thought that there were friezes incorporating human figures and other motifs, and that the ceilings were decorated with geometric patterns of some form.

The realistic architectural forms and *trompe l'oeil* treatment of the wall-decorations are very reminiscent of the Second Pompeian Style, which had passed out of fashion in Italy about two centuries previously. It is very rare in the Second Style, however, to find the particular formula used here: a continuous podium supporting semi-columns and pilasters attached to a closed wall. The nearest parallel is in Room IV of the House of the Griffins on the Roman Palatine (*c.* 90-70 B.C.), where however the upper surface of the podium is barely indicated, the semi-columns are not attached to pilasters, and there is no clear articulation of semi-columns and intervening panels (in fact it is possible to argue that free-standing columns, and not semi-columns, were intended).[1] Again, although it is not uncommon in the mid Second Style to find torches, branches and other objects resting on the podium between columns,[2] the surrealist notion of a plant growing from the podium is totally alien to that style.

The decoration clearly belongs to one of the phases of revival or variation of the earlier styles which characterize Roman painting of the post-Pompeian period. Detailed discussion of the parallels and dating must await the full publication of the Dover building. There are certain similarities with the decoration of a house discovered in Via Merulana in Rome in 1960, perhaps datable *c.* 140-160; this employs a similar colour-scale (red, yellow and purple predominate) and shows a similar continuous podium and, in the main zone, a similar combination of flat, framed panels and flanking columns. But its execution is much neater and more delicate, its ornamental detail much richer (including small animals and still-life vignettes), and its polychromy more evenly spread but at the same time less logically and coherently used.[3] A rather better parallel might be the painting of the Paedagogium on the Roman Palatine, dated to the Severan period or a little later.[4] Here the podium is occupied by large-scale standing figures, but the treatment of the architecture, with its freer execution, stronger modelling, and predominantly light ground, is very reminiscent of the Dover decorations.

Another resemblance between Dover and these second- and third-century paintings in Rome is the fact that the light-source in both is at the centre of the wall, whereas in the true Second Style the light generally (though not invariably) falls from the sides, often in accordance with the real source of light in the room.[5]

The column-bases are interesting in that, though sketchily rendered, they seem to belong to the type used in the eastern Empire: the upper torus is shallow and set well back from the lower one, apparently on the line of the top of the intervening scotia.[6] Slightly similar in form are the bases from the legionary baths in Bridge Street, Chester; but there the scotia has become a simple cavetto, and we cannot think of them as in any true sense a parallel.[7] The Dover painter, if not himself an immigrant artist, has clearly taken the base-type, along with the whole of the decorative framework, from imported pattern-books — unlike his colleagues in Verulamium (No. 44, A) and York (No. 52, A), whose column-bases are closer to local types.

References: J.M.C. Toynbee, in *Kent Archaeological Review*, 29 (Autumn 1972) pp. 262-4; *Britannia*, iii (1972), p. 351, pl. XXVIII B; iv (1973), p. 322; *Current Archaeology*, iv (1973-74), pp. 84-5; v (1975-77), pp. 304-5; B.J. Philp, *The Roman Painted House at Dover* (guide-book, n.d.), *passim.*
Excavator: B.J. Philp, Kent Archaeological Rescue Unit.

[1]Engemann, p. 15 and n. 9, pls. 1, 2; 2, 1. Generally on the motif of columns on pedestals or podia in the early Second Style, *ibid.*, pp. 15-27.
[2]E.g. in the villa at Oplontis (Andreae and Kyrieleis, figs. 4-10, 17, 23).
[3]Via Merulana paintings: De Vos 1969, pp. 149-65, pls. LXIII-LXVI; H. Mielsch, in *Affreschi*, pp. 38-41, pls. XI-XV. Cf., for a comparison with true Second-Style painting, Barbet 1978, pp. 105 f.
[4]Wirth, pp. 125-9, pls. 29-31; W. Helbig, *Führer durch die öffentlichen Sammlungen klassischer Altertümer in Rom*, ii (4th ed., 1966), pp. 858-61 (no. 2076). On the dating Mielsch 1978, p. 170, n. 75. Another provincial decoration with an illusionistic podium, the garden-paintings in Room 36 of the House of the Consul Attalus at Pergamum (Asia Minor), is probably to be dated to the second half of the second century: Strocka, p. 100.
[5]Cf. Engemann, plates; Barbet 1978, p. 105. The same lighting is employed in the tablinum of the Inn of the Peacock at Ostia (*Mon. pitt. ant.* iii. Ostia iv. G. Gasparri, *Le pitture della Caupona del Pavone* (1970), p. 19).

[6]On the distinction between eastern and western Roman Ionic bases see L. Shoe Merritt, 'The geographical distribution of Greek and Roman Ionic bases', *Hesperia*, xxxviii (1969), pp. 186–204.

[7]Blagg, p. 60 and fig. 4.4. Mr. Blagg informs us that he does not regard the upper moulding in this example as the equivalent of the normal Ionic upper torus, but rather as an astragal *above* the main part of the base (which would thus have only one torus).

No. 15.   ★DROITWICH, Worcs.   Villa. Late second or third century (the building was destroyed by fire at the end of the third century). Now in Birmingham, City Museum and Art Gallery (on loan). PL. XLIII.

Fragments of painted plaster were found in hypocausts on either side of the central apsidal room (1967 excavations). The best pieces have been partially reconstructed at the University of Birmingham and mounted in slabs by conservators at the Museum.

(A) Restored panel *c*. 42 × 68 cm.[1] Fragments of a curly-haired Cupid painted in shades of brown and purple on a white ground. His left arm seems to have been lowered, his right raised.

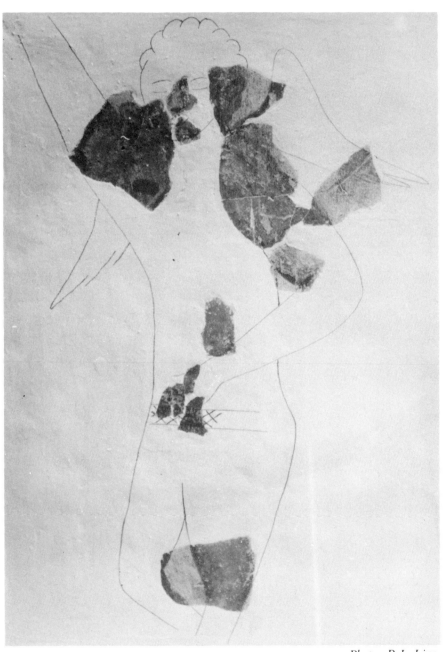

XLIII   No. 15 (A)   Droitwich, fragments of Cupid.   *Photo: R.J. Ling*

The painting is crude, with flat washes of colour and heavy contours; the wings are uncomfortably disposed, the left one splayed out above the left shoulder, the right one hanging behind the right shoulder. The positioning of the smaller fragments, which are assigned in the restoration to the torso and legs, is uncertain. From the east hypocaust; ascribed to the apsidal room.

(B) *c.* 48 × 36 cm. Part of a garland of red and purple pointed leaves, with yellow and green tendrils curling off to either side, all on a white ground. The treatment is fully two-dimensional. From the same source as (A) above. The surface is concave, and the piece should therefore be ascribed to a vault, or perhaps to the back of the apse of the central room.

(C) (i) 29 × 31 cm. (ii) 23 × 21 cm. Two groups of fragments showing swags suspended between vertical lines of purple. The first shows the right end of a garland, whose lower half is red, and the upper half pale green, fastened by a red ribbon whose ends float above. The second shows the left end of a red swag adjacent to three purple lines. From the west hypocaust.

(D) Various fragments of panel-frames, green, red, purple and yellow on a white ground; the angles are ornamented in the normal manner with pyramids of red or purple spots. Included is a column (?) sketched in pale green on a white ground; it is decorated with veins of marbling (?) or spiralling tendrils (?). A distinctive feature of the frames is a green band decorated with darker green spots (cf. Wroxeter, No. 51, and Introduction, pp. 50 f.). From the west hypocaust.

References: *JRS* lviii (1968), p. 187; D.F. Freezer, *From Saltings to Spa Town. The Archaeology of Droitwich* (n.d.), p. 5 and cover illustration.
Excavators: L.H. Barfield and R.A. Tomlinson, University of Birmingham and Department of the Environment.

¹The measurements could not be taken directly and are copied from the Museum labels.

No. 16. EAST BRENT, Somerset. Villa? Dating uncertain. Now in possession of J. Sheppard, Mark Causeway. PL. XLIV.

Pieces restored from fragments recovered during the construction of the M5 motorway in 1970.

(A) 57 cm long × 20 cm high. Part of a frieze with a scroll on a white ground. The scroll, set between black lines, consists of a series of thick green S-curved elements leaning against thin black volutes; each volute encloses a green leaf-ornament. Yellow zone above.

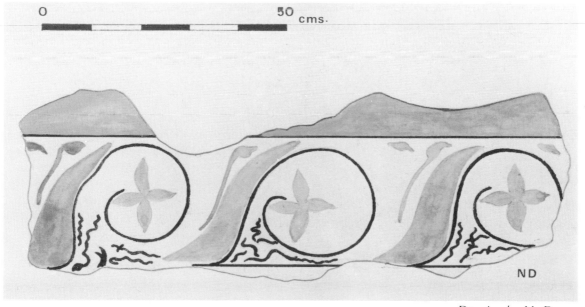

Drawing by N. Davey

XLIV   No. 16 (A)   East Brent, restored piece of plant-scroll.

(B) 22 cm × 27 cm. Corner of a panel bordered by a pale green frame (on one side 4.5 cm wide, on the other incomplete) between white lines. The interior of the panel is divided by a diagonal white line into yellow and red areas.

(C) 26.5 cm × 27 cm. Corner of a panel bordered by a black frame 5.5 cm wide between white lines. The interior of the panel is again divided by a diagonal white line into yellow and red areas.

The unusual form of the restored frieze and the unusual diagonal colour-divisions within the panels shed no light on the dating; we have been able to find no adequate parallels.[1]

Unpublished.

Excavators: J. Sheppard and P. Slocombe, M5 Research Committee.

[1]The diagonal colour-division perhaps represents a joint at the corner of a border, as in a much earlier decoration at Glanum in Gaul, where however there is no white dividing-line: Barbet 1974 a, figs. 24, 26, pl. VIII (first century B.C.). For a diagonal white line between two areas of the *same* colour, Drack, fig. 21 (Augst); cf. our Appendix, No. 2 (Aldborough).

No. 17. *FISHBOURNE, Sussex. Early palace (Period 1C). *c.* 60–70 (late Neronian period). Now in Fishbourne Museum. PL. CXIII.

Fragments of wall-plaster found in the make-up layers for the Period 2 palace. It is likely that the schemes included yellow and red fields with green interspaces. The latter sometimes carried richly-painted candelabra; one large group of fragments (approx. 36 cm wide × 24 cm high) shows a detail with a red plate from which hang white tassels and fillets and on which rest yellow fruits, each with a white highlight and orange shadows.

One tiny fragment carries a delicately painted shrimp (?) on a turquoise ground (approx. 4 cm × 4 cm). The shrimp has a yellow underside and orange back with white and purple rings.

Fragments with eight-petalled, star-like rosettes painted pink, red or green within inscribed circles may well derive from a ceiling-decoration like those in the entrance-passage of the Forum Baths at Pompeii and the vestibule of the Palaestra at Herculaneum.[1]

Reference: Cunliffe, i, p. 67 f.; ii, pp. 52–56, figs. 27, 28.
Excavator: B.W. Cunliffe, Chichester Civic Society.

[1]Barbet and Allag, pp. 997–9, figs. 28, 29 *a*.

No. 18. *FISHBOURNE, Sussex. Palace, Period 2. *c.* 75–100 (Flavian period). Now in Fishbourne Museum. PL. XLV.

Among the innumerable fragments of wall-plaster from the Flavian and later periods, the most remarkable is part of a landscape painting found in the filling of a ditch to the west of the north wing. The fragment (approx. 13 × 14 cm) comes from the top left corner of the picture and shows a black border 1.3 cm wide and a yellow surround, perhaps part of one of the main fields of the wall-scheme. In the picture-field the ground is pale blue with white squiggles; at the bottom is a dark red-purple building with a white entablature supported by thin white stalk-like columns and surmounted at the middle by a white pediment with blobs at the angles. Places where the paint has flaked reveal the sequence in which the colours were applied: the surrounding yellow originally covered the whole surface, the blue of the picture-field was painted over it, and finally the purple and white of the building were applied over the blue.

The impressionistic style is reminiscent of numerous landscape paintings of the Neronian and Vespasianic periods in Italy, including the well-known harbour-scene from Stabiae; but it would be rash to argue that the Fishbourne picture is by the same artist or school as any surviving examples.[1]

Reference: Cunliffe, i, p. 141 f.; ii, p. 57 f., pl. XIV.
Excavator: B. W. Cunliffe, Chichester Civic Society.

XLV No. 18 Fishbourne, fragment of landscape from Flavian palace.

[1] As suggested in the excavation-report (see bibliography). For the Stabiae harbour-scene see e.g. A. Maiuri, *Roman Painting* (1953), p. 123; and for other impressionistic 'villa landscapes' *Röm. Mitt.*, xxvi (1911), pls. VII, VIII; W.J.T. Peters, *Landscape in Romano-Campanian Mural Painting* (1963), pls. XXXV-XXXVIII; G. Picard, *Roman Painting* (1970), pls. XLVI, LVII.

No. 19. GADEBRIDGE, Herts. Villa. Second half of second century (late Antonine period). Now in Verulamium Museum. PL. XLVI. FIG. 24.

Area of ceiling-decoration reconstructed from fragments found in well.

91 cm × 85 cm. A pattern of square coffers containing acanthus rosettes set in medallions. The paths between the coffers are decorated with guilloche, and their points of intersection masked by simple rosette-like discs with four pawn-shaped shadows converging on a central circle; the coffers themselves have an inner border formed by a pair of lines connected by diagonal strokes. Apart from the outlines of the coffers and of the guilloche, which are rendered in red, the only colour used is greyish-yellow. The monochrome is clearly intended to reproduce the effect of coffering in stone or stucco relief, the guilloche being shaded on both sides, and the inner border on one, in both areas to suggest volume. A similar effect is sought in the hexagonal pattern of a ceiling from Collingham, Yorks. (No. 12, A).

The idea of using guilloche as a framing element may ultimately derive from mosaic floors,[1] but the immediate prototype for our decoration are the soffits of stone arches such as those of Titus in Rome and Trajan at Benevento,[2] and stuccoed vaults such as that of the recently excavated four-way arch at Herculaneum (Vespasianic).[3] In all these examples coffers containing rosettes are separated by a guilloche or spiral pattern along the dividing strips, and in the last-named its intersections are masked by discs similar to ours. Another painted imitation, though with narrower guilloche and more broadly spaced inner frames, occurs in a vault in Hadrian's Villa at Tivoli (117–138).[4]

The inner border with diagonal strokes is reminiscent of the simplified 'rope'-moulding found, variously positioned, in architectural carving in Italy and the eastern provinces during the Imperial period.[5] In Britain examples occur on second- and third-century altars and tombstones.[6]

Photo: Verulamium Museum.

XLVI   No. 19   Gadebridge, restored piece of ceiling plaster.

References: Davey 1972, p. 265 and fig. 12; Neal 1974, pp. 27, 200-3, fig. 89.
Excavator: D.S. Neal, Hemel Hempstead Excavation Society.

[1]For an early example of a mosaic pavement with square panels framed by a guilloche, Becatti, p. 226 f., no. 427, pl. LXII (beginning of first century A.D.); cf. Morricone Matini, p. 90 f. A similar two-ply guilloche is established as a framing element in the later mosaics of Pompeii (before 79): Blake 1930, p. 108, pls. 26 (1), 27 (4), 30 (2), 36 (3, 4), 39 (1), 42 (2).
[2]F.J. Hassel, *Der Trajansbogen in Benevent* (1966), pl. 33 (1, 2).
[3]Mielsch 1975 a, pp. 49 f., 133, pl. 32.
[4]Wirth, fig. 28; Borda, fig. on p. 95.
[5]For early-Imperial examples see De Vos 1975, p. 57 and n. 17. Further examples occur in the later second and third centuries, e.g. in the theatre at Philippi (between architrave and frieze), the Captives Façade at Corinth (architrave), the nymphaeum at Laodicea on the Lycus (architrave), and the arch of Septimius Severus in Rome (corbels).
[6]*Corpus Signorum Imperii Romani. Great-Britain*, i, l. E.J. Phillips, *Corbridge. Hadrian's Wall East of the North Tyne* (1977), nos. 230, 247, 258, 270.

FIG. 24   No. 19: Gadebridge, restoration of part of ceiling-decoration. Diagram showing
position of original fragments. Scale 1:8.

(Drawing by Yvonne Brown)

No. 20. ★†HARPHAM, Yorks. Villa. Dating uncertain. Now in Driffield, private
museum.

Fragments of painted plaster found in excavations in 1950 show various-coloured roundels
containing rosettes; clusters of leaves are grouped at points round the circumference. In the
most elaborate motif a yellow flower is surrounded by concentric rings of red, yellow, green
and red, with black spokes radiating towards a series of external ornaments with small
medallions containing birds and, in one place, a human figure.

The fragments suggest a ceiling-decoration or decorations like that from the market-hall in
Leicester, in which roundels were connected by plant-forms running parallel or diagonally to
the axes of the pattern (No. 23). The motif with radiating spokes is particularly closely related
to elements from another East Yorkshire villa, that at Brantingham (No. 4, C).

Reference: Liversidge 1969, pp. 139, 147, fig. 4.6.
Excavator: E. Mellor, Augustinian Society, Bridlington.

No. 21. KINGSCOTE, Glos. Building, part of a settlement of uncertain interpretation.
Late third or early fourth century. Now (1979) in site museum.| PLS. XLVII–XLVIII, CXX.

Large areas of decoration of south wall of Room 1, reconstructed from fragments found
(1976) collapsed within the room. Reconstruction is still in progress and many details remain
uncertain. Apart from a dado formed by panels of imitation marbling (white with blue, pink
and grey veins) framed by green bands, the whole wall was occupied by a figure-painting over

Photo: E.J. Swain

XLVII   No. 21   Kingscote, head of Cupid.

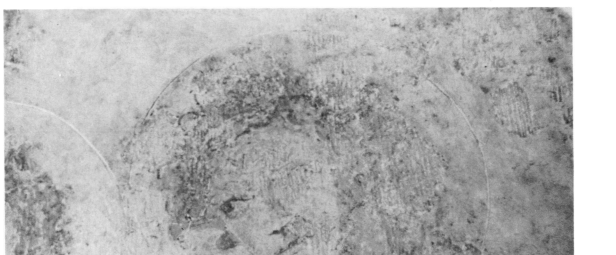

Photo: E.J. Swain

XLVIII   No. 21   Kingscote, head of female figure with nimbus.

two-thirds life-size. The over-all dimensions of the painting, which was framed by a purple band 9 cm wide set about 9 cm from the corners of the wall, would have been approximately 1.50 m high by 3.50 m long.

The background is a neutral greenish white; the only indications of a setting are a slight darkening to suggest the ground-surface at the bottom of the picture and traces of purple flowers visible on some fragments. The colours used are predominantly oranges, greens and purples. Flesh is pinkish-orange with red-purple shading, and drapery pale purple with dark purple shadows or pale green with dark green shadows. Other details are carried out in cream (e.g. the nimbi), slate-grey (the wing of the cupid), or pale blue (the enrichment round the rim of the seated figure's shield). In execution the work is skilful. Forms are normally modelled by shading, although in one or two places a more linear technique is employed, with strong red lines marking out the contours of the flesh. Some of the heads are almost impressionistic, their features being rendered in quick strokes of brown and purple. An individual quirk of the artist is his treatment of hands, which are given strikingly long and spindly fingers.

Four main areas have been reconstructed.

(A) 1.37 m wide × 1.15 m high (including frame). At the top, the upper parts of three female figures with nimbed heads; below, the upper part of a flying cupid. Of the female figures the central one is in frontal view, with a green drape hung from the left shoulder; she seems to bend her right arm to the side. The right-hand figure, of which only the head and shoulders are preserved, seems to be at a slightly higher level than its companion and leaning back towards her, as if seated and turning to see what the other is doing. She has a few traces of drapery, probably again green. The left-hand figure, which had a purple cloak slung across the bosom and over the left shoulder, is shown in profile to our right. It seems probable that its right arm was extended towards the adjacent figure; the restoration of these traces as a trumpet is problematic. The cupid below is flying in three-quarters view to our right with his head turned back and slightly lowered. A purple drape hangs from his left arm, while his right arm, to judge from a photograph taken at the time of excavation, passed across his chest.

(B) 1.81 m wide × 1.01 m high. At the left, the legs of the flying cupid; in the centre, the lower part of a seated figure; at the right, more uncertain traces. The cupid has his left leg advanced, with the end of his purple drape hanging over the thigh. (The back of his right leg has recently been reconstructed along with — a short distance to the left — the leg of an adult figure with purple drapery hanging to one side, perhaps seated on a stool.)

From the direction of the cupid, and perhaps held by him, a pale green ribbon runs diagonally down to the right, passing behind the thighs of the seated figure. The latter, its head and shoulders missing, is in three-quarters view to our left with its right leg extended and left arm hanging at the side; purple drapery hangs down the figure's back, passes under the left leg, and is gathered over the right. Against the seat, hiding it, rests an oval shield painted white with a pale blue bead-and-reel enrichment round the rim; the central boss is decorated with a design in black consisting of a quatrefoil of heart-shaped leaves enclosed by pelta-ornaments.

(C) 56 cm wide × 78 cm high. Part of the torso of a standing (?) figure, perhaps female. Whitish-green drapery hangs from the left shoulder and is gathered over the left forearm; the hand holds a reed.

(D) 50 cm wide × 1.32 m high. Adjacent to the vertical frame at the right end of the wall comes the left side of a seated figure with pale green drapery gathered over the forearm. The hand passes behind what appears to be a *calathus* containing red flowers (compare the *calathi* in the scenes of flower-picking Psyches in the great dining-room of the House of the Vettii at Pompeii).[1]

Further work remains to be done on the unplaced fragments and, until this has been completed, attempts at an interpretation are perhaps premature. But the scene was clearly mythological, and certain basic ingredients can be recognised: notably a seated martial figure and a cupid apparently flying towards it. We must look for a myth containing a love-element (appropriate enough in a room whose mosaic pavement featured a bust of Venus) and involving a martial deity or hero. Further, the seated figure has the long drapery of a female figure, but exposes the left leg in a gesture which would be quite unseemly in a martial goddess like Minerva.

The most convincing interpretation at the moment is that originally suggested by Professor J.M.C. Toynbee: Achilles in female dress on Skyros. The seated figure would be Achilles himself, the female figures would be the daughters of Lycomedes, and the cupid would symbolise the love between Achilles and one of the daughters, Deidameia. Further, the female figure holding a reed might possibly be Thetis, spying from the sea to observe her son's progress at court.[2]

There are, admittedly, problems with this interpretation. It is odd that the daughters of Lycomedes should be given nimbi, attributes more appropriate to goddesses and personifications than to mere princesses.[3] More serious, in other representations of the Skyros episode, Achilles is normally shown either seated with a lyre or on his feet in agitated movement, brandishing the shield and sword (or spear) which Odysseus and Diomedes have brought to lure him to war.[4] Here, however, although still seated, Achilles lacks the lyre and is provided with a shield whose position suggests that it is his own property rather than a newly-arrived temptation.

If the Skyros interpretation is retained, there are two alternatives: either Achilles has not yet responded to the call-to-arms and revealed himself, or this is a later scene in which he sits with, or takes his leave of, Lycomedes and family.

In the first, the shield remains a difficulty. Professor Toynbee, citing a scene on the Kaiseraugst silver dish in which Achilles, newly arrived on Skyros, conceals his nakedness with a shield,[5] argues that in some versions of the story he retained a shield throughout his sojourn on the island. Yet it seems odd that the hero, while nominally disguised as a woman, should vaunt his military potential by sitting with a shield at his side. It is easier to assume that the shield has been put there by Odysseus and his party. There is some support for this view on a sarcophagus from Crete in the British Museum, whose main face carried a relief which is reminiscent of our painting.[6] Achilles is seated with his drapery hanging behind him and gathered over his thighs so as to leave his extended left leg bare, as at Kingscote; he holds a helmet in his right hand, a shield rests against his legs, and a sheathed sword against his left arm. He looks back regretfully at Lycomedes and his daughters who are on the right, while the Greek warriors and a trumpeter blowing the call-to-arms are on the left. It appears that Achilles has been given his armour but lingers a moment on his throne, as though reluctant to be carried to war. Only the sound of the trumpet will galvanise him into action.

This could be the version depicted at Kingscote. Although there is no evidence in the restored parts of the painting for the presence of Odysseus, Diomedes or the trumpeter (the restored trumpet being problematic), some of the other elements in our scene can be paralleled in representations of the call-to-arms. The flying cupid appears on some of the sarcophagi which depict the subject;[7] while the figure with a reed may not be Thetis but a personification of a local stream rather like the possible river-god in the scene on the so-called Capitoline puteal.[8]

The second possibility is that Achilles has already been discovered and is now conversing with or taking his leave of Lycomedes. There is no Roman work of art which, to the knowledge of the writers, shows this precise moment in the story, but a series of gold reliefs from fourth-century B.C. *goryti* (Scythian bow-and-arrow cases) from South Russia presents a Greek cycle of scenes from Achilles's life in which a leavetaking or conversation-piece seems to follow the hero's self-betrayal.[9] These reliefs are arranged in two friezes. In the top frieze, after a scene showing the boy Achilles learning the use of the bow, there is a group of six figures which is best interpreted as Achilles revealing himself among the daughters of Lycomedes. He is advancing in agitated movement to the left, clutching an object like a scabbard in his right hand and looking back towards a female figure who is either dancing or fleeing in alarm, rather like the frightened girl in the Pompeian paintings of the subject.[10] The next scene, which begins at the end of the upper frieze and continues in the lower frieze, shows Lycomedes enthroned and holding a sceptre, Achilles seated facing him, and a group of four onlooking women, three seated and one standing, presumably the queen and three daughters. Achilles here is very similar to the seated figure at Kingscote. His drapery falls behind his shoulders, exposing the upper part of his body and his left leg, but covering his right; a shield lies behind him. In his right hand he holds a sword.

The next scene on the bow-case, showing a similar figure seated between two standing bearded men, who are evidently conversing with him while another bearded figure sits watching at the left, has been interpreted as Achilles's meeting with Agamemnon;[11] but it could possibly represent Lycomedes watching in distress while Odysseus and Diomedes persuade Achilles to return with them to Troy. If so, we would have an unattested early version of the story in which the unmasking of Achilles took place before the Greek deputation came to seek him.[12] This is, of course, speculation and does not seriously affect the interpretation of the two previous scenes.

Whether the Kingscote painting represents the moment before Achilles takes up the arms or a later stage of his sojourn on Skyros must remain an open question which only further reconstruction will resolve. But, in the present stage of the evidence, an interpretation based on some aspect of the story of Achilles on Skyros seems the most attractive available.

Among the many loose fragments of plaster from the wall still in storage is a group with what seems to be part of a painted Greek inscription, not yet deciphered.

References: Kingscote Archaeological Association. *The Chessalls Kingscote Excavations, 1975-76,* pp. 12, 23 f., fig. 6 (early reconstruction); *Britannia,* viii (1977), p. 413 and fig. 25 (early reconstruction); E.J. Swain, in *Glevensis,* xi (1977), p. 29; *Britannia* xii (1981).

Excavator: E.J. Swain, Kingscote Archaeological Association.

[1] E.g. A. Mau, *Pompeji in Leben und Kunst,* 2nd edn. (1908), p. 355, pl. IX (4), fig. 188; Reinach, pp. 94 (12, 13), 95 (1, 3, 4).

[2] We are deeply indebted to Professor Toynbee for discussing, in correspondence, her ideas on the Kingscote paintings. She does not necessarily agree with all the views expressed here.

[3] But for the range of mythological personages who might wear the nimbus see e.g. Levi 1947, p. 289 and n. 12. On the history of the nimbus, M. Collinet-Guérin, *Histoire du nimbe* (1961), and especially, for the Roman period, pp. 203 ff., 263 ff.

[4] Achilles on his feet: Strocka, pp. 107 f., n. 380; cf., for the sarcophagi, F. Baratte, 'Un sarcophage d'Achille inédit', *MEFRA,* lxxxvi (1974), pp. 773-812 (with bibl. on representations in other media, pp. 809 ff.). Seated with lyre: *ibid.,* p. 782 f.

[5] R. Laur-Belart, *Der spätrömische Silberschatz von Kaiseraugst* (1967), fig. 1.

[6] C. Robert, *Die antiken Sarkophagreliefs,* ii (1890), p. 31 f., no. 23.

[7] Examples in the Louvre (Baratte, *art. cit.* (note 4), figs. 1, 8 and *passim*), the Vatican Museum (*ibid.,* fig. 11), and the Villa Pamphili in Rome (Robert, *op. cit.* (note 6), ii, no. 33). Cf. Baratte, *art. cit.,* p. 787.

[8] H. Stuart-Jones (ed.), *A Catalogue of the Ancient Sculptures Preserved in the Municipal Collections of Rome. The Sculptures of the Museo Capitolino* (1912), p. 46 and pl. 9 top left (figure reclining on an urn and holding a sceptre).

[9] On goryti in general see W. Rätzel, 'Die skythischen Gorytbeschläge', *Bonner Jahrbücher* clxxviii (1978), pp. 163-180, and for the Achilles series *ibid.,* pp. 172-6; cf. V. Schiltz, in *Revue archéologique,* 1979, pp. 307-9; P.G.P. Meyboom, *Meded. Rome,* xl (1978), pp. 64 f., pl. 33, figs. 30, 31. For another, somewhat different, version of Achilles's leave-taking see possibly an Attic red-figure volute-krater by the Niobid Painter: E. Simon, *AJA,* lxvii (1963), pp. 57-61.

[10] See especially the version from the House of the Dioscuri (Naples Museum inv. 9110): Curtius, fig. 124.

[11] Originally by B.V. Farmakovsky: cf. Ratzel, *art. cit.* (note 9), p. 174; Meyboom, *art. cit.* (note 9), p. 65.

[12] This interpretation presupposes that Achilles's sex was originally unknown to Lycomedes and his daughters, as in Statius's version of events (*Achillaid* i); but surviving earlier writers do not adopt a clear position on whether the family of Lycomedes was privy to the concealment or not.

No. 22. LEICESTER. Insula XVI, courtyard house. Mid second century. Now in Leicester, Jewry Wall Museum. PLS. XXII, XLIX-LI, CXXI. FIGS. 25-27.

Three areas of wall-decoration from the peristyle of the courtyard, reconstructed partly from plaster found *in situ* (at the bottom of the wall in A), partly from jumbled fragments (collected according to a grid system). The house was built in the early second century, but the paintings are ascribed to a later renovation. Excavations in 1958.

(A) West wall (to left of central door).

(i) Lower part of the wall (2.71 m long × 87 cm high). Above a brownish-red baseboard at least 12 cm high is an illusionistically projecting podium, painted yellow, with a curving recess in the right half. The front face of the podium, about 67.5 cm high, has projecting mouldings at top and bottom: at the bottom, above a pale green fascia, a cyma recta decorated with leaf-and-dart painted in dark reddish purple with white details, and a beading decorated with diagonal purple lines (compare the similar moulding imitated in the Gadebridge ceiling, No. 19); at the top another cyma (?) and a fascia decorated at intervals with sets of three vertical strokes (purple, white, purple). The vertical face between the mouldings shows indecipherable traces of imitation reliefs, painted (purple, white and red) with the aid of a pair of horizontal guide-lines scored in the plaster. At the right the podium is bevelled inwards, then gives way to the curving back-wall of the recess; here the lower mouldings are omitted, but the upper are continued, the fascia being decorated with a spiral motif (perhaps intended to indicate S-curved modillions seen at an angle). On the floor of the recess there are traces of unidentifiable angular objects.

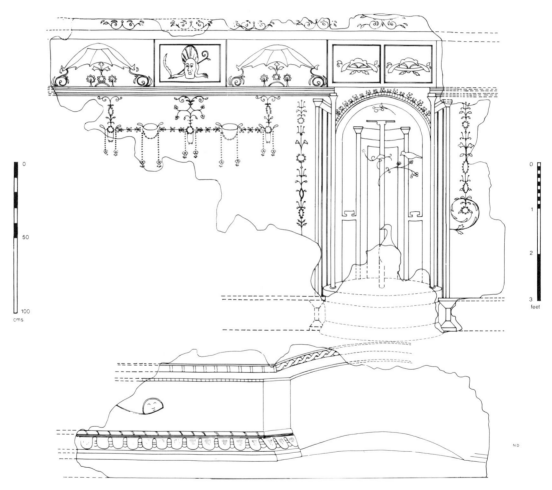

FIG. 25 No. 22 (A): Leicester, restoration of painted plaster from west wall of peristyle in courtyard house in insula XVI. Scale, 1:25.

(Drawing by N. Davey)

The treatment of perspective seems somewhat clumsy, especially as regards the upper mouldings, whose exact profile cannot be determined. The lighting, too, is not entirely successful; the bevelled face is painted yellow-white as if catching the light, yet the immediately adjacent back-wall of the niche is brownish-orange, suggesting shadow.

(ii) Upper part of the wall (3.03 m long × 2.08 m high). In the main zone a pair of large red fields separated by a columnar aedicula on a black ground; above this, a black frieze divided into rectangular panels containing various motifs.

The aedicula, which corresponds in position to the recess in the podium, presents uncertainties in some details but is safe in its main essentials. Its main framing elements are a pair of slender yellow-green columns (61.5 cm apart) which reach up to the lower edge of the frieze and are crowned by simple bevel-capitals with snake-like volutes projecting inwards. These capitals play no real supporting role but are engaged to the imitation mouldings running above the red fields. Between the columns is a lofty arch in pale blue, pale yellow, and brown, surmounted by delicate palmette and volute ornaments in yellow; and within the arch, forming the central axis of the aedicula, is a single fluted column set in a curving bay framed by two

Photo: Oxford Institute of Archaeology

XLIX   No. 22 (A)   Leicester, restored plaster from west wall of courtyard in house
in Blue Boar Lane, central aedicula.

further, slenderer columns. The central column, coloured yellow with white highlights and brown shadows, seems to have had objects attached to it, including a blue shield (?), and to have been encircled by a spiralling plant-tendril, parts of which remain, embellished with green leaves, white fruits, and white and blue honeysuckle-like flowers. Perched on a side-branch at one point is a bird (a dove?) delicately painted in white, purple, and blue. Another bird, long-necked and rather larger, stands lower down, immediately next to the column. A graffito identifies it as a peacock.[1] The two columns of the bay are olive-green, and the upper edge is formed by a concave purple band which links the capitals (which are again of simple bevel type); a broad red band forms an inner border. Connecting this two-columned bay with the framing arch is a short curving cross-piece, one at each side.

To left and right of the main aedicula, overlapping the edge of the red field, projects a wing supported by another olive-green column. The column at the right preserves a pedestal with strongly projecting bevel-mouldings at top and bottom, while that at the left casts a purple shadow on the background; on each side the space between the column and the edge of the main aedicula is framed by a purple band.

Within the red fields stood human figures; part of one such, wearing pale blue drapery with white highlights, has survived (set in the left field). The surface of each field was framed by delicate ornamental candelabra at the sides and an elaborately-decorated horizontal rod suspended above. Of the candelabra only those immediately to left and right of the aedicula remain. The one at the right is shown rising from a blue flower at the centre of a volute which grows bracket-like from the edge of the neighbouring column; the bottom of the other one is not preserved. In each the stalk and main elements are white and yellow, and the ornaments are chosen from the same basic repertory: a plate with three vertical prongs rather like a trident, a pair of green leaves on yellow stalks, a pale blue disc with white outline sometimes embellished with bobbles, a pale blue almond-shape with yellow volutes growing from the sides. The horizontal rod is preserved only above the left-hand field. It is suspended from the upper frame at three points by elaborate ornaments similar to the candelabra but incorporating volutes and, in the case of the central one, carrying trefoil leaves; and to it is attached a pair of large oval

Photo: Oxford Institute of Archaeology

L   No. 22 (A)   Leicester, restored plaster from west wall of courtyard in house in Blue Boar Lane, detail with mask and shell-ornament.

shields (?), whitish-yellow in colour at the top and bluish below. On either side of each shield and of the small blue discs which mask the three points of suspension is a long pendant fastened with a loop above and ending in a trefoil below. The rod itself is formed by a chain of stylised yellow flowers ('cross-key' ornaments) and leaves. The volute-ornaments above it, the pendants, and the side-candelabra all cast purple shadows to the left.

Above a series of horizontal stripes in various colours which suggest a series of mouldings comes the frieze. The section above the aedicula is divided into two identical panels, each framed by pale blue borders, and each containing an ornament consisting of two yellow dolphins leaping to left and right above a short curving red-purple band with leaves hanging below it; a green ribbon with a wavy upper edge arcs above. The only other part of the frieze restored is the section above the left-hand field of the main zone. This is divided into a central panel with a reddish-brown border and two longer, unframed side-panels. The side-panels contain shell- or 'umbrella'-like canopies, pale green and yellow, fastened by volutes at the corners and supported at the centre by a short candelabrum resting on a blue semicircle and flanked by a pair of yellow flowers on short stalks. In the central panel there is a tragic mask. Its face is pale blue with purple shadows and white highlights, while its *onkos* and trailing hair are reddish-purple. Behind it slopes a yellow *pedum*, possibly indicating that the subject is Dionysus. The light falls from the right, as in the decoration below.

The frieze is crowned by a horizontal yellow band, above which comes a zone with yellow double-volute ornaments on a red ground.

(B) North wall (section beginning about 6 m from north-west corner). 4.49 m long × 2.13 m high. This section is more fragmentary and the designs less well preserved than in (A), so the reconstruction was more difficult and the detail more uncertain. Generally speaking the scheme is identical, large red fields alternating with black-ground architectural 'Durchblicke', the whole ensemble surmounted by a black-ground frieze and a pink zone with double-volute ornaments; but the architectural forms are more complicated and apparently less logical (for example there are perspectival ceiling-coffers along the tops of the red fields) and the frieze carries stretches of repeating candelabrum-ornaments rather than individually-treated panels.

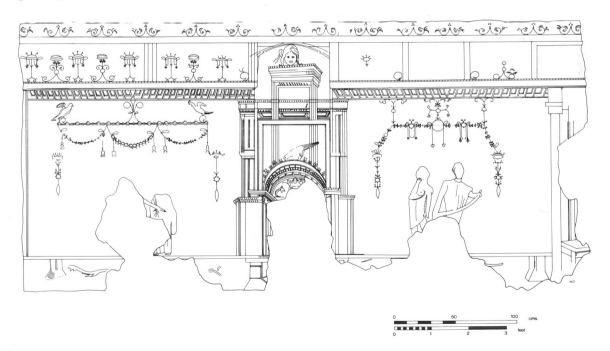

FIG. 26   No. 22 (B): Leicester, restoration of painted plaster from north wall of peristyle in courtyard house in insula XVI. Scale, 1:30.

(Drawing by N. Davey)

No part of the socle remains, but parts of a black predella about 27 cm high have been reconstructed. This predella is interrupted by the green and white pedestals which supported the columns of the aediculae and was decorated with pale and dark green sinuous forms (dolphins? or plant-tendrils?).

In the main zone there are two complete red fields with the intervening aedicula and traces of another at the right. The principal feature of the more complete aedicula is a coffered arch supported by jutting entablatures and containing a frontal Cupid or Psyche, a *pedum* in the right hand (PL. CXXI). The painting is sketchy and the colouring unnaturalistic. The arch is pale green and red with white highlights; the Cupid or Psyche has crimson hair and pale blue wings, and is otherwise pale blue and brown with touches of white and crimson. Above the arch, set between delicate yellow palmettes, is a pecking bird, again sketchily painted, this time in pink and brown with purple shadows and white highlights. The upper part of the 'Durchblick' juts into the frieze and contains the entablature of a pavilion supported by two white pillars; on top of the cornice, much faded, rests another theatrical mask with high reddish-brown *onkos*. The relationship of this pavilion to the arch below remains uncertain, and it is curious that the pavilion is shown in perspective from the right while the arch is apparently represented frontally. Once again the architecture of the 'Durchblick' overlapped on to the red fields to left and right: delicately-painted green and white columnar structures have been restored in three stories.

The candelabra and ornamental rods in the red fields incorporate many of the same motifs as the decoration of the west wall (A) but in some respects show important differences. Thus in the right field the rod seems to have been linked to the tops of the candelabra by diagonal swags; while in the left it is simplified to a white line with bobbles above it and three swags hanging below, but is given the additional embellishment of a yellow cockatoo perched at either end. This second rod casts a purple shadow underneath, and a similar shadow appears to left of the columns which overlap the left field. No shadows are visible in the right field.

There are tantalising traces of the figures which stood within the fields. These seem to have been deliberately mutilated in antiquity,[2] and their restoration is thus particularly difficult; but the fragments discovered belonged to at least three personages, all shown in frontal view. One wore green drapery and had a curving white band passing in front of the right shoulder; a second wore a short white cloak slung from the left shoulder and apparently had the right hand raised to the chin; the third was also dressed in green and held the end of a white band or fillet in his or her left hand. These figures, as the fragments make clear, were expertly painted with a confident use of white highlights on the yellow and pink of the flesh.

(C) West end of north wall. 85 cm wide × 74 cm high. Fragments restored to form part of a black vertical strip adjacent to a red field. Within the black strip, which is framed by pale green foliate borders, there are remains of an elaborate ornament incorporating yellow tendrils and volutes, whitish-green trefoil leaves, and, most striking, a large disc seen in perspective with a raised rim decorated with a fringe of bobbles. The interior of the disc is red, the rim is pale green, and the bobbles are white along the near rim, pale blue along the far rim. The interstices within the volutes and tendrils are filled, as in the similar ornaments in the frieze and main zone of (A) and (B), with flat washes of red or pale blue.

Discussion. The illusionistically projecting podium is similar to the contemporary or slightly later examples in the painting at Dover (No. 14) and is reminiscent in its solidity of the Pompeian Second Style; but the decoration of the main zone is much closer to the Fourth Style. The alternation of large flat fields and 'Durchblicke' containing slender and unreal architectural forms; the motif of a plant spiralling up a column; the delicate ornamental borders inside the main fields; the device of volutes and tendrils with interstices filled with solid colour; and (in the frieze) the shell- or 'umbrella'-ornaments — all can be more or less closely paralleled in the wall-decorations of Neronian or Vespasianic Italy.[3] But the general two-dimensional treatment of the frieze, with its framed panels and more or less stylised ornaments, again recalls an earlier phase, namely the late Second and early Third Styles.[4] We are once again dealing with a

Photo: Oxford Institute of Archaeology

LI No. 22 (C) Leicester, restored plaster from north-west corner of courtyard in Blue Boar Lane house.

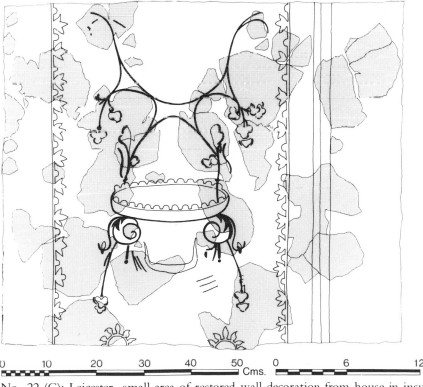

FIG. 27 No. 22 (C): Leicester, small area of restored wall-decoration from house in insula XVI. Diagram showing position of original fragments. Scale, 1:8.

(Drawn by Christine Boddington)

second-century decoration in which themes and motifs not normally found together in the Pompeian period are mixed to create a new 'eclectic' manner.

The particular scheme used here, which depends upon an alternation of red fields and black 'Durchblicke', is clearly derived from the simpler red and black schemes popular in Britain and the other north-western provinces during the Flavian and Trajanic periods (see Nos. 2; 8; 28 and introduction, pp. 33–5). The closest parallels occur in House XXI, 2 at Verulamium (No. 41, A–C) and probably in a fragmentary decoration at Winchester (No. 47). In both of these the red fields carry delicate candelabra which are painted in the same colours (yellow with blue, green, and white accessories) and include many of the same floral and foliate motifs as ours (cf. also fragments from Colchester (unpublished) and Scampton (No. 32)). Neither, however, has the elaborate architectural pavilions or the human figures of the Leicester decoration.

Outside Britain there are interesting parallels, though with different colour-schemes, in Antonine decorations at Rome and Ostia. At Ostia, in Rooms V and VI of the House of the Yellow Walls, yellow fields alternate with red intervals carrying slender architectural structures which overlap, like the Leicester ones, on to the fields to left and right; the yellow fields, moreover, are framed by floral candelabra and rods of the Leicester type, here painted red.[5] At Rome the same system of yellow fields and red intervals containing flimsy overlapping architecture occurs in a house beneath the basilica of S. Giovanni in Laterano. Here the vertical candelabra are lacking, but horizontal ornaments of Leicester type remain, and there are also figures in the yellow fields.[6] Despite the differences in colour, these decorations clearly represent the same artistic phase as those from Blue Boar Lane.

It is unfortunate that we do not have a more complete stretch of the decoration. The surviving sections from the north and west walls show differing treatments of the pavilions, of the ornamentation in the red fields, and of the frieze; while there are differences of treatment even within the same section, for example in the forms of the candelabra and horizontal rods of the two red fields from the north wall. It is therefore difficult to understand what rules of symmetry or parataxis applied to the decorations as a whole. In peristyles at Pompeii the wall-decorations normally employ a broadly paratactic arrangement with a rhythmic alternation of roughly identical 'Vorhänge' and 'Durchblicke', as in the Houses of the Vettii and of the Dioscuri (both Neronian).[7] The perspective of the architecture in the 'Durchblicke' may be treated in mirror-image in the two halves of a wall,[8] but there is no fundamental change in the architectural forms. It is, however, possible to find examples with somewhat more complex arrangements, such as the late Claudian decoration in the upper peristyle of the Villa San Marco at Stabiae, where one of the fields (the central one?) is singled out for more elaborate treatment than the rest and is framed by architectural 'Durchblicke', whereas the adjacent pair of fields is separated by a flat fascia with a scroll-ornament.[9]

Possibly some form of axio-symmetrical arrangement obtained on the walls at Leicester. All the visible shadows cast by vertical elements fall to the left; so, since section A certainly and section B probably lay within the left half of their walls, the shadows would be consistent with a central light-source, as at Dover. The perspective is certainly more complicated, at least on the north wall, where some architectural elements are viewed frontally, some from the right; but any detailed interpretation is rendered difficult by the uncertainties imposed by the difficulties experienced in the reconstruction and is best not attempted.

The painting of the main zone shows a masterly hand or hands using quick and confident but at the same time delicate brushwork. Some passages are almost impressionistic (e.g. the Cupid or Psyche). On the west wall, however, it is noteworthy how much heavier and less careful is the painting of the podium in comparison with the main zone and frieze.

Several further, unplaced fragments from this decoration remain in storage at Fortress House, London.

References: *JRS* xlix (1959), p. 113, pl. XVII (1, 2); Toynbee 1962, p. 195, no. 173, pl. 199; Toynbee 1964, pp. 215, 218, 219; Davey 1972, pp. 262–4, figs. 8–10, pls. XX, XXI (A), XXII (A); Wacher, pp. 56, 348, pls 65–66; Liversidge 1977, pp. 80–83.
Excavator: J.S. Wacher, Leicestershire Museums.

[1] *JRS* lii (1962), p. 197 (no. 34, *e*).

[2] We are grateful to Mr. Wacher for his opinion on this point.

[3] The alternation of flat fields and 'Durchblicke' is one of the commonest themes in Fourth-Style decoration: see e.g. the 'sacellum' in the House of Loreius Tiburtinus at Pompeii, where the "Durchblicke' have a black ground, as at Leicester (T. Kraus and L. von Matt, *Lebendiges Pompeji* (1973), pl. 252). Plant spiralling up column: e.g. House of the Vettii at Pompeii, Room *k* (Peters, pl. 90, fig. 65; pl. 92, fig. 70); Villa Varano at Stabiae (*Röm. Mitt.* lxxxiv (1977), pp. 66 (fig. 7), 69 f. (figs. 8, 9), pls. 35 (1), 36 (2), 40 (3), 41 (1); House of the Centenary at Pompeii (Kraus and von Matt, *op. cit.*, pl. 309); House of the Gilded Cupids at Pompeii (Schefold, pl. 124; cf. pl. 117 (2, 3)). Ornamental borders: e.g. the Sala degli Uccelletti in Nero's Golden House in Rome (E. Nash, *Pictorial Dictionary of Ancient Rome* (1961), i, fig. 414). Volutes and tendrils filled with colour: e.g. a fragment of unknown provenance in the Louvre (Tran Tam Tinh, p. 44 f., no. 21, fig. 23) which also has a shell-ornament and another device found in our decoration, a candelabrum growing from a flower at the centre of a volute (cf. the socle of the decoration reconstructed in Elia, folder A).

[4] Cf. e.g. House of Obellius Firmus at Pompeii, oecus 3 (Schefold, pl. 31); Pompeii I 11, 14 (De Vos 1975, pl. 11, fig.8; pl. 12, fig. 10).

[5] *Mon. pitt. ant.* iii. *Ostia,* i–ii. B.M. Felletti Maj, *Le pitture delle Case Volte Dipinte e delle Pareti Gialle* (1961), pls. IX, X (1).

[6] *Boll. d'Arte* i (1965), fig. 68. On the dating De Vos 1969, p. 170, n. 119; Mielsch 1975 b, p. 122.

[7] Peters, pp. 108 f., pls. 75, 76; L. Richardson, in *MAAR* xxiii (1955), pp. 55–60, pls. XI–XIII. Cf. the House of the Centenary (K. Schefold, *Die Wände Pompejis* (1957), p. 276).

[8] Cf. H. Eristov, in *Latomus* xxxvii (1978), pp. 628 f.

[9] Elia, *loc. cit.* (note 3). For the Claudian date F.L. Bastet, *BABesch.* xlvii (1972), pp. 83 f.

No. 23. LEICESTER. Insula XVI, market-hall. Late second or third century. Now in Leicester, Jewry Wall Museum. PL. LII. FIGS. 4, 28.

Area of ceiling-decoration reconstructed from scattered fragments found in 1958 excavations. 1.21 m × 1.20 m. The pattern is formed by an alternation of two elements, each based on roundels.

The larger roundel (diameter 17 to 18.5 cm) consists of a white central medallion surrounded by a broad yellow border between pinkish-red lines. The central medallion contains eight radial almond-shapes, dark blue with a pale blue bar across the widest point. Round the outside of the roundel there are alternating pale green and yellow-green plant-forms, the former a large tuft-like palmette growing along the diagonals, the latter a simple lotus-bud crowned by a pink circumflex. The palmettes are crowned by large boomerang-shaped elements, dark blue along the outer margin, and pale blue along the inner.

The smaller roundel (diameter 12 to 13 cm) has a central medallion, half pink and half purple, enclosed by a broad purple border. The line separating the central medallion and the border alternates from one row of roundels to the next, being either white or black; the outer contour is always black. From the roundel radiate alternately pale green trefoils (along the diagonals) and leaf-sprays the colour of which alternates from roundel to roundel, now pale green, now yellow.

Scored guide-lines radiate from the small roundels along the diagonals and axes of the scheme. There are also compass-drawn guide-lines round the large roundels, corresponding roughly to the tips of the palmettes. Despite the care taken in marking out the scheme, the painting of details seems to have been rather irregular and may have included mistakes; for example some leaf-sprays seem to have grown inwards towards the roundels rather than out-wards. The distance between centres of small and large roundels is 38 to 39 cm.

This type of ceiling-design, in which a basically geometric design is concealed beneath a repeating pattern of small curvilinear shapes and diagonal and/or axial leaf-ornaments, is a favourite in Roman painting, occurring for instance in various forms in Nero's palaces at Rome.[1] The surviving metropolitan parallels are first-century in date, but later examples are known from the provinces, for instance from sites in Austria, Switzerland, and France.[2] In Britain fragments from Silchester (No. 33), Greetwell (Appendix, No. 8), and Harpham (No. 20), all showing medallions with plant-forms radiating from them, may have derived from similar schemes. For purely rectilinear panel-schemes with foliate frames compare Nos. 41, D (Verulamium) and 50 (Witcombe).

0   10   20   30   40   50 Cms.   0   6   12 Inches
                                                                                CB

FIG. 28   No. 23: Leicester, restored area of ceiling-decoration from market-hall in insula XVI. Diagram showing
          position of original fragments. Scale, 1:8.

(Drawing by Christine Boddington)

References: Davey 1972, p. 264, fig. 11; Wacher, p. 348 and pl. 67.
Excavator: J.S. Wacher, Leicestershire Museums.

[1]Domus Transitoria: F.L. Bastet, in *BABesch*. xlvi (1971), pp. 157-60, figs. 7-9. Domus Aurea: *Ant. Denkm.* iii, 2 (1912-13), pls. 16-18; Dacos, figs. 23, 29, 33. Cf. M. Pallottino, in *Bull. Comm.* lxii (1934), p. 49, pl. II (first-century tomb in Rome). For similar patterns at Pompeii, mainly on walls, Barbet and Allag, p. 1000 and fig. 29; W. Zahn, *Die schönsten Ornamente und merkwürdigsten Gemälde aus Pompeji, Herkulanum und Stabiae*, ii (1842), pl. 39. Similar patterns are common in North African mosaic pavements, but, since they are lacking in British and Gaulish mosaics, it is difficult to postulate any direct influence of floor-decoration upon ceilings.

[2]Austria: H. Brandenstein, in *Carnuntum Jahrbuch* 1961-62, p. 11 f., pls. III*d*, IV *o* (Carnuntum, probably first half of third century); Praschniker and Kenner, pp. 175 f., 221 f., figs. 154-6, pl. I (Virunum, wall-decoration, late third or fourth century). Switzerland: Drack, pp. 21, 39, Beil. 5 (Allaz, wall-decoration? third century?); cf. *ibid.*, fig. 18 (Augst); unpublished decoration at Avenches (information from Alix Barbet and Michel Fuchs). France: J.-L. Massy, in *Revue du Nord* lv (1973), pp. 29-31, pl. IX (Amiens, second half of second or first half of third century); unpublished decoration from villa at Sarreinsming (Moselle) (second half of second or third century: information

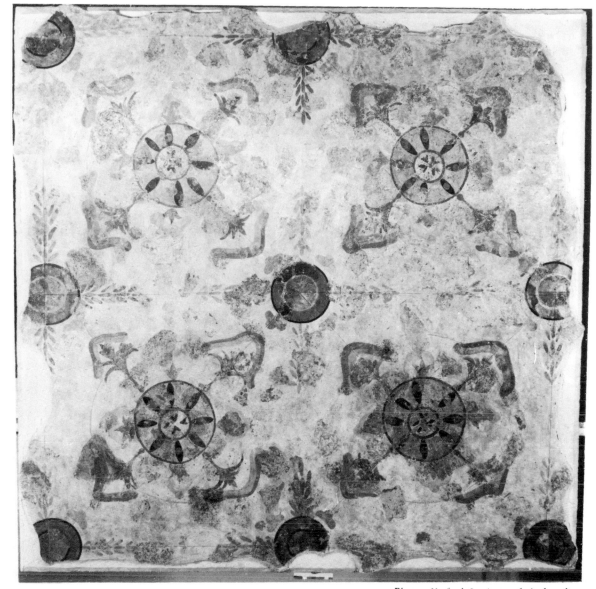

Photo· Oxford Institute of Archaeology

LII No. 23 Leicester, restored piece of ceiling-plaster from market hall.

from Alix Barbet and Dominique Heckenbenner) On 'Tapetenmuster' in general see W.J.T. Peters in *Berichten van de Rijksdienst voor het Oudheidkundig Bodemonderzoek*, xv–xvi (1965–66), pp. 140–2.

No. 24 ★LEICESTER. House outside west defences. Dating uncertain (third or early fourth century?). Now (1979) in Leicester, Newarke Houses Museum (in storage).

Abundant fragments of painted plaster from opposite sides of a wall of unbaked bricks, found collapsed from an upper storey into a cellar (1979 excavations, Norfolk Street). The decorations are currently being reconstructed.

(A) The side which landed uppermost is less complete and has been less intensively studied. It was predominantly white-ground and carried panels with red, yellow and green frames, some with pyramids of three red spots at the corners. The most striking feature is a horizontal garland with green leaves and orange fruits (peaches? or oranges?), painted along a scored guideline. Its precise position in the decoration is as yet uncertain.

(B) The decoration of the lower face is largely complete, except that the left end of the wall was not excavated. Large red and green fields alternate, separated by illusionistic columns. If the length of the wall corresponded to the length of the cellar into which it fell, there would have been three red and two green fields; the section salvaged contains two complete red ones, one complete green one, and a part of another green one. The area is approximately 5 m × 3m.

The unusually elaborate dado consists of a pink baseboard about 40 cm high, splashed with black and white, and of a much broader zone of marbled panels, alternately long and short, set in a green and white streaked surround 5.5 cm wide. The long panels beneath the red fields have a white ground with green, yellow and blue streaks and blobs overlaid by red scribbles. Those beneath the green fields are yellow with red and white streaks and blobs overlaid by red scribbles. The narrow panels beneath the columns are alternately (a) green and grey with white scribbles, (b) grey with green, blue, and yellow blobs.

This zone is surmounted by a continuous pale yellow band 15.5 cm wide, above which comes the main zone.

The red fields have a pair of white inner border-lines, a purple band (2.5 cm) round the edge, and a band of blue frit (about 6 cm) round that. The corresponding elements in the frame of the green fields are respectively yellow, white, and red. Within the fields are decorative motifs: a green garland hanging across each of the red fields, from top corner to top corner, and at the middle of the complete green field a small picture-panel. The latter, which is framed by yellow bands overlapping at the corners in such a way as to suggest a wooden picture-frame, is unfortunately fragmentary, but it seems to have had a pale blue ground, and there are traces of a wavy object vividly painted in purple, white, and red.

Of the columns four survive, that against the right end of the wall being broader than the rest. The shafts are modelled in pink and purple, and round them spirals a white vine-scroll; the Corinthian capitals are yellow. Despite the painter's concern to suggest volume, there seems to have been no consistent light-source: the lighted side in each case is that towards the red fields.

Above the main zone runs a large-scale imitation ovolo (8 cm high), painted in pink and purple on a white ground; and above this in turn there are fragments of horizontal garlands with green, white and yellow leaves on a purple ground.

An important technical detail is the evidence for the use of a fresco method of painting. Seams marking the divisions between 'giornate di lavoro' (areas of fresh plaster) can be distinguished: for example, along the upper edge of the red border of the complete green panel, along the left edge of the left-most surviving column, and along the top of the pale yellow band below the main zone. The colour and texture of the plaster vary slightly on either side of these seams.

Good external dating evidence for the decoration is lacking, but the marbling in the dado-panels is of a schematic type more usual in the later Roman period. Its combination of oblique bands of colour and superimposed scribbles is reminiscent of panels in the dado of the wall-decoration from York Minster, dated to the early fourth century (No. 52). The York decoration also contained, in the upper zone, an ovolo somewhat similar to ours. For the general syntax of the scheme, namely flat fields alternating with plastically-rendered columns, the nearest parallel is an undated decoration from Water Newton drawn by Artis in the nineteenth century (Appendix, No. 11).

Unpublished.

Excavator: J.E. Mellor, Leicestershire Museums.

No. 25. LINCOLN. House underlying west defences. Early second century. (A) Present whereabouts unknown, (B-D) Now (1979) in London, Fortress House (in storage). Excavations 1973. PL. LIII. FIG. 29.

†(A) Fragments of polychrome floral and related ornaments. One (approximately 12 cm × 11 cm) seems to show part of a candelabrum like those from Leicester (No. 22, C) and Verulamium (Nos. 41, A-C; 44, B) with a disc carrying a yellow volute with red filling on a black ground.

(B) Two fragments (14 cm × 17 cm; 11.5 cm × 13.5 cm) restored to form spindle-shaped floral ornaments, red with black borders and sepals.

Drawing by N. Davey.

LIII No. 25 (A) Lincoln, fragments of floral ornaments from house under east defences.

(C) 16.2 cm × 24 cm. Fragment of creamy-yellow panelling with red and blue splashes.

(D) 33 cm × 45 cm. Fragment of decoration of bands and stripes in different colours, probably from a frieze above a panel-system. The upper part is intended to suggest profiled mouldings, including a dentillated enrichment represented illusionistically in purple with white highlights and purplish-black shadows. Somewhat similar enrichments appear in wall-paintings

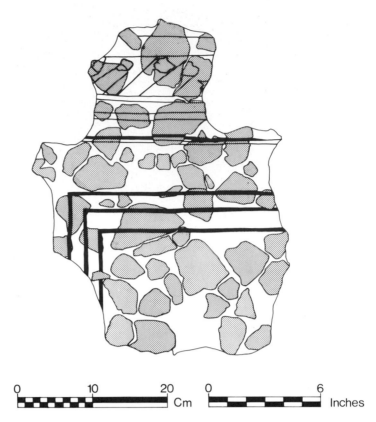

FIG. 29 No. 25 (D): Lincoln, restored wall-plaster from house beneath east
defences. Diagram showing position of original fragments. Scale, 1:5.
(Drawing by Diane Dixon)

of the Fourth Pompeian Style, for example in the House of the Vettii at Pompeii and in a
painting from Herculaneum in the Louvre.[1]

References: *Britannia*, v (1974), p. 421; *Antiq. Journ.*, lix (1979), p. 83.
Excavator: J.S. Wacher, Department of the Environment.

[1]Peters, pl. 59, fig. 2; pl. 71, fig. 23; pl. 74, fig. 27, etc.; Tran Tam Tinh, p. 61, fig. 44; cf. Barbet 1977, p. 113,
fig. 3B.

No. 26. ★LULLINGSTONE, Kent.   Villa, so-called 'Deep Room'. Last quarter of second century. *In situ*. PLS. LIV, LV.

Wall-painting on back of arched niche in south wall. This niche was later blocked, and part of
the blocking-rubble and mortar remains at the right. Maximum dimensions of visible part of
back wall: 64 cm wide × 92 cm high. Excavated 1957.

On a white ground framed by a red band are a group of three female figures, apparently
water-nymphs. Only the central and left-hand figures are at all well preserved, but both have
lost their middle portions, and the face of the left-hand one is badly damaged. It seems that the
central figure was standing, or possibly sitting at a high level, while the others were seated at
the sides in roughly symmetrical postures, the upper parts of their bodies more or less frontal
and the lower parts in three-quarters view. The central figure is frontal, but with the head
turned and slightly tilted to our left. Apart from a purple drape visible on the left-hand nymph's
left shoulder, the two surviving figures were nude from the hips upwards; but their legs were
swathed in cloaks, the left figure's blue-green with black linear shadows and white highlights,
and the central figure's a foldless yellow. Of the right-hand figure a knee covered with reddish-
brown drapery remains. Between the knees of the two side-figures, overlapping the yellow
dress of the central one, is a lozenge-shaped area, blue-green with black outlines, which looks

Photo: R.J. Ling

LIV No. 26 Lullingstone, painting of nymphs in Deep Room.

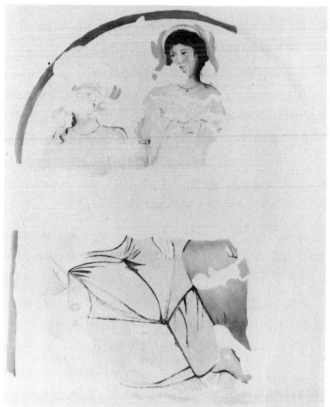

Drawing by J. Thorn, Department of the Environment.

LV No. 26 Lullingstone, water-colour of nymphs in Deep Room.

like drapery but cannot easily be associated with any of the figures. It is also difficult to know who owned the hand on the left nymph's knee: from its form it would seem to be a right hand and therefore to belong to the standing figure.

The attributes of the figures are most clearly visible in the central one. She wears a blue necklace round her throat and purple armlets on her upper arms; an orange nimbus or diadem rests on her purple-brown hair, and green foliage flanks the head; most strikingly, spurts of blue water emerge from the breasts. Her left hand is laid beneath the breasts, possibly pointing to the flow of water. There can be no doubt over the identification of the figure: the motif of the water-pouring breasts is unparalleled in surviving art but occurs in a literary description of nymphs in a painting,[1] and the nimbus and leafy framing of the head appear in other representations of water-nymphs.[2] The left-hand figure also wears a blue necklace, and there are traces of leaves next to her head. Whether her right hand rested on an overturned flagon, as claimed in early accounts of the scene, cannot now be determined.

In style, despite the generally flat, linear treatment of the drapery, the bodies are fully classical, the flesh being modelled with white highlights and orange shadows.

The remaining wall-decoration in the late second-century phase of the Deep Room consisted of coloured panels, red, yellow and green, and stylised date-palms with yellow fronds and red fruit. Nothing of this survives in situ.

References: Meates 1955, pp. 72 f., 99, fig. 7 (a); Liversidge 1958, p. 384; Meates 1962, pp. 11-15; Toynbee 1964, p. 220 f., pl. LIII; Liversidge 1969, p. 149 f; Meates 1979, pp. 32-35. Excavator: G.W. Meates, Darent Valley Archaeological Group and Department of the Environment.

[1]Philostratus the Elder, Imagines ii, 4, 3.
[2]E.g. in a representation of Hylas and the nymphs on a mosaic from the vicinity of Rome now in Leningrad (S. Korsunska, 'Mosaik mit Hylasdarstellung', Röm. Mitt. xlv (1930), pp. 166–71, pl. 52). Here and in other Hylas-representations, however, the nymphs have reeds growing from their hair rather than the more bushy foliage of the Lullingstone painting.

No. 27. LULLINGSTONE, Kent. Villa, Christian rooms. Second half of fourth century (perhaps datable to reigns of Valentinian I and Valens, 364-378).[1] Now in London, British Museum (C and D in storage). PLS. LVI-LIX. FIG.30.

Parts of walls restored from fragments found collapsed in Deep Room underneath.[2] Much of the initial work of reconstruction was carried out by C.D.P. Nicholson. Further fragments await reconstruction (C, D). Excavations 1949-51, 1956-57.

(A) West wall of Room A (chapel?). 4.27 m × 2.24 m high (discounting projecting moulding at foot). A marbled dado is surmounted by a series of six figures, approximately one-third life-size, standing between columns.

The marbling of the dado, which is continuous and is restored to a height of 88 cm, takes the familiar 'fried-egg' form, with reddish-orange, brownish-black, and yellowish-brown splodges enclosed by reddish-brown or purple wavy lines, all on an off-white background. A purple and an orange-red band, the first 5 cm wide, the second of uncertain width, form a border above and at the sides; while along the foot of the wall is restored a projecting moulding coloured pale green.

The forms of the columns in the main zone vary according to a symmetrical arrangement. The central one is the most elaborate. Above a three-stepped base in which the two lower steps are fluted and the upper is decorated with a pair of S-volutes, the shaft is divided into horizontal bands, alternately narrow ones containing sets of three rosettes, and broader ones with sets of three vertical hook-motifs above a wavy line. The capital has a sagging Ionic volute-member above a pair of echini, the lower of which is decorated with a wavy line, and the upper with a series of loops. The outline of the column is black, reinforced by a white line, while the internal detail is carried out in bold contrasts of white and purple on a brown ground.

The columns to left and right of the central one are considerably simpler in form. Pale blue to dark blue in colour, with all detail rendered in white, they had vertical fluting formed by chains

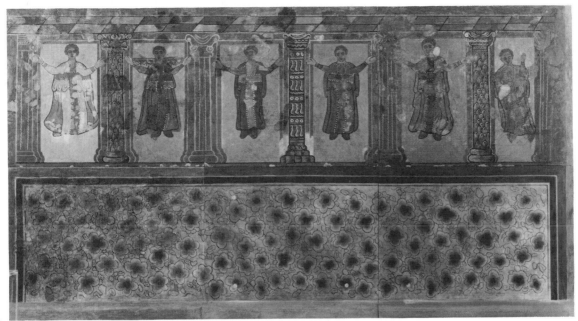

Photo: British Museum

LVI   No. 27 (A)   Lullingstone, *orantes* from west wall of house-church, restored.

of comma-like strokes. The capitals are difficult to decipher from the surviving fragments (the right-hand example) but seem again to have consisted of sagging volute-members above a pair of echini (decoration uncertain). The bases were apparently formed by a thick torus surmounted by a quarter-round moulding.

The next balancing pair of columns, the last complete ones, have a scale-decoration carried out in purple on an orange-red ground; each scale carried a black or purple spot near the top and vertical white strokes at the middle and left to suggest highlights. The left-hand capital apparently had three volute-members, one above the other; but its counterpart at the right was apparently closer in form to the capital of the central column (see above). The form of the bases is more or less identical to that of the blue columns, though here modelled by white highlighting and purple shading, in accordance with the stronger colouring of this pair of columns as a whole.

The three-quarter columns which conclude the series at either end repeat the general form and colouring of the blue ones.

Within each intercolumniation there is a white ground framed by a pair of coloured borders. The outer border, always red, varies in width from 3 to 5 cm; the inner one, alternately purple and ochre, from 1.5 to 2.5 cm. The width of the intercolumniations, as restored, ranges from 52 cm (the second from the left, established by joining fragments) to 58 cm, except for the last intercolumniation at the right, which is only 36 cm wide.

At least four and probably five of the figures within the niches seem to have been shown with their arms extended in the gesture of *orantes*, their hands overlapping the coloured borders. The sixth, that of the narrower right-most niche, seems to have been smaller, and lacked the space for the praying gesture; the position of the arms is uncertain (the raised left arm shown in the restoration is conjectural).

It is difficult to discuss the figures in detail, since the remains are fragmentary and the colours have often been altered by exposure to fire.[3] But certain generalisations can be made. The hands were mostly huge and misshapen; the arms emerged uncomfortably from the middle of the chest; the heads (only two of which are at all well-preserved) had brownish-red hair low over the eyes, thick eyebrows, and wide eyes in which the irises showed white highlights; and all the figures wore full-length robes. The main garment, a long-sleeved tunic, is distinguished by a cross-shaped element consisting of broad bands framed by white beads running vertically from neck to foot and horizontally across the chest beneath the arms; the sleeves have bands of ornamentation at the wrists, and there is an overfold indicated by a series of pouches at the hips.

Some at least of the figures also wore cloaks (unfastened *lacernae*) on their backs, indicated by different-coloured folds down the left and right sides. It is uncertain whether the feet were originally visible.

The best-preserved figure is the second from the left. A young man, he wears a brown robe with blue bands. He was apparently distinguished from the other figures by being shown against a curtain, which hangs from a rod running behind his head; his hands, to judge from early reconstructions of the fragments,[4] may have been represented as clenched, instead of with the fingers extended.

The next figure to the right is also male and beardless, but has his hands open, palms outwards. What little remains of his tunic suggests that it was pale blue or greyish-purple with pink bands. The cloak was probably brown.

The only other figures of which more than minimal fragments survive are the last two at the right. The penultimate figure, which was perhaps female, also held the hands palm outwards and wore a pale purple tunic with dark purple bands. The other (that in the narrow inter-columniation) had an orange tunic with pale blue bands and wore over it a grey-yellow cloak.

Photo: M.B. Cookson

LVII   No. 27 (A)   Lullingstone, fragments of second figure from west wall, before restoration.

Photo: M.B. Cookson

LVIII   No. 27 (A)   Lullingstone, fragments of right-most figure from west wall, before restoration.

Above the figures, supported by the columns, ran a double tier of roof-tiles or ceiling-coffers shown with sides receding obliquely upwards to the right. Colours varied from coffer to coffer. It is impossible, from the surviving fragments, to determine the arrangement of the colours, but they apparently included purple, yellow, pink, brown, and pale blue, mostly with horizontal white or purple strokes at the ends to suggest highlights and shadows.

The coffers are surmounted by a continuous reddish-brown band which turns vertically down the wall at the right end (and possibly originally at the left end too), forming a frame about 12 cm wide. Beyond this vertical frame runs a pale green stripe 2.5 to 3.5 cm wide.

★(B) Panel from south wall of Room A: Chi-Rho monogram set within wreath. Restored by P. Shorer and others.

Total measurements of modern panel: 1.52 m wide × 1.22 m high. Outer diameter of wreath 93 cm; inner diameter 68 cm.

The Chi-Rho is red on a white ground and contained the letters Alpha and Omega between its lateral arms (part of the Omega remains). Of the wreath the inner edge is painted in a farrago of red, grey or pink, the outer edge is pale blue, and the central part is a dirty greyish-yellow delimited by purple and white spiky leaves. On this central band are set red, white and blue fruits, quickly sketched with bold shadows and highlights.

To left and right, columns with double-volute capitals similar to those of the west wall support an entablature which passes behind the top part of the wreath. The columns are garishly painted, the ornament of their capitals and the fluting of their shafts being rendered in white and purple against, respectively, a dirty yellow and a reddish-brown ground. White and purple are also used in diagonal strokes to indicate highlights and shadows on the shafts. The entablature seems to change colour from one side to the other. On the right it is coloured like the column-capitals, on the left it is formed by grey-blue and purple stripes on a white ground. Over it hang what look like purple strings.

The spandrels above the entablature are white, with a purple band acting as a border. Above them run continuous horizontal bands of pale yellow, darker yellow, and red.

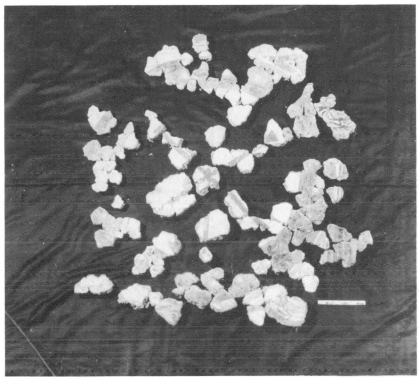

Photo: M.B. Cookson.

LIX   No. 27 (B)   Lullingstone, fragments of Chi-Rho from south wall of house-church, before restoration.

At the bottom, in the spandrels between the wreath and the column, a white field framed by a greenish-yellow band contained birds, one perched on each side on an orange ribbon fastened to the lower part of the wreath. The right-hand bird is preserved, somewhat clumsily drawn with a purple outline and a reddish body overpainted with white and yellow. In front of its beak floats a purple dot-rosette. Of the corresponding group on the other side only the dot-rosette survives.[5]

Finally, beneath the left-hand orange ribbon, there is a fragment of a series of dark blue and white stripes interrupted at the right by a volute, possibly part of another column-capital.

The position in which the fragments of this ensemble were discovered suggests that it decorated the west end of the south wall. If so, it was framed by at least one other column at the right, since a large corner-piece showing a shaft and capital was found immediately beneath the south-west angle of the room. This piece, measuring approximately 34.5 cm by 43 cm, still exists in fragments; the column, which is similar in colouring to those framing the wreath (orange with purple and white detail), is separated from the actual angle by vertical bands of red and reddish-brown (respectively 9 cm and 7.5 cm wide).[6]

★(C) Large areas of the decoration of the ante-chamber (Room B) have been reconstructed by Frances Weatherhead.[7] The elements included panels framed by purple lines on a white ground, with spots at the corners, and a further Chi–Rho monogram set within a wreath. The latter has now been mounted on a panel (1.34 m × 1.27 m). The Chi–Rho here too is red against a white ground, and there is again evidence for the presence of an Alpha and Omega within the lateral arms of the cross. The wreath is again formed by three concentric bands of colour: the inner edge is grey with a black border, the outer edge red, and the central part, which carried the fruit and the foliage, yellow. Its style of painting once again is sketchy: the leaves are indicated by V-shaped purple ticks along the edge of the yellow band, and the fruit by splodges of red, purple and blue along the spine.

FIG. 30 No. 27 (C): Lullingstone, detail of wall-decoration in ante-room of Christian chapel (reconstruction drawing). The Chi–Rho is painted red. Scale, 1:25.
(Drawing by Frances J. Weatherhead, adapted by R.J. Ling)

The wreath was set within a rectangular frame formed by a chain of lozenges, alternately grey, yellow and white, arranged concertina fashion. This motif, similar to a device which recurs in the fourth-century paintings from Rudston (No. 31, B), is framed by coloured bands, red on the inside, purple on the outside, and is further enriched by pyramids of spots growing outwards from each angle of the concertina. White pyramids adorn the re-entrant angles, black the salient. In addition each lozenge has at least one inner frame of purple, and some have two. The whole framing motif was 23 cm wide, and was accompanied by an additional orange band 5 cm wide on the inside.

The spaces above and below the wreath were outlined by purple lines, from which rows of dots ran into the angles between wreath and frame.

★(D) Thousands of further fragments from Room A have been sorted and give some idea of the remaining motifs within the decoration; features have been allocated to the various walls, and hypothetical restorations of the schemes attempted by Miss Weatherhead. Material perhaps ascribable to the south wall includes a colonnade in perspective, fragments with basketwork and chair-legs, and parts of two small figures in skirts. From the north wall perhaps come more columns, buildings shown in perspective, peacocks' feathers (?) in purple on a pink ground, wheat-sheaves, fruit and foliage, the head of a dog, a hand resting on a cuirass of scale-armour (?) or a basket (?), and parts of human limbs. From the east wall come fragments of a third Chi-Rho and more columns and figures. Finally there are pieces of plaster probably from the ceiling which carry intersecting roundels formed by reddish-brown bands between purple border-lines.

Many of the figures and other motifs on fragments ascribed to the north, south and east walls are on a considerably smaller scale than the figures of the west wall; it is highly probable that the north and south walls at least, and probably the east wall too, included representational scenes, perhaps in a landscape setting.

Discussion. The Lullingstone paintings are of great importance, both as an example of later fourth-century painting in Britain, and as a testimony to the spread of Christian worship in the province. The *orans* type, though inherited from the pagan repertory, is one of the commonest motifs in early Christian art. The sacred monogram, in the form adopted here, is closely paralleled on a number of Passion and Resurrection sarcophagi (also of the fourth century), in which a wreath-enclosed Chi-Rho rests on a cross, a pair of doves peck the fruit of the wreath, and a pair of Roman soldiers, guardians of Christ's tomb, sit below.[8] This whole motif is a symbol of the Resurrection and the victory of Christianity; the birds are Christian souls absorbing the fruits of the new life.

The style of the paintings is best judged from the *orantes* and their architectural framework. It is somewhat crude and simplified, as shown for instance by the heads and hands of the figures. The artist relies generally on strong outlines and linear detail rendered in boldly-juxtaposed light and dark tones. The figures here again provide a good example, their flesh (painted white over an orange undercoat) being left totally unshaded within black or reddish-brown outlines, and the folds of their drapery being indicated only by vertical purple and white lines. Such modelling as does occur is rudimentary, being expressed by quick horizontal strokes of white and purple, as in the coffers and in the bases of the scale- and rosette-columns. Generally speaking, the light comes from the left, that is it falls towards the door of the room rather than away from it; but this rule is not consistently followed. The coffers seem to be lit now from one side, now from the other, and sometimes from both sides; the flutes of the two lower elements in the base of the central column seem to be lit from opposite directions.

The pattern-like treatment of architectural forms and the bold and garish colouring are reminiscent of the decoration from the *principia* at York (No. 52); but the schematisation has here progressed considerably further (see especially the two-dimensional column-shafts and the multi coloured ceiling-coffers). The whole handling of space is unrealistic. Despite attempts at modelling and perspective in some details, the overall effect is of a flat framework encompassing a series of flat panels — an effect which is emphasised by the way in which the figures seem to float in the middle of their intercolumniations. All these features, together with the frontal postures, wide eyes and linear style of the figures, accord with a date in the middle or second half of the fourth century.[9]

The device of representing figures in the intervals between columns is also characteristic of the fourth century. It occurs in a series of early Christian sarcophagi which continue the pagan Asiatic tradition of the second and third centuries; the most famous and elaborate example is the sarcophagus of Junius Bassus (359), where the architecture is in two tiers and the columns are either spirally fluted or decorated with vegetal ornament.[10] The mosaic dome-decoration of the mausoleum at Centcelles (near Tarragona, Spain), datable to the mid fourth century, has, in its second zone, a series of Christian scenes separated by spirally-fluted columns.[11] Smaller works of art with figures set between framing columns are the ivory consular diptychs and the illustrations of the calendar of 354, where some of the columns have a scale-decoration similar to two of the examples at Lullingstone.[12]

Three details of the west wall require some further comment.

First the scale-decoration just mentioned. This type of decoration is employed on real stone columns, for instance the second- and third-century Jupiter-columns of the Rhineland and smaller votive columns in Britain; but the monumental examples generally had down-hanging scales, at least on the upper two-thirds of the shaft, whereas the Lullingstone scales grow consistently upwards.[13] Moreover in none of the stone-carved examples are there internal markings like those at Lullingstone. It is possible that our imbrication may owe something to stylised date-palms like those in the second-century paintings of the Deep Room in the same villa.[14] The palm-shaft motif goes back in painting at least to the first century A.D., when it occurs for instance in a Third Style decoration from Commugny, Switzerland.[15]

Secondly the dress of the *orantes*. Such figures are almost invariably shown wearing dalmatics or (as here) long-sleeved tunics; but the decoration of the Lullingstone tunics is unusually elaborate. Normally the garment has merely a pair of vertical stripes *(clavi)* running from the shoulders to the lower hem. Occasionally these *clavi* are richly embroidered, for instance in the painted female orants of the catacomb of Thraso in Rome, dated about 300, where a ribbon interweaves between white spots recalling the Lullingstone 'pearls';[16] but there is no parallel, to our knowledge, for the different colouring of the central part of the garment,[17] for the addition of a transverse band, or for the row of pearls on each shoulder.

The third noteworthy feature is the curtain behind the second figure from the left. Although the remains are too fragmentary to reveal whether there were similar curtains behind the first and fourth figures, it is certain that none existed behind the third and fifth, and probable that none existed behind the sixth. Why the second figure should be singled out in this way (and, if his hands were originally clenched, he would be doubly distinguished) is a matter for conjecture. Professor Toynbee's suggestion that the curtain indicates the fact that the orant in question is a dead person remains the most likely explanation: portraits of the dead are frequently set in front of curtains on late Roman sarcophagi.[18]

References: Meates 1955, pp. 72 f., 126-42, 146-53, figs. 10-12, 13 (b), pls. 42-46; Liversidge 1958, p. 384 f.; Meates 1962, pp. 29-33, 37 f.; Toynbee 1962, pp. 195 f. (nos. 175-6), pls. 204-5; Toynbee 1964, pp. 213, 221-7, pls. LIV, LV; Liversidge 1977, p. 75; Meates 1979, p. 53. Excavator: G.W. Meates, Darent Valley Archaeological Group and Department of the Environment.

[1]Meates 1962, p. 29.

[2]The description has been assisted, for A and B, by photographs and paintings of the fragments before restoration. Neither the photographs (by M.B. Cookson) nor the paintings (by D.S. Neal) are fully published.

[3]Meates 1955, p. 130.

[4]Cf. the painting by D.S. Neal (Meates 1962, p. 31).

[5]The bird visible in the early drawing and photograph is not preserved.

[6]Meates 1955, pl. 45.

[7]We are extremely grateful to Miss Weatherhead and to Dr. I.H. Longworth and his staff in the British Museum's Department of Prehistoric and Romano-British Antiquities for their help in the study of this material. The results of Miss Weatherhead's work will be incorporated in the forthcoming publication by her and Miss Liversidge, to appear in the second volume of G.W. Meates's excavation-report.

[8]E.g. Wilpert 1929-36, pls. XVI (1-2), XVIII (5), CXXXVII (4), CXLII, CXLVII, CCXVII (7), CCXXXIX, CCXLI (1); Grabar, p. 265, figs. 295-6; cf. fig. 294.

[9]Mielsch 1978, pp. 191 ff., 204.

[10]E.g. Grabar, pp. 246-9, fig. 273; cf. figs. 276 ff.

[11]*Madrider Mitteilungen* ii (1961), pp. 124 ff., fig. 3, pls. 18, 19, 29, 30, 32.

[12]Diptychs: R. Delbrück, *Die Consulardiptychen und verwandte Denkmäler* (1929), nos. 1, 38, 43, 51, 52, 63, 64. Calendar: J. Strzygowski, *Die Calenderbilder des Chronographen vom Jahre 354* (1888), esp. pls. XXX, XXXIV, XXXV.

[13]Rhineland: *Germania romana*, 2nd edn., iv (1928), pp. 33 f., 35, pls. VII (figs. 1-4), IX (fig. 1); H. Schoppa, *Römische Gotterdenkmäler in Köln* (1959), pls. 20-21. Gaul: H. Walter, *La colonne ciselée dans la Gaule romaine (Annales littéraires de l'Université de Besançon* (cxix) (1970), pp. 21-41, pls. I-V, XXVII (1), XXVIII. Britain: VCH *Shropshire*, i

(1908), p. 253 and fig. 23 (Wroxeter); *JRS* l (1960), p. 218, pl. XXII, fig. 2 (Catterick); cf. Toynbee 1964, pp. 145-7. In the Catterick example and one or two others which Mr. T.F.C. Blagg has kindly brought to my notice the scales (or leaves) appear to be growing upwards. An unpublished fragment from Caerwent has 'crinkled' leaves, but the markings are not very close to ours.

[14] Meates 1955, pp. 72 f., 99, fig. 7 (a); 1962, pp. 11 f., 15. For palm-trees framing an *orans* on a sarcophagus see Wilpert 1929-36, pl. XCII, 1.

[15] Drack, p. 70, pl. v, Beil. 1 (fig. 154).

[16] Wilpert 1903, pls. 174, 176; Grabar, fig. 118; for the date, Mielsch 1978, p. 163 n. 52. On the decoration of tunics and dalmatics Wilpert 1903, pp. 93 ff.

[17] A possible exception is the Madonna in the Coemeterium Maius in Rome: Grabar, fig. 232. Cf. (a more schematic figure) one of the *orantes* on mosaic panels from Tabarka in Tunisia: *Inv. mos.* ii. P. Gauckler, *Afrique proconsulaire (Tunisie)* (1910), no. 953.

[18] E.g. Grabar, fig. 126; Wilpert 1929-36, *passim*.

No. 28. ★MALTON, Yorks. Fort, building inside north-east defences. Late first or early second century. To be displayed in Malton Roman Museum.

Fragments of a predominantly red and black wall-decoration (1927-30 excavations). These were set in the 1930s in slabs of plaster of paris and some were covered with a coat of modern red paint, but all have now been disentangled and are being cleaned and studied by the Yorkshire Museum.

Proportionately the largest group of fragments is those with a red background; several carry parts of a thick black and green garland or garlands, from which dangle pairs of delicate white pendants ending in discs and bobbles. There are also a number of pieces with vegetal candelabra, yellow with white highlights, white side-shoots and green leaves, on a black ground; some of them apparently abutted on a door-jamb. Fragments of framing elements suggest that the red and black areas were separated by a band of blue-green 4 cm wide, enclosed between white lines. It is possible, therefore, to postulate a scheme of red panels with coloured borders and black intervals carrying candelabra — the familiar Flavio-Trajanic scheme paralleled, for example, at Boxmoor and Cirencester (Nos. 2; 8).

Further elements can be assigned to a dado. One crucial fragment implies the presence of a rectangular panel containing a lozenge, a motif which recurs in later decorations in Yorkshire, for instance at Aldborough (Appendix, No. 1), Catterick (No. 5, C) and York (No. 52, A). The lozenge would be red, the corners of the rectangular panel pale blue, and the surrounding surface of the dado yellow.

Among the numerous other fragments the most interesting show rosettes with sets of eight triangular petals, red or cream on a black ground, which give the appearance of having been applied with stamps, a feature paralleled in the paintings from Collingham, also in Yorkshire (No. 12).

Reference: P. Corder, *The Defences of the Roman Fort at Malton* (1930), p. 37.
Excavator: L.G. Rowland, Malton and District Excavation Committee.

No. 29. ★MALTON, Yorks. Vicus, so-called 'Town House'. Fourth century (the house was perhaps built *c.* 300 and destroyed soon after 350). Now in Malton Roman Museum. PLS. LX-LXI.

(A) Numerous heterogeneous fragments from the 'mosaic room', showing mainly panel-framings and floral and vegetal elements (1949-52 excavations). There are also pieces with parts of human figures and faces about half-lifesize. The faces are painted in a skilful, impressionistic style, pink with purple shadows and pale pink and white highlights. Some of them, notably that of a mature, bearded man, have pale blue nimbi. The trays of fragments, many of which show remains of an earlier decoration, are labelled R32.2912 ('Town House').

(B) Another face was found in a pit in the *vicus*. Composed of joining fragments (total measurements: 18 cm wide × 22 cm high), it is on a much larger scale (slightly over lifesize) and in a much coarser style than those from the Town House; the nose, mouth and eyes are

Photo: R.J. Ling

LX   No. 29 (A)   Malton, fragments of parts of human faces from 'Town House'. Scale, 1:3.

indicated by red outlines, the pupils of the eyes by large black blobs. Though not itself labelled, it is displayed with some other joining fragments in the same style labelled R32.52.

References: N. Mitchelson, in *YAJ* xli (1963–66), p. 219; cf. L.P. Wenham, *Derventio (Malton)* (1974), p. 37.
Excavator: D. Smith, Department of the Environment.

No. 30.   ★OTFORD, Kent.   Villa (?), corridor. Second half of first or second century?[1] Now in British Museum. PLS. LXII–LXIII.

Fragments of wall-plaster, evidently from a Virgilian scene or scenes (1927 excavations; presented to the British Museum in 1928).

(A) 10 cm wide × 11 cm high. On a black ground the right arm and side of a figure holding a spear; flesh skilfully painted in tones of red and pink, spear yellow.

(B) 19.5 cm long × 12 cm high. The words BINA MANV in white, again on a black ground: a yellow stripe above. These words open three lines in the *Aeneid*; but the vertical stroke which remains of the first letter of the next word effectively reduces the options to two (i, 313; xii, 165), since it suggests 'L' for 'LATO' rather than 'F' for 'FVLVOS' (vii, 688). The full line would

Photo: R.J. Ling.

LXI No. 29 (B) Malton, fragments of a face found in a pit in the *vicus*.

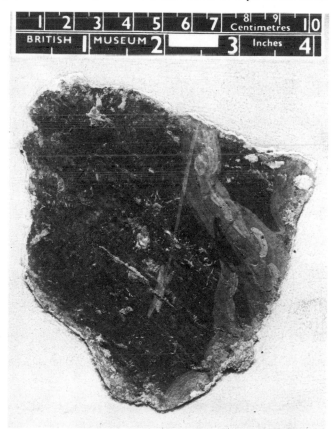

Photo: British Museum

LXII No. 30 (A) Otford, fragment showing spearsman.

Photo: British Museum.

LXIII   No. 30 (B)   Otford, fragment of Virgilian inscription.

then be *bina manu lato crispans hastilia ferro*, which refers in one context to Aeneas exploring the land round Carthage in company with Achates, in the other to Turnus coming forward in his chariot for the final reckoning with Aeneas. One can postulate a series of scenes from the *Aeneid*, perhaps a continuous frieze, with a commentary in the form of quotations from the poem; the quotations would probably have been placed above the heads of the figures, like the hexameters above the heads of the seven sages in the Baths of the Seven Sages at Ostia.[2] Whether the arm with the spear belongs with the BINA MANV quotation is, of course, an open question.

Subsequent excavation in 1927 revealed wall-plaster with bands of cream, pink and red; more letters of Latin inscriptions; and fragments showing 'parts of two male figures and a large variety of coloured patterns' (now in Maidstone Museum?).

References: *JRS* xvi (1926), pp. 238, 244, fig. 68; B.W. Pearce, *Arch. Cant.*, xxxix (1927), pp. 153, 154 f.; M.V. Taylor, in VCH *Kent*, iii (1932), p. 122, pl. XXV above; Hinks, p. 56 (no. 84), fig. 64 (upside down); Liversidge 1958, p. 380; Toynbee 1964, p. 220; Liversidge 1969, p. 144 f., pl. 4.6, 7.
Excavator: B.W. Pearce, Sevenoaks Society.

[1]The style of the paintings and the associated finds (see Taylor, *loc. cit.* in bibl.) are against the fourth-century dating accepted by Toynbee *(loc. cit.)* and Smith 1969, p. 91.
[2]E.g. Van Essen, p. 166, fig. 6.

No. 31.   RUDSTON, Yorks.   Villa, house 8. Fourth century (the plaster does not belong to the first phase of the structure but is perhaps contemporary with the mosaics, dated stylistically to the early fourth century).[1] Now in Hull, Transport and Archaeology Museum. PLS. LXIV-LXVII. FIGS. 31-34.

Fragments of wall-decoration recovered in 1971-72 from Room 2 (room of the charioteer mosaic) are ascribed to the north and west walls. From the north wall are four pieces restored by Dr. Davey.

(A) 1.80 m wide × 74 cm high. A kind of perspectival recess rendered in pale green and reddish purple on a white ground. The angles of the recess are marked by vertical bands 2.6 to 3.2 cm wide, green between black lines. These are interrupted by a broad horizontal zone, green with two bands of reddish purple, each 6 to 7 cm wide, enlivened with white and purple inner detail (oblique strokes and horizontal squiggles). On the side-walls of the 'recess' this zone diverges from the horizontal and adopts lighter colours (red and white detail on a pink ground) to give the effect of depth. The back-wall of the recess, restored as 72.5 cm wide, contains an arching motif formed by chains of purple lines enclosing a purple floral ornament, and above it, hanging from the horizontal zone, a pair of hook-like volutes in purple and pink.

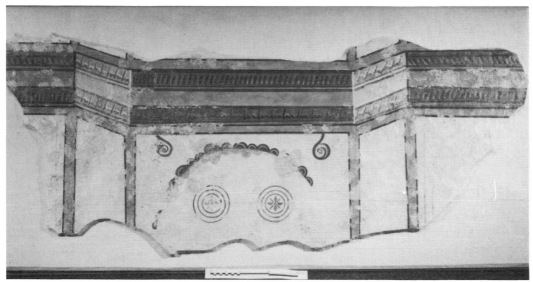

Photo: Department of the Environment: Crown Copyright reserved

LXIV   No. 31 (A)   Rudston, restored painting of perspectival niche.

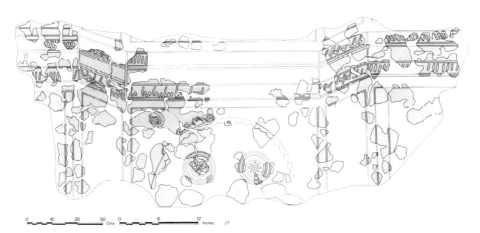

FIG. 31   No. 31 (A): Rudston, restoration of architectural perspective. Diagram showing position of original fragments. Scale, 1:15.

(Drawing by J. Thorn)

(B) 84 cm long × 41 cm high. A series of white and yellow lozenges arranged concertina-fashion. Along the series, zig-zagging in sympathy with the concertina, runs a pair of stripes, each approximately 1.4 cm wide, coloured red on the yellow lozenges, pink on the white. The whole motif is set in a band 27 cm wide, whose background is red on one side and dark purplish-blue on the other. Beyond this the colours are exchanged, a red zone lying adjacent to the blue, and vice versa.

LXV   No. 31 (B)   Rudston, restored concertina ornament.

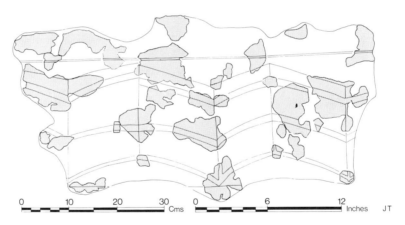

FIG. 32 No. 31 (B): Rudston, restored concertina ornament. Diagram showing position of
original fragments. Scale 1:8.

(Drawing by J. Thorn)

(C) 91 cm long × 32 cm high. On a white ground a series of plants and, above these, a
fence. The plants, all painted pale green, form three well-defined types: on the left a shrub with
long forking fronds like seaweed, at the centre a close clump of club-shaped leaves reminiscent
of certain types of cactus, and at the right a cluster of almond-shaped leaves arranged according
to no organic principle. The fence, painted greyish-yellow, is 7.5 cm high and consists of a pair
of horizontal bars, a series of uprights surmounted by triple-knobbed finials, and, in the intervening spaces, cross-shaped struts. Above this is the lower edge of a brownish-red zone
decorated with little diagonal strokes of dark purple.

(D) One face 20 cm wide × 75 cm high; the other 39 cm wide × 82 cm high. An angle-piece
ascribed to the north-west corner of the room. Along the angle runs a broad red band, flanked
on each wall by a band of pale green or grey framed by black lines. Beyond this, on a white
background, is set a broad horizontal band, purplish-red with a decoration of repeated white
and purple volutes.

LXVI   No. 31 (C)   Rudston, restored fence and plants.

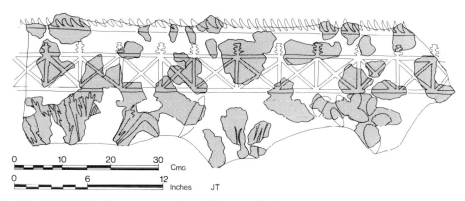

FIG. 33 No. 31 (C): Rudston, restoration of fence and plants. Diagram showing position of original
fragments. Scale, 1:8.

(Drawing by J. Thorn)

Other fragments ascribed to the north wall (1971 excavations) include a large floral motif in
purple with touches of pink and part of a window-splay in white framed by red. To the west
wall are ascribed pieces with the same purple and green horizontal band as in A, in one group of
fragments with a red fillet and ribbons hanging beneath it, in another ending against a vertical area
of pink decorated with purple veins. A third area shows the same pink, purple-veined element
(a column with scale-pattern?).

Further fragments came from Room 3, including small white flowers on a yellow ground,
purple buds or stalks on a pink ground, and panel-frames in green, pink, red and yellow.

Discussion.   From the material available it is not profitable to attempt a reconstruction of the
decorative scheme. The actual reconstructed pieces are rather hypothetical, since Dr. Davey did
not receive all of the plaster recovered from the room. In the case of Piece A, Miss Valery
Rigby, who was present at the excavation, feels that the right half of the restored recess should
be set to the left of the left half and indeed that some of the material discovered in 1971,
including the possible column or columns with scale-pattern, may belong to a central structure
between them: in other words Piece A may comprise parts of two recesses from opposite ends
of the wall. It would be attractive to postulate a counterfeit recess of some form at the centre of
the wall, since it would there have overlain a real recess which had subsequently been blocked.
The fence and plants (C) should be set, not high on the wall, as suggested in the excavation-
report (see bibliography below), but somewhere near the bottom: although fences are sometimes used to suggest balconies in the upper zones of wall-decorations,[2] there is no place for
plants in this position.

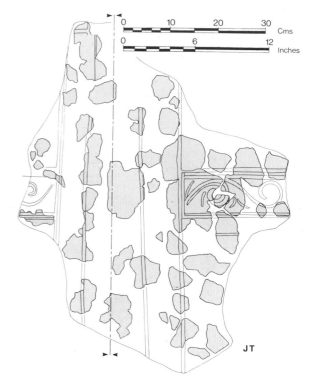

FIG. 34 No 31 (D): Rudston, restored piece of plaster
from angle of wall. Diagram showing position
of original fragments. Scale 1:8.
(Drawing by J. Thorn)

LXVII   No. 31 (D) Rudston, restored plaster at
angle of wall.
*Photo: Department of the Environment: Crown
Copyright reserved.*

Of the other pieces little can be said. Piece D comes from the angle of the room, but its level on the wall is indeterminable. The concertina motif (B) recalls a framing-element in the fourth-century paintings from Lullingstone (No. 27, C), but its alternation of light and darker colouring gives it a plasticity wholly lacking in the Kentish villa. This does not exclude its coming from a vertical rather than a horizontal concertina (in which case the 'light' presumably falls from above, as at Dover, No. 14); but the direction of the brush-marks suggests that the orientation was horizontal.[3]

Apart from the Lullingstone concertina, it is difficult to find meaningful parallels for the Rudston motifs. The colouring and the ornament of the painted recess are unique, and, if the restoration is correct, the lighting is also curious; we have an alcove in which both the receding side-walls catch the light while the back-wall remains in shadow. A slightly similar effect is achieved in a fourth-century painted alcove in House VII S at Caerwent (Appendix, No. 4), but there the difference between side- and back-walls is one of colour (the side-walls are yellow, the back-wall red) rather than of lighting. In both one is reminded of the somewhat unrealistic, pattern-like treatment of architectural forms found in the Lullingstone chapel (No. 27).

The fence and plants recall a favourite fourth-century theme, found in the paintings both of Rome and of the provinces; but there is no true parallel, since the fences found elsewhere are on a large scale and are set *in front of* the plants, which are often visible through the lattice.[4]

Reference: J. Liversidge, in I.M. Stead, *Rudston Roman Villa* (1980), pp. 141-5, figs. 89-91.
Excavator: I.M. Stead, Department of the Environment.

[1]Smith 1976, p. 5.

[2]E.g. the House of the Silver Wedding at Pompeii (F. Niccolini, *Le case e i monumenti di Pompei disegnati e descritti* (1854-91): 'Nuovi scavi', pl. XVIII); the House of the Amazons at Pompeii (*ibid.*, 'L'arte in Pompei', pl. XV); the house in Villa Negroni in Rome, *c.* A.D. 134 (*Röm. Mitt.* xxxiv, 1919, pl. I); the stucco frieze in Domitian's villa at Castelgandolfo (E.L. Wadsworth, in *MAAR* iv (1924), pls. XIII, XIV, XV, 1). Cf. our No. 42 (Verulamium).

[3]The same motif is used as a framing-element in a mosaic pavement from Lillebonne in North France (for ref. see Introduction, n. 98).

[4]Cf. Mielsch 1978, pp. 162, 168, 169, 192, 206, pls. 83 (2), 88 (2), 98 (1) (with further bibl. in footnotes). The scale of the fence and plants is more consonant with examples in dados of the first century, e.g. in the tablinum of the House of M. Lucretius Fronto in Pompeii: B. Andreae, *Römische Kunst* (1973), fig. 60.

No. 32. SCAMPTON, Lincs. Villa(?). Dating uncertain (the excavation, in 1973, was in the nature of a salvage operation, and proper recording was impossible; such pottery as was recovered belonged to the fourth century). Now in Potterne (in storage).

Fragments of a panel-system awaiting reconstruction.

The dado evidently contained at least two types of rectangular panel: (a) purple-red with white spots (porphyry) set in a white surround with pink scribbles; (b) dark grey with black inner border-stripes. The two types are separated by a black line and surmounted respectively by a black line (the white surround of the porphyry panel) and a white line (the dark grey panel). Along the top of the dado ran a yellow band 6.5 cm wide, crowned by a white stripe. Possibly another yellow band ran along the bottom.

Other elements which may have been set between the dado and the main zone or may possibly have belonged to a frieze above the main zone are: (a) a grey band 13.5 cm wide carrying five black stripes of varying thickness; (b) a purple-red band 4.5 cm wide between white stripes; (c) a black band of uncertain width (at least 5.5 cm) between white stripes.

The main zone contained red fields framed by pale green bands between white lines, and many fragments show parts of floral swags and candelabra which were evidently painted within the red fields. The effect was probably similar to the Antonine walls from Blue Boar Lane at Leicester (No. 22, A-B) and House XXI, 2 at Verulamium (No. 41, A-C).

There are also fragments showing a column or columns with scale-decoration.

Unpublished. See: *Britannia*, v (1974), p. 424.
Excavator: J.S. Wacher, Department of the Environment.

No. 33. ★SILCHESTER, Hants. Insula XIV, House 1. Second century? Now in Reading. Museum and Art Gallery (in storage). PL. LXVIII. FIG. 35.

Fragments of painted decoration found (1895) in a rubbish deposit north of Room 22, some of which were restored by Fox in a panel 1.09 m × 55.5 cm.

On a reddish purple ground is a repeating pattern or patterns based on roundels and squares.

The roundels (outer diam. 19 cm; inner diam. 10 cm) were formed by two white lines and an inner yellow line. At the centre of each was a white four-petalled rosette (the fruit-like cluster shown by Fox's restoration is formed by a group of heterogeneous fragments: the true appearance can be gauged from the example mistakenly set outside the roundel). The eye of the rosette was pierced by the point of the compass with which the circles were drawn, and incised guide-lines radiated outwards, dividing the roundel into eight equal sectors. From the circumference, continuing the radial lines, grew yellow 'fleurs-de-lis' and green triple-leaf ornaments, apparently in alternation.

The squares (outer measurement approx. 19 cm) had an outer grey border 3.5 cm wide, flanked by white lines, and an inner border-line of yellow, each side of which ended in a brief volute at the corners. At the centre (probably, though not certainly) was painted a white ring with external bobbles. The 'fleurs-de-lis' and triple-leaf ornaments were repeated round the exterior, again apparently in alternation. The surviving fragments suggest that the former grew

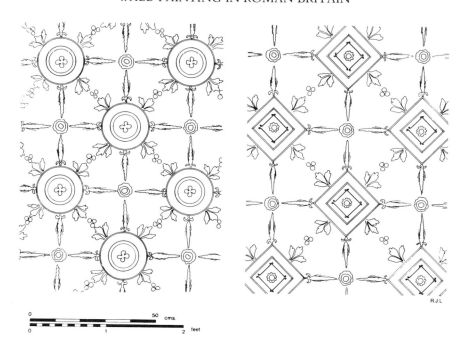

FIG. 35   No. 33: Silchester, ceiling-patterns (reconstructed). Background reddish-purple,
pattern white, yellow, grey and green. Scale, 1:15.
(Drawing by R. J. Ling)

from the corners, the latter from the mid-points of the sides (*contra* Fox's version, which has
leaves on only two sides).

Further fragments indicate that the 'fleurs-de-lis' were in fact the bases of barley-ear ornaments, the central member forming the stem, and the side-parts being flanking volutes. Four
barley-ears seem to have converged on a green rosette with a circular white highlight. From
still further fragments it appears that pairs of the triple-leaf ornaments grew towards each other,
being separated only by a cluster of three round fruits, yellow with white highlights.

Fox's reconstruction, the earliest known attempt in Britain to put together part of a fragmentary painted decoration, is a careful and intelligent piece of work; but his belief that the pattern
belonged to a dado is certainly wrong, since dadoes were never so decorated in antiquity. The

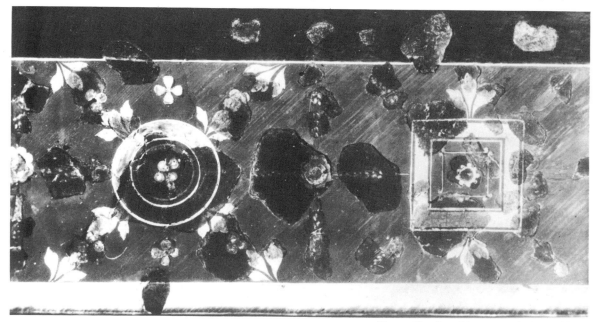

Photo: Reading Museum and Art Gallery.

LXVIII   No. 33   Silchester, Fox's restoration of plaster from Insula XIV, 2.

elements indicate an all-over pattern of the type found most commonly on ceilings (cf. Nos. 23; 41, D; 50).

The data available, however, make it difficult to accommodate both squares and roundels in a single pattern. A single pattern would only be possible either if the squares measured 19 cm along the diagonal rather than along the side or if the larger of the intervening motifs (the barley ear) grew from the side of the square rather than from the angle. It is accordingly suggested in the drawing that there were two closely related but separate patterns, one based on squares, the other on roundels. These might have derived from adjacent or balancing rooms, or even from different parts of the same room; the use of related patterns in different parts of one ceiling is well-attested in Roman interior decoration, for instance in the cryptoportico of Nero's Golden House in Rome, in the *oecus* (Room 8) of the House of the Smith at Pompeii, and in the baths at St. Romain en Gal.[1]

References: W.H.St.J. Hope and G.E. Fox, *Archaeologia* lv (1896–97), pp. 249 f., fig. 5; F. Haverfield, *The Romanization of Roman Britain*, 4th edn. (1923), fig. 14; Boon 1957, p. 150 and fig. 29; 1974, p. 212 and pl. 29.
Excavators: W.H.St.J. Hope and G.E. Fox, Society of Antiquaries.

[1]Golden House: *Ant. Denkm.* iii, 2 (1912–13), pls. 16–17; Dacos, fig. 23. House of the Smith: *Not. Scav.* 1934, p. 282, pl. X. St. Romain en Gal: information from Alix Barbet.

No. 34.   SOUTHWELL, Notts.   Villa, bath-building, *frigidarium*. Late second or early third century. Now in Southwell Minster (B and C in storage). PLS. LXIX–LXXI, CXIX.

Areas of wall- or ceiling-decoration restored from fragments found in 1959 sealed beneath a later floor.

(A) 1.79 m wide × 2.38 m high. The piece is here described as it is displayed in the Minster; for differences between the authors on the orientation and interpretation see below. A Cupid, virtually lifesize, (PL CXIX) is shown in three-quarters view to our right in a marine environment. His right arm is raised and his left arm is lowered; his wings, pale blue with gold rims, are extended behind his shoulders; and a short red-brown cloak, held by a cord which passes from the right shoulder to the left armpit, swirls round his left arm and spreads out behind him. The forms of the body have been skilfully rendered with modelling achieved by white highlights and reddish shadows. On the greenish blue background, to left and right of the Cupid, two fat fish are shown. At the left, beneath the fluttering cloak, a grey and brown fish dives diagonally to the right; at the right, next to the Cupid's (missing) left hand, a pale green fish with a white belly carrying red markings plunges straight down.

To the right of this scene runs a broad vertical border consisting of a pink band about 4 cm wide and a broader green band shading into a second pink band (total width about 25 cm). Beyond the border comes another green band, this time decorated with small yellow elements carrying white highlights, possibly the remains of a frieze of sea-monsters set perpendicularly to the main figure-scene. The central creature looks like a sea-horse or deer, its forelegs ending in fins, swimming to the right.

In the lower part of the panel, forming a continuation of the scene with the Cupid, is a large area of plaster containing reddish-brown, grey-blue and white elements on the greenish-blue background. The reconstruction is problematic, but there are possible remains of another fish and of a female arm with a reddish-brown scarf flying from it.

(B) Two joining pieces (44 cm × 90.5 cm; 91 cm × 1.51 m). Two nude figures stand arm in arm against a pink and green border identical to that in Piece A. The right-hand of the two figures, which have yellowish flesh and are probably both male, seems to hold a club or stick beside his left leg. Beyond the border a pale blue green ground carries fronds of seaweed, pink with purple veins.

(C) Four small pieces showing marine fauna and flora on a blue ground. One seems to be slightly curved, suggesting derivation from a vault.

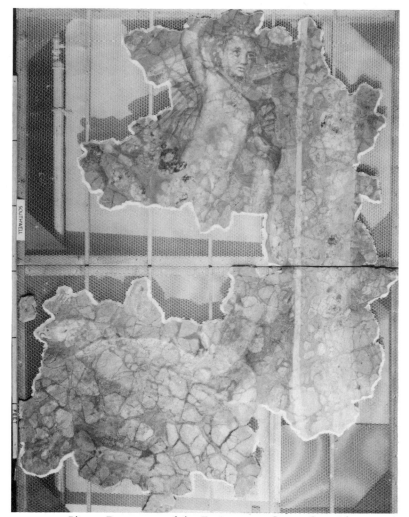

LXIX   No. 34 (A)   Southwell, restored plaster showing Cupid in marine environment.

A large quantity of plaster remains in the Department of the Environment stores at Avebury, which if restored might throw further light on this decoration.

The main focus of interest in the decoration is the finely painted Cupid and its relation to the marine context.

Marine subjects are a favourite motif in the decoration of baths, and there are parallels for our fish in the painted decorations of bath-suites in the villas at High Wycombe, Lullingstone, Sparsholt (No. 37, C), Winterton (No. 49) and Witcombe (No. 50), as well as in a set of suburban baths at Verulamium.[1] When painted on the walls and vaults of the plunge-baths in *frigidaria*, such creatures would be reflected in the water and would thus create a marine environment for the bathers, as in the *frigidarium* of the City Baths at Herculaneum, where the painted dome shows sea-eels, mullets, garfish, and an octopus, all on a bluish ground.

But the occurence of Cupids generally betokens a more elaborate sea-scene. In a mosaic pavement from Cirencester, now lost but drawn by Lysons in the early nineteenth century, they are shown riding a dolphin and clinging to a wheel, presumably a remnant of Neptune's chariot, while around them swim sea-creatures of every description.[2] Similarly the marine mosaics of the Hadrianic Baths of Neptune at Ostia include Cupids riding on dolphins or flying, torch in hand, before a sea-horse carrying a nereid.[3] As winged creatures, Cupids seem uncomfortable in an aquatic context and must generally be conceived as above the surface of the water, whether on the wing or on dolphin-back. But sometimes, as in the Cirencester mosaic, the media air and water are inextricably confused; and sometimes Cupids actually appear to be swimming: for example on a number of sarcophagi and on the lower part of a mid third-century mosaic from Utica in North Africa (now in the Louvre).[4]

Photo: R.J. Ling

LXX No. 34 (B) Southwell, detail of restored plaster showing two nude figures.

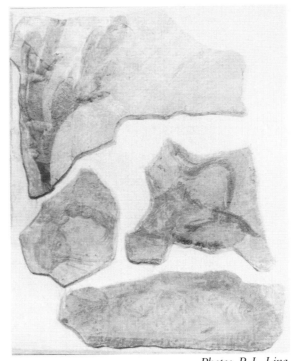

Photo: R.J. Ling

LXXI No. 34 (C) Southwell, restored pieces of plaster showing marine life.

The Southwell painting too shows a confusion of air and water: the Cupid's posture and his extended wings suggest flight, but fish swim round his legs. The most anomalous feature, however, is the spreading cloak. In all the examples cited the Cupids are shown naked, and the same applies even where Cupids are merely standing in the water, as in the third-century mythological painting in the house under the church of Ss. Giovanni e Paolo in Rome, or are merely attending Venus Anadyomene against a backdrop of marine fauna (the Baths of the Seven Sages at Ostia).[5] We have as yet found no example of a Cupid in marine surroundings, still less swimming, who wears a cloak.

A further problem concerns the orientation of the figure. Of the present writers one (N.D.) believes that the piece, as displayed, is wrongly oriented. The Cupid was shown swimming on his back, and the bands of pink and green above him represented the surface of the water, the graduations of colour perhaps being intended by the artist to represent the irridescent effect of light striking it. To enhance this effect the artist depicted rays of light falling obliquely from above. Upon the surface of the water, which it is logical to expect to be horizontal, were the fragments of yellow creatures and in the water were several fishes. Piece B joined Piece A at the right and the pink and green bands curved upwards round the two nude figures, who thus appeared on an island, approaching the water in the foreground.

The other writer prefers the present orientation; he feels that the Cupid is unlikely to have been shown swimming on his back with cloak spreading and wings extended. If the creatures beyond the green and pink bands were oriented differently, another explanation must be sought. Perhaps the plaster had fallen from the ceiling, in which case apparent inconsistencies in orientation are only to be expected: compare the birds and feline heads of the Verulamium ceiling (No. 41, D).

References: Toynbee 1964, p. 219; C.M. Daniels, in *Trans. Thoroton Soc.* lxx (1966), p. 21; Davey 1972, pp. 265 and 268, figs. 14, 15, pl. XXII (B).

Excavator: C.M. Daniels, Department of the Environment. Lifted by Nan Shaw.

[1] High Wycombe: J. Parker, *The Early History and Antiquities of Wycombe* (1878), p. 3 (undated). Lullingstone: Meates 1955, p. 97 (last quarter of second century). Verulamium: unpublished (Antonine: I am grateful to C. Saunders for letting me see the material). Cf. for Continental examples Kapossy, *passim*, esp. pp. 39–41.

[2]Lysons 1813–17, ii, pl. 7; Toynbee 1962, p. 197 (no. 182), pl. 213. On Cupids and the sea in general see R. Stuveras, *Le putto dans l'art romain* (1969), pp. 153–64.

[3]Becatti, pls. CXXIV ff.; cf. a mosaic from Ciciliano (*Not. Scav.* 1948, p. 298, fig. 2) and other, later Ostian mosaics (Becatti, pls. CXLVIII, CLIV ff.).

[4]Sarcophagi: e.g. *Die antiken Sarkophagreliefs*, v, 1. A. Rumpf, *Die Meerwesen auf den antiken Sarkophagreliefs* (1939), pls. 8 (29), 19 (75, 76), 24 (73), 26 (68), 36 (95), 40 (116). Mosaic: *Corpus des mosaïques de Tunisie*, i, 3. *Utique, mosaïques sans localisation précise et El Alia* (1976), pp. 40–42 (no. 288), pls. XXII–XXIII, XL; F. Baratte, *Catalogue des mosaïques romaines et paléochrétiennes du musée du Louvre* (1978), p. 53 f., fig. 39.

[5]House under Ss. Giovanni e Paolo: e.g. Borda, p. 320 and col. pl. facing. Baths of the Seven Sages: Van Essen, p. 60 f. and fig. 2; Dorigo, col. pl. 5.

No. 35. SPARSHOLT, Hants. Villa, Building 1. Second century. Now in Winchester, City Museum. PL. LXXII, FIG. 36.

Piece restored from fragments of wall-plaster found (1971–72) packed in the foundations of the aisled house which replaced Building 1, possibly in the early third century.

1.10 m long × 54 cm high. Painted imitation of a mosaic border, probably from the foot of a wall (as is suggested by the straightish edge and slight splaying at the bottom). Above a plain red band 6 cm wide comes a pair of guilloches, one above the other, between a pair of white bands 8 or 9 cm wide. In the lower guilloche (12 cm wide) each ply is formed by strands of four colours: from top to bottom, purple, brick-red, white, and purple again. A single white 'tessera' is set at the eye of each plait. The upper guilloche is more complex, with purple, red,

Photo: Department of the Environment: Crown Copyright reserved

LXXII   No. 35   Sparsholt, restored mosaic pattern.

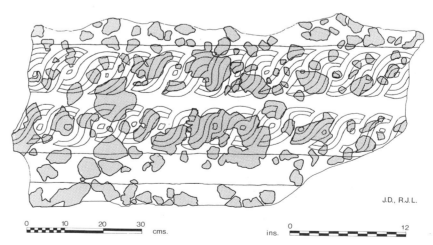

J.D., R.J.L.

FIG. 36   No. 35: Sparsholt, restoration of part of painted mosaic pattern. Diagram showing position of original fragments. Scale, 1:10.
(Drawing by Judith Dobie, adapted by R.J. Ling)

yellow, white and purple strands in each ply; the extra strand results in a width of 13 cm. Single 'tesserae' again mark the mid-points of the plaits. The guilloches are set on a purple background, represented by a double row of 'tesserae' between them and a single row above and below. The white borders are each five rows of tesserae wide.

The whole motif is rather carelessly painted, the tesserae varying in size from a minimum of 0.7 by 0.9 cm to a maximum of 1.3 by 2.5 cm. The interstices are painted purple, except in the case of the purple 'tesserae', which are outlined in red.

The motif of imitation mosaic is virtually confined to Britain, where it has been found on three other villa-sites, all in the south and west: Bignor (Appendix No. 3, B), Compton Abdale (Gloucestershire) and Lufton (Somerset) (Introduction, FIG. 2).[1] The first and last of these sites yielded the same guilloche motif, white, grey, red, yellow and blue at Bignor, yellow, red and black at Lufton. We may possibly have here a local motif, favoured by a workshop operating in the south and west of the province. Unfortunately there is no firm dating evidence available for any of these parallels. On the Continent imitation mosaic of a rather different sort has been found in the baths at St.-Romain-en-Gal, France:[2] here, in addition to 'fish-tail' patterns in white 'tesserae', there are elements in which isolated 'tesserae' or clusters of 'tesserae' are set on an otherwise plain coloured background, recalling a favourite type of opus signinum floor-decoration.[3]

It is interesting that the colours of the 'tesserae' are those of floor-mosaics rather than wall-mosaics. In each case, however, the borders in question may have come from the foot of a wall and may have been inspired by actual floor-mosaics carried up the lower part of the wall: a well-known example of such a mosaic wainscoting, decorated with a vegetal scroll, is known from Büelisacker in Switzerland (second century).[4]

Unpublished. Reference: D.E. Johnston in M. Todd (ed.), *Studies in the Romano-British Villa* (1978), p. 82.

Excavator: D.E. Johnston, Department of the Environment.

[1]Liversidge 1969, p. 134 and fig. 4.1 *b, c, d*. The Compton Abdale piece, recorded as being in Cheltenham Museum, is now apparently missing.

[2]Unpublished. We are grateful to Alix Barbet for showing us the fragments, which are awaiting restoration at Soissons.

[3]E.g. Blake, pp. 25 ff.

[4]Von Gonzenbach, pp. 225 f., pl. 4; Sear, p. 179 (No. 283), pl. 71, 2.

No. 36. SPARSHOLT, Hants. Villa, Room 7. Third or fourth century. Now in Winchester, City Museum. PL. LXXIII.

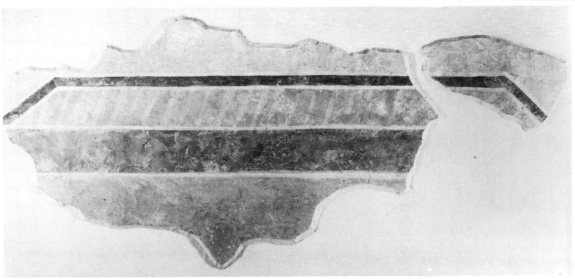

Photo: Department of the Environment: Crown Copyright reserved

LXXIII   No. 36   Sparsholt, restored piece of plaster from Room 7.

Two pieces reconstructed from fragments found (1965-66) in the main reception room (Room 7).

1.13 m wide × 63 cm high; 37 cm wide × 23.5 cm high. The larger piece shows the upper part of a fawn-coloured dado, speckled with white, green and yellow splashes. Above this comes a dark red band 11 cm wide between white stripes, and above this in turn an orange-brown zone surmounted by a purple band 2.5 cm wide between white stripes. This crowning band bends obliquely down at the left to abut against the dark red band below; and on the smaller piece it is shown repeating this angle in mirror-image. Above it comes a pale green surface. Both the orange-brown and pale green surfaces carry oblique stripes in a watery white.[1] Granted that the restoration is correct, these pieces may show the floor of a stylised alcove or alcoves painted in perspective, similar to the fourth-century examples from Caerwent (Appendix, No. 4) and Rudston (No. 31, A).

Unpublished.

Excavator: D.E. Johnston. Department of the Environment.

[1] This unusual motif is paralleled at Caerwent, where a fragment found in trenches south of House II S showed oblique white stripes on a pink ground (unpublished drawing in Newport Museum).

No. 37. SPARSHOLT, Hants. Villa, baths. Third or fourth century. Now in Winchester, City Museum. PLS. LXXIV-LXXVII. FIGS. 37-40.

Pieces restored from fragments found (1966-67) in various parts of the baths.

†(A) Arch with a portion of the supporting wall or jamb, from the doorway leading into the bath-house. On a blue band between red zones a pair of white lines is punctuated at regular intervals by pairs of white knobbles.

(B) Part of the jamb of the doorway between Rooms 17 and 18 *(tepidarium/caldarium* and *frigidarium)*. 59 cm wide × 58.5 cm high (bevelled at both edges). A woman's bust set in a roundel. The interior of the roundel is pale blue, and it is framed by a light green band 6.5 cm

LXXIV   No. 37 (B)   Sparsholt, female bust in medallion.

FIG. 37   No. 37 (B): Sparsholt, restoration of female bust in medallion from baths. Diagram
showing position of original fragments. Scale, 1:5.
(Drawing by Judith Dobie)

wide between white enrichments reminiscent of a bead and reel (the reel is reduced to two pearls). The inner enrichment (diam. approx. 36 cm) is reinforced by a black line. The frame overlaps the vertical frames of the door-jamb, which are also light green. The spaces above and below are red.

It is difficult to judge the style of the head, since only a few fragments of the original painting remain. These show that the flesh was brownish-pink with orange-red shading and purple contours, that the hair had a fuzzy outline, and that the eyes were wide with purple irises carrying white highlights. The motif of a bust within a medallion recalls the *imagines clipeatae* of triumphal and sepulchral art (cf. Brantingham, No. 4, A); some actual carved examples have similar bead-and-reel frames.[1] In painting the best parallels are from France, where wall-paintings from Mercin-et-Vaux (Aisne) and Martizay (Indre), admittedly at least a century earlier in date, contain very similar bust-medallions.[2] At Mercin-et-Vaux the busts (probably representing deities) were painted against a black ground and had green borders set between an inner enrichment of pearls and hearts and an outer enrichment of pearls and spindle-shaped beads (apparently one of each, whereas at Sparsholt there were two pearls for every bead). At Martizay the framing and colouring were identical to those of the Sparsholt medallion, except that the inner field was red instead of blue. In addition to these Gallo-Roman parallels, there is a medallion-bust of Christ with a similar (though less broad) frame painted in the Coemeterium Maius in Rome (fourth century).[3]

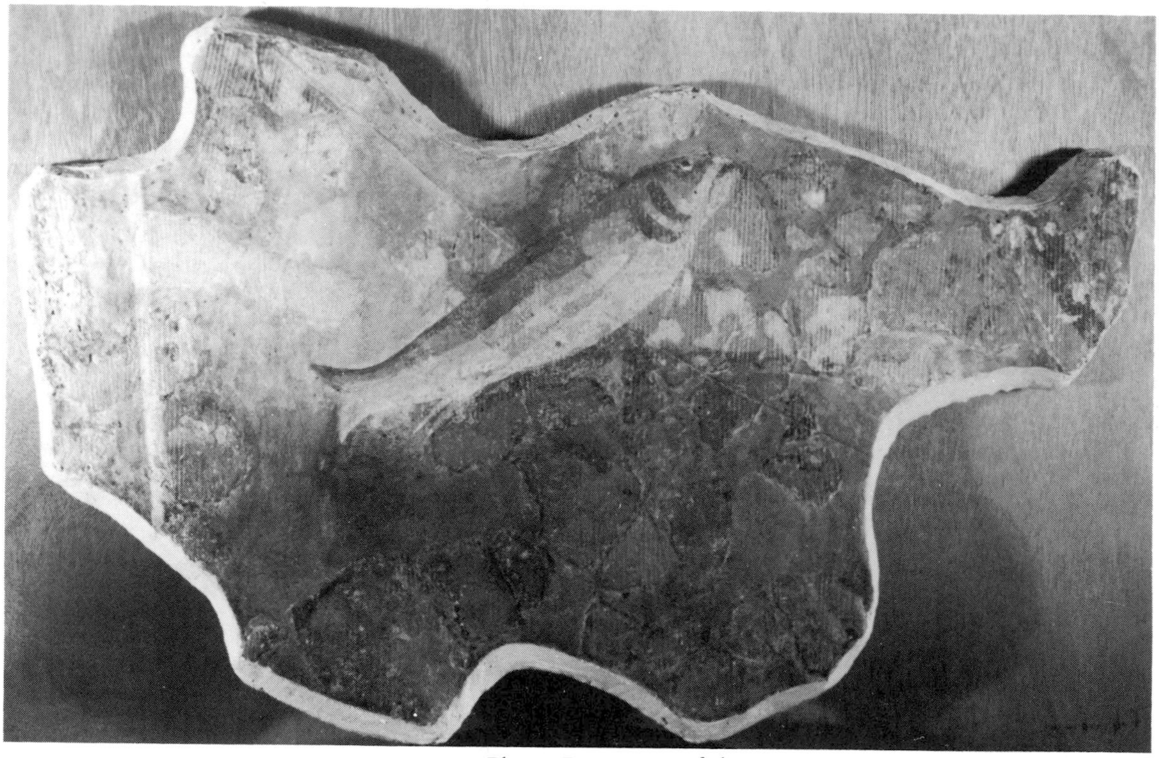

Photo: Department of the Environment: Crown Copyright reserved

LXXV No. 37 (C) Sparsholt, restored fragment with fish.

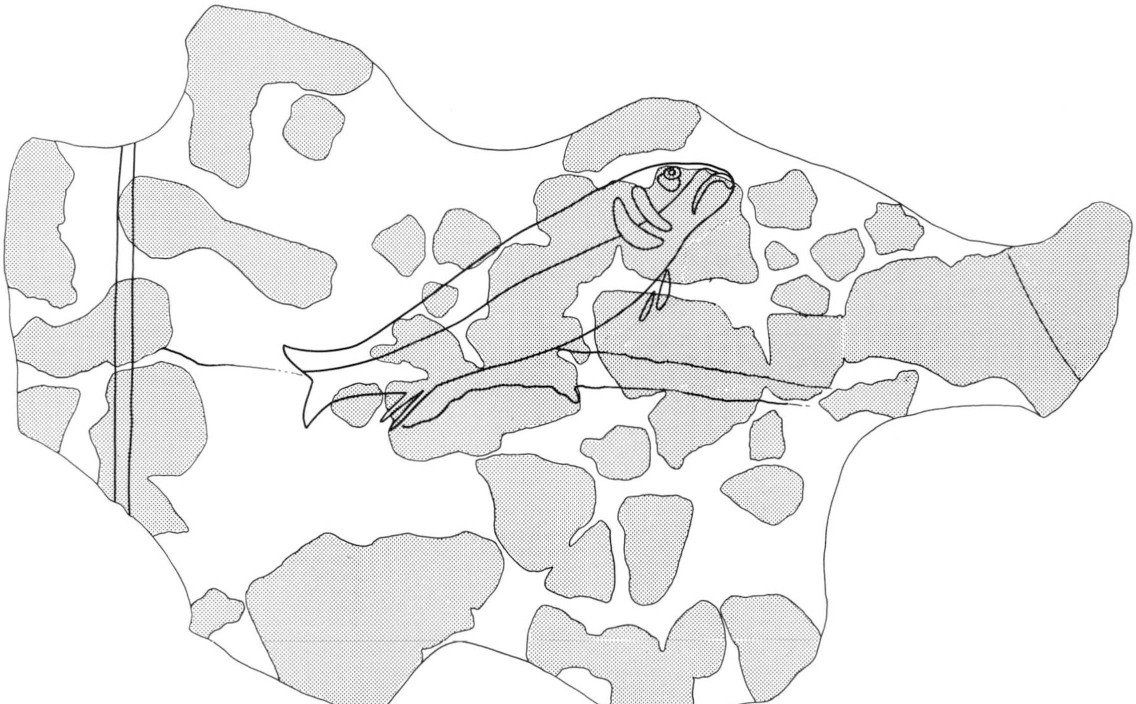
J.D.
0 10 20 Cms
0 6 Inches

FIG. 38 No. 37 (C): Sparsholt, restoration of part of painted vault of plunge-bath (Room 18). Diagram showing position of original fragments. Scale, 1:5.

(Drawing by Judith Dobie)

(C) Piece of painted vault of plunge-bath (Room 18). 73 cm × 48 cm. On a background grading from sea-green (pale green over a blue undercoat) below to sky-blue above, is a fish with white belly and brown back. The mouth, eye and gills are preserved on one fragment, and much of the belly with two white filaments apparently representing the anal fin also survive; only the tail has had to be significantly restored. A vertical white stripe runs a short distance to the left of the fish's tail. For the popularity of marine fauna in the wall- and vault-decoration of plunge-baths see No. 34 (Southwell) and the parallels there cited.

(D) 21.5 cm wide × 72 cm high. A thick, straight garland growing from a yellow container (also from Room 18). The container is restored as cylindrical with a broad curving base seen from above and a broad curving rim seen from below; the background, and the interior of both rim and base, are pale purple. The garland itself is formed by a dark purple band, jagged at the

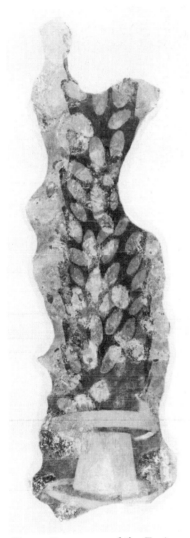

Photo: Department of the Environment: Crown Copyright reserved

LXXVI No. 37 (D) Sparsholt, restored garland.

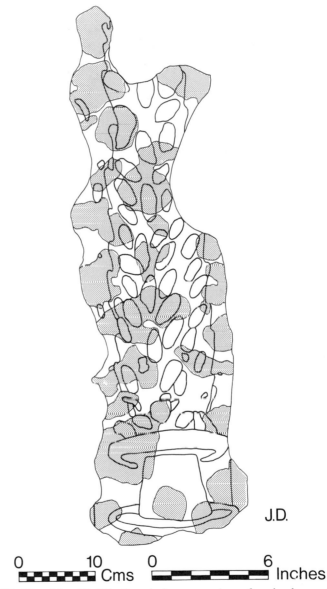

J.D.

0   10   0   6
Cms   Inches

FIG. 39.   No. 37 (D): Sparsholt, restoration of garland growing from vase, from Room 18 in baths. Diagram showing position of original fragments. Scale, 1:5.
(Drawing by Judith Dobie)

edges, carrying a profusion of pale green elliptical leaves. At the bottom, left and right of the container, there are traces of pale whitish-blue zones beyond the purple background. The role of this garland within the decoration is uncertain, but the presence of the container indicates that it is vertical rather than horizontal (unlike the example in the newly-excavated decoration at

Photo: Department of the Environment: Crown Copyright reserved
LXXVII   No. 37 (E)   Sparsholt, restored laurel-garland.

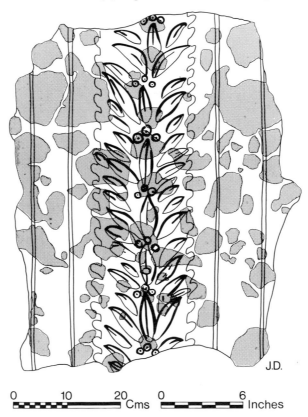

FIG. 40   No. 37 (E): Sparsholt, restoration of garland from Room 18 in baths.
Diagram showing position of original fragments. Scale, 1:7.

(Drawing by Judith Dobie)

Leicester: No. 24, A).[4] Possibly it decorated the interval between panels on the wall; possibly it spanned a vault, like the stucco garland decorating a rib in the House of the Cryptoportico at Pompeii.[5]

(E) 53 cm wide × 67 cm high. Part of a somewhat similar garland to the last (also from Room 18), but with a different arrangement of leaves and different framing colours. The purple band of the garland, here decorated with regular knobbles along the edges, carries almond-shaped leaves, each of which has part of its spine and one edge picked out in yellow or white; large leaves grow along the axis, alternating with clusters of three berries outlined in white, and both large and small leaves grow out to the sides. The genus of plant intended is perhaps laurel.

The garland is set on a yellow background, which is separated by turquoise bands 6.3 cm (as restored) and 7.7 cm wide from orange-red zones beyond. The yellowish tinge of all the main colours implies that the whole surface was initially painted yellow and that the other colours were painted over this; the turquoise would have been achieved by an over-painting of blue, the orange-red by an over-painting of red.

The curvature of the reconstructed panel suggests that it came from the soffit of an arched opening or recess.

References: D.E. Johnston, in M. Todd (ed)., *Studies in the Romano-British Villa* (1978), p. 82. Idem, *Roman Villas* (1979), pl. I.

Excavator: D.E. Johnston, Department of the Environment.

[1]E.g. Winkes, pl. III *b, c* (Corinth, Hadrianic-Antonine).

[2]Mercin-et-Vaux: Barbet 1974b, pp. 112, 117, figs. 4, 5 (late first or early second century). Martizay: Barbet 1975, p. 105, fig. 5 (first century?). Plain (?) roundels with bead-and-reel frames similar to those at Sparsholt occurred also in the baths of the villa at Münsingen in Switzerland: Kapossy, p. 13, figs. 1, 24, 25.

[3]Wilpert 1903, pl. 164, 1.

[4]For the motif of a vertical garland growing from a vase cf. Drack, pl. I and Beil. I (fig. 153) (Commugny, Switzerland: first century).

[5]Spinazzola, pls. XXIV-XXV; Ling, p. 35, pl. XV *a*.

No. 38. ★TARRANT HINTON, Dorset. Villa, Building II. Fourth century. Now in Wimborne (in storage). PLS. LXXVIII-LXXIX, CXI.

Large quantities of fragments (approx. 500 kg.) were collected in Room 1 in the excavations of 1970-71. These are being studied and assembled by Lt.-Col. G.E. Gray; the most important element to emerge is a scene or scenes with almost lifesize figures on a pale turquoise ground. At present there are three main assemblages.

(A) The bottom left-hand corner of a figure-scene. At the left edge a vertical reddish-purple border at least 10.5 cm wide, bisected by a vertical yellow line. At the bottom a reddish-purple band 4 cm wide above a white band 8 cm wide which in turn surmounts a zone of imitation marble, yellow with red veins. In the picture-field an undulating ground-surface, reddish-brown in colour, carries the right foot of a male figure in three-quarters view to our right; next to this rests a rectangular block on which is seen a flesh-coloured detail, presumably the figure's other foot. The preserved foot is strongly modelled, with red and purple shading and pink highlights, both rendered in diagonal brush-strokes. The block is shown in a 'foreshortened frontal setting',[1] as if from the right, its vertical face being purple, and its upper surface grey-white. Width of the ankle 8 cm.

(B) The head and right shoulder of a (seated?) male figure with long hair and an effeminate face tilted languidly downwards in three-quarters view to our left (PL. CXI); behind it, at the right, rises a staff or spear, purple with a yellow highlight along the left edge. The colouring is similar to that of the foot, and the paintwork shows the same predilection for modelling with diagonal strokes of colour. To the right of the staff, at a higher level and on a slightly smaller scale than the first head, is a second head, this time in profile. It apparently rests, disembodied, on the top left corner of a rectangular grey block, and is thus presumably a carved embellishment of a fountain or the like; its paler colouring and less firm modelling distinguish it from

Photo: R. J. Ling

LXXVIII   No. 38 (A)   Tarrant Hinton, fragments of foot of human figure.

the real head below. It has full lips and is perhaps intended to depict a satyr. To the right of it, above the block, is a confused area of pink and purple, perhaps a layer of unworked stone crowning the 'fountain'.[2] The turquoise background gives way, above the first head, to an arching pink surface of uncertain significance. Height of the first head 24 cm.

(C) Fragments of a dado (?) (if they do belong to a dado, they belong to the upper part of it, since a dark green zone 45 cm high was seen *in situ* at the bottom of the wall). A pattern of imitation veneering in which a roundel is set in a square from which horizontal bands lead off at the sides. The roundel consists of a central tondo, about 33 cm in diameter, painted purple-red with pink splashes to simulate porphyry, and a framing band 4 cm wide, grey with green mottling, enclosed between white stripes. The enclosing square is grey with white and pink splodges, framed by a white stripe and a black line; the bands leading off it continue the marbling pattern and the white and black frames, and have a total width of 8 cm. Above (and presumably below) these bands ran bands of imitation porphyry (6.5 cm wide) which seem to have bent like a meander round the squares; and beyond these in turn, separated from them by a white stripe, were bands of imitation giallo antico (cream with yellow and orange mottling and red veins: 5 cm wide). It is possible that the last bands were identical with the zone of yellow marbling below the picture-field in A.

It is unlikely that the motif described belonged to a repeating series, as suggested in the published reconstruction-drawing (see bibliography below); other fragments show details which could not be accommodated in such a scheme, for example (1) adjacent corners of areas of porphyry, one with a giallo antico border, the other with a grey-green border, each approximately 4.5 or 5 cm wide between white stripes, (2) the corner of an area of giallo antico with a porphyry border. Perhaps the panel with the roundel was set at the central point of the wall and simpler panels succeeded it on either side.

Discussion.   The Tarrant Hinton figure-paintings are, in quality, the finest yet discovered in Britain; their importance is thus very great. An interpretation must await further reconstruction; but already some ideas suggest themselves. In area B the effeminate face of the main figure, the angle of the head and shoulder, and the presence of what could be a spear, all bring

Photo: R. J. Ling

LXXIX No. 38 (C) Tarrant Hinton, fragments of marbled dado.

to mind the iconography of Narcissus, who is frequently shown seated, his weight supported on one arm, his head languidly tilted to catch the reflection of his face in the spring below, and his hunting-spear or spears resting against his arm or shoulder.[3] The fountain, if such it is, would be appropriate in the context, presumably representing the source of the water which gave the reflection.[4] In area A the motif of a figure with one foot on a block is too non-specific to permit the identification of the subject, but one is reminded of the postures of Perseus or Argos in the early Imperial paintings of the tribulations of Andromeda and Io perhaps based on works by Nicias,[5] and (more forcibly) of a stucco relief in the Underground Basilica at Porta Maggiore in Rome. Here a male figure stands in three-quarters view with his left foot resting, as at Tarrant Hinton, on a rectangular block. His arms are crossed on the raised thigh and he seems to be watching or speaking to a female figure seated at the left, who holds a statuette (the *palladium*?) in one hand, and rests her head on the other in the conventional gesture of grief or anxiety. The subject is uncertain.[6]

Every indication supports a date in the first half or middle of the fourth century. The presence of large-scale mythological scenes, apparently above a marbled dado; the technique of shading with short diagonal strokes; and to some extent the range of colours employed — all recall the frescoes from Kingscote, which are dated to the late third or early fourth century (No. 21). The treatment of the eyes, which are large and semicircular in shape with the iris set against the upper lid, is particularly closely related to Constantinian art and can be compared to that of the eyes of the figures in the ceiling-paintings from the palace beneath the cathedral in Trier.[7] The fully plastic treatment of form would accord, in metropolitan contexts, with a date after about 315.[8] Another element, the dark, bumpy ground-surface in A, which gives no real spatial setting and looks almost like a cross-section, is found in Rome and Ostia in paintings of the second half of the century; but it is there combined with a much harder and more two-dimensional figure-style.[9] That stage is represented in Britain by the Christian paintings at Lullingstone (No. 27). The Tarrant Hinton paintings are clearly earlier, and we should be safe in accepting a date between *c.* 315 and *c.* 360. The imitation of marble veneering in the dado, including at least one roundel, is a characteristic fourth-century feature (see Bignor, No. 1).

Other fragments from the Tarrant Hinton figure-scenes show more parts of staffs or spears like that in area B (one has a trumpet-shaped mouth or terminal, another seems to emerge from behind a head). There are also folds of drapery in turquoise, white, and purplish red, and one piece has, on a green ground, a yellow medallion (diam. 11.5 cm) with a *gorgoneion* quickly sketched in white and purple.

Room 1 also yielded numerous fragments of a different, softer plaster containing bits of a white material, perhaps chalk. This plaster probably came from the ceiling, since some pieces have imprints of reeds on the reverse. The decoration includes wreaths or garlands (white and green leaves against yellow and red grounds) and roundels (one example is red with a green border between white lines).

The corridor outside Room 1 yielded a piece of wall-painting *in situ*. A dark red or brown dado was surmounted by the lower part of a white or yellow panel with red veining.

References: R.M. Tanner and A.G. Giles, *A Guide to the Excavations at Barton Field, Tarrant Hinton, Dorset*, 1st edn. (1971); 2nd edn. (1972), *passim* and fig. VI, pls. I-V.
Excavators: R.M. Tanner, A.G. Giles, Wimborne Archaeological Group.

[1] For this term J. White, *Perspective in Ancient Drawing and Painting* (1956), p. 13 f. and *passim*.

[2] A type of 'rustication' used, for example, for Hellenistic statue-bases on the island of Rhodes: H. Lauter, in *Ant. K.* xv (1972), pp. 51-3.

[3] E.g. Reinach, pp. 196-7; Schefold, pls. 175 (4), 176 (4), 178 (3). An alternative possibility is Endymion (Reinach, p. 54 (2, 4)).

[4] Several of the Narcissus paintings (see last note) contain pillars, pedestals and other block-like structures, but there is no clearly identifiable fountain.

[5] See e.g. Curtius, pl. III, figs. 153, 155-7. Cf. Pliny, *NH* xxxv, 132.

[6] G. Bendinelli, in *Mon. Ant.* xxxi (1926), cols. 691-4, pl. XXIII, 1: variously identified as Odysseus and Helen, Orestes and Electra, or Orestes and Iphigenia.

[7] T. Kempf, in Reusch, pp. 236-43. Datable to the 320s or 330s: Mielsch 1978, p. 174. Cf. the orants in the catacomb of Thraso in Rome: e.g. Grabar, fig. 118.

[8] Mielsch 1978, pp. 173 ff.

[9] *Ibid.*, pp. 195, 199, pls. 97 (3, 4), 99 (2).

No. 39.   ★TARRANT HINTON, Dorset.   Villa, Building III, Room 1, Second or third century? (earlier than No. 38). Now in Wimborne, Priest's House Museum. PL. LXXX.

Numerous fragments of a vault-decoration executed on a fine white chalky plaster: an all-over pattern of medallions connected by bands running across and along the vault. The medallions (approximate diameter 14 cm) alternated in colour, having either a grey central tondo and a yellow border, or a yellow central tondo and a grey border; in each case the borders were framed by black lines. The connecting bands were red and were accompanied by a pink stripe on each side (the total width being 3.4 cm). The intervening spaces created by this pattern had a white ground. Each was outlined by a single brown line and contained a square field with a central ornament consisting of blobs arranged in X-formation. The colour-scheme again alternated: yellow frames enclosed green ornaments, green frames reddish-brown ornaments. The frames were each in two shades, darker outside and paler inside, with a brown line along the exterior and a further brown line set a short distance inside.

Some fragments of half-medallions abutting against a broad purple-red band presumably come from the edge of the vault.

The pattern of medallions and connecting bands is a favourite in Roman ceiling-decoration, particularly in the second century, and particularly in stucco relief, where it sometimes includes squares in the intervening spaces, as here.[1] A somewhat crude painted example of a similar pattern, though without the square panels, is used in the vault of the well-known fourth-century tomb at Silistra in Bulgaria.[2]

A reconstruction drawing has not been attempted, owing to uncertainties about the spacing of the medallions and the size of the squares.

Reference: R.M. Tanner and A.G. Giles, *A Guide to the Excavations at Barton Field, Tarrant Hinton, Dorset*, 2nd edn. (1972), fig. VII, pl. VIII.

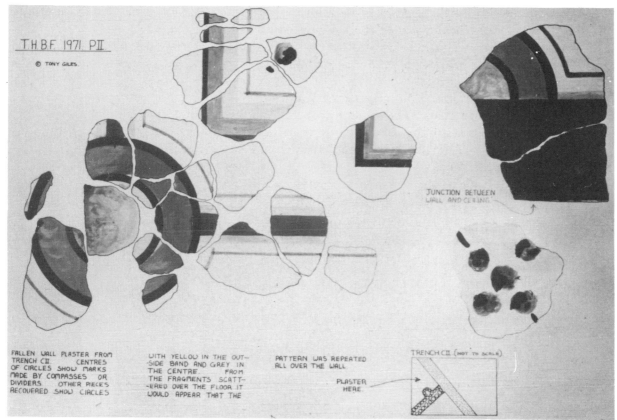

Drawing by A.G. Giles

LXXX   No. 39   Tarrant Hinton, water-colour drawing of fragments of ceiling-plaster.

Excavators: R.M. Tanner and A.G. Giles, Wimborne Archaeological Group.

[1] E.g. in Tomb 87 at Isola Sacra (alternating with octagons): Mielsch 1975a, pp. 81 f., 162, pl. 76, 2.
[2] A. Frova, *Pittura romana in Bulgaria* (1943), *passim*.

No. 40. VERULAMIUM (St. Albans), Herts. Insula XIX, possible bath-building.

Between 49 and 60/61 (the plaster belongs to a phase which was sealed by a layer of burning best associated with the Boudiccan destruction). Now in Verulamium Museum. PLS. LXXXI, CXV-CXVI.

Excavations of 1974 on the Six Bells site revealed a corridor or portico which had part of a painted dado in position on the south-west wall and contained fragments of fine-quality polychrome decoration fallen from a higher part of the wall.

The dado, which ran continuously along the wall and round each of a series of pilasters which were attached to it, was white with purple, black, yellow and orange splashes, and was divided by vertical black lines. The most interesting of the fragments from the main part of the decoration are the following:

(A) 15 cm wide × 19.5 cm high. Part of a still life (PL. CXV), reconstructed from smaller fragments. A lyre, quiver and bow painted on a red ground with a grey-green stripe beneath. The lyre is yellow with white highlights; the bow yellow; the quiver pink with yellow-white highlights.

(B) Fragment of a pink object with a yellow fillet (?) hanging beside it, also on a red ground. Perhaps another quiver? or an incense-burner *(turibulum)*?

(C) 13 cm wide × 16.5 cm high. Upper corner of a yellow panel or border surmounted by a green frieze 4.5 cm wide carrying yellow quatrefoils and white S-modillions which support a white cornice above (PL. LXXXI). The modillions have shadows at the right.

Photo: R. J. Ling

LXXXI   No. 40 (C)   Verulamium XIX, upper corner of panel and S-modillion.

(D) 41 cm wide × 19.5 cm high. Fragments of an element similar to the last, except that the modillions have shadows on their opposite sides (PL. CXVI).

This decoration is interesting for its early date, earlier even than the Period 1C fragments at Fishbourne (No. 17). Unfortunately too little survives for the scheme to be reconstructed, but the predominant colour among the fragments is red, and one possibility is that the main fields were red and that each contained one of the still lifes (A, B), set like a vignette at the centre. Still lifes appear frequently in the middle of fields in Neronian and Vespasianic decorations at Pompeii, though usually occupying a little framed panel rather than in the form of a vignette.[1] The still life A shows attributes of the god Apollo, and thus fits in a familiar category of paintings showing groups of symbols associated with particular deities.[2]

Reference: *Verulamium Museum. Rescue Excavations 1974-75* (1976), s.v. 'Six Bells, St. Michael's' and pl. 3.
Excavator: C. Saunders, St. Albans City and District Council.

[1] E.g. in the House of the Vettii: Peters, pls. 60, 88, 89, 90 (fig. 64).
[2] Apollo: Reinach, p. 347, nos. 6, 9. Dionysus: J.-M. Croisille, *Les natures mortes campaniennes* (1965), pp. 31 (no. 15), 54 (no. 100), 92 (245 C), pls. CI, LXXXVII (168); Reinach, p. 358, no. 3. Jupiter: Croisille, *op. cit.*, p. 70 (no. 161 B), pl. CXVIII (224); Reinach, p. 362, nos. 1, 3, 5. Isis: Croisille, *op. cit*, p. 93 (no. 250, 2). A later still life in Rome with attributes of Mercury: H. Mielsch, in *Affreschi*, p. 40, pl. XII, 2.

No. 41. VERULAMIUM (St. Albans), Herts. Insula XXI, Building 2 (courtyard house). *c.* 180. (A) Now in British Museum (on loan from the Earl of Verulam). (B, C, D, E, F) Now in Verulamium Museum. PLS. LXXXII-LXXXIX, CXII. FIGS. 41–44.

Areas of wall- and ceiling-decoration in the north-west and south-west wings, reconstructed mainly from collapsed fragments (though parts of the dados of B and E were found *in situ*). Pieces A, B and D were reconstructed by Dr. Davey; C, E and F by the Institute of Archaeology, University of London.

(A) Part of frieze from the north-west wall of the courtyard, probably beneath a verandah (found 1956).

Photo: British Museum

LXXXII   No. 41 (A)   Verulamium XXI, 2, restoration of wall with peopled scroll in British Museum.

3.63 m long × 99 cm high. On a yellow ground a 'peopled' scroll, of which four spirals survive. The main stem of the scroll, delicately painted in green and black, undulates regularly, sending off in-curling volutes on either side, at the centre of which are set alternating fauna, a frontal panther's head in each of the upper ones, a long-tailed bird (peahen? — not a pheasant as claimed in earlier publications) in each of the lower ones. Both panthers and birds are brown-purple in colour with pale purple and black details (the facial markings of the former, the feathers of the latter). The scroll itself is richly embellished. In addition to pale green leaves, almond-shaped, heart-shaped or trifid, it has sets of disc-like nodes and sends off spiralling mini-tendrils in black, notably in the interstices next to the volutes. Most striking are the floral ornaments set in the forks between the main stem and the volutes. From cornet-shaped calyces coloured alternately pale green (the upper ones) and pale yellow (the down-hanging ones) rise triple flame-like crests grading in colour from red-purple at the tips to yellow at the roots. Each

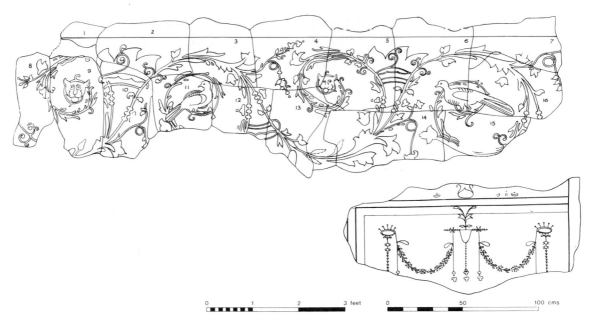

FIG. 41   No. 41 (A): Verulamium XXI, 2: restoration of the 'peopled'-scroll frieze and part of the panelling below it
from the north-west wall of the courtyard. Diargram showing areas as reassembled. Scale, 1:25.
(Drawing by N. Davey)

calyx is decorated near the mouth by a curving band and round the actual rim by a three-lobed fringe (formed by a side-shoot wrapping itself round the calyx). Bands and fringes are green with black outlines, except in the left-most calyx, where they appear brownish.

Above the frieze runs a brownish-red zone, preserved to a height of 13 cm, which reached to the angle of the ceiling. The lower part of the frieze is missing, but its original width can have been barely greater than the existing 86 cm.

Fragments of the wall-decoration below the frieze reveal a system broadly identical to that in the corridor of the south-west wing (Pieces B and C, described below). The main differences are that the red fields seem to have had a slightly more elaborate framing (a pale green border 3 cm wide edged with white lines, and an inner border-line in yellow) and that the one field of which part is preserved ends at the right against a chamfered surface painted yellow, presumably a door- or window-reveal. Above this red field is preserved part of the black surround, containing isolated yellow volute-ornaments: in the middle an inverted heart-shaped motif, with its interior painted blue and with little volutes growing from the sides, and at the right faint remains of a double volute with a central vertical. The whole height of the wall has now been restored in imitation of the decorations from the south-west corridor.

The presence of the green border-band and inner yellow border-line stresses the continuity from Flavio-Trajanic red-and-black decorations like those of Boxmoor and Cirencester (Nos. 2; 8); but the delicate ornamentation of candelabra and festoons within the red fields is fully in the Antonine tradition (see below). What is unique about this wall is the yellow-ground peopled scroll in the frieze. Although the motif of the peopled scroll is familiar in Roman sculpture and painting,[1] the yellow ground, the frontal panther's head, and more particularly the 'flame'-crested floral ornament are all unparalleled in this context. The latter is slightly similar to motifs set in the same position in scrolls represented on mosaic pavements, for example at Cirencester, Dorchester, Silchester and Chichester;[2] but the mosaic examples are much simplified and stylised compared with our painted version. They consist at the most of a white calyx with a yellow bar surmounted by a red three-lobed fringe (or the same in pale and dark blue). At Fishbourne in a second-century mosaic an even simpler calyx-ornament, plain red in colour and flat-topped, gains a little interest because one of the spirals of the scroll contains a stylised bird; but the bird is an isolated phenomenon, a kind of artist's signature, and the scroll as a whole, with its bare volutes and simple leaf- and floral ornaments, is very remote in style from ours.[3]

Photo: M.B. Cookson

LXXXIII   No. 41 (A)   Verulamium XXI, 2, bird in peopled scroll.

Photo: M.B. Cookson

LXXXIV   No. 41 (A)   Verulamium XXI, 2, panther's head in peopled scroll.

The use of a scroll to decorate the upper part of a wall is common in the Roman world[4] and is found again in the same house (see B below) and elsewhere in Verulamium (House XXVIII, 3: No. 44, A).

(B) Restored area from the south-west wall of the corridor in the south-west wing (Room 3). The bottom of the dado still adhered to the masonry sleeper-wall, but the rest of the dado and the main panels were found (1956) lying face downwards in the corridor. The upper part of the decoration, a red frieze carrying a spiral scroll of dark tendrils, had struck the opposite wall and doubled back; it was poorly preserved and has not been reconstructed.

Total dimensions: 3.16 m wide × 2.39 m high. Dimensions of preserved ancient plaster: 2.92 m wide × 2.33 m high (including a gap of uncertain width in the lower part of the dado). The main areas of modern restoration are at the left and right extremities of the design.

The main zone consists of red fields separated by black intervals which merge with horizontal bands at top and bottom; the dado of rectangular panels, long black ones coming beneath the red fields, narrow purple ones beneath the intervals. Of this scheme a length corresponding to one complete red field and two-thirds of each of its neighbours has survived.

At the foot of the wall is part of a purple baseboard (restored to a height of 10 cm). The dado-panels are bordered by white lines and set on a continuous yellow background which forms bands from 7 to 9 cm wide between, above and below them. The purple panels are 28 cm wide and the central black one over 80 cm; they are restored to a height of 31 or 32 cm, but in no case is the bottom edge preserved in the original plaster. The colours are badly faded, and the ornamentation which they probably contained (cf. C below) is not discernible.

In the main zone there are traces of volute-ornaments in the black bands above and below the red fields, and of elaborate candelabra in the vertical spaces between them. All the interstices in the volute-ornaments seem to have been filled with solid colour (red, blue or purple). The candelabra grew from a symmetrical pair of volutes, the triangular space between them coloured red, and the interior of the volutes themselves pale blue; otherwise nothing of the shafts is visible apart from occasional green leaves, purple plates, and volutes of uncertain colouring.

The intervals containing the candelabra are respectively 27 cm and 30 cm wide. The red field between them, the only one whose complete dimensions are preserved, is 96 cm wide and 1.63 m high.

Each of the red fields was edged by a white line. At the centre, on a short base-line, stood a

Photo: British Museum

LXXXV   No. 41 (B)   Verulamium XXI, 2, restored section of red wall in Corridor 3.

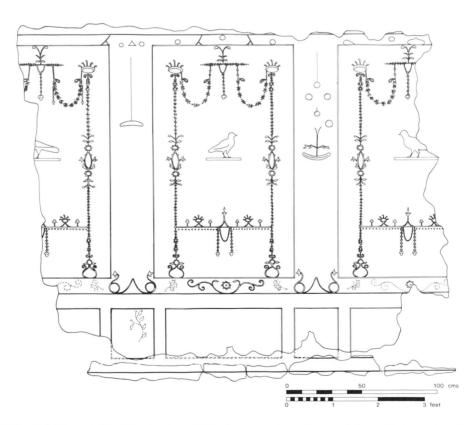

FIG. 42   No. 41 (B): Verulamium XXI, 2: restoration of part of the wall-decoration from
the south-west wall of corridor, Room 3. Scale, 1:25.
(Drawing by N. Davey)

bird (a dove?) painted entirely in shades of green. The one in the middle panel, which is almost
complete, faces to the right; the other two, which are only partially preserved, faced to the left.
Framing each of them was a delicate structure of candelabra, rods and festoons very reminiscent
of those within the comparable fields in the Blue Boar Lane decoration at Leicester (No. 22,

A–B). At each side a slender yellow candelabrum grows from an onion-shaped volute-ornament with a blue-white interior. The stem of the candelabrum is flanked by little side-shoots (as in the framing lines of the ceiling: D below), which grow downwards in the lower half and upwards in the upper; dividing the two halves are almond-shaped insets and a pair of medallions with blue-white interiors. At the top of the candelabrum rests a plate with blue-white underside and five vertical prongs. Between the umbels in each field, and connected to them by garlands, is a short horizontal rod suspended by another vegetal stalk from the upper edge of the panel. A trefoil pendant hangs beneath it. Finally the lower parts of the candelabra are connected by a second horizontal rod, decorated with various pendants below and ornaments on stalks above.

The details of this ornamentation vary slightly between the central field and the two side-fields, which seem to have been a little narrower. For example, in the central field the two garlands are composed of a simple chain of yellow-white leaves and 'cross-key' ornaments, while in the side-fields they receive an impressionistic treatment in greenish white and have a trefoil pendant at either end. But the basic structure and most of the constituent elements are identical. The over-all effect is simpler than that of the Leicester examples, but it is striking how many of the same ornamental details recur: pale blue almonds in the candelabra, pale blue tambourine-like medallions framed by a white line with bobbles, pairs of yellow stalks carrying green leaves, crown-like plates with pale blue undersides, yellow trefoil pendants, yellow loops marking the fastening-points of pendants, yellow 'cross-key' ornaments. Similar details appear on red-ground fragments from Scampton (No. 32), Winchester (No. 47) and Colchester (unpublished). It is obvious that a certain formal vocabulary was widely available to wall-painters in Britain during the second century.

Despite the similarity of motifs, the workmanship of the Verulamium wall is generally less delicate than at Leicester. The framing lines are uneven and do not follow the colour-boundaries closely; the ornaments are quickly and roughly painted and not always regularly spaced.

★(C) Another restored area from the same wall (1959–60 excavations).

Total dimensions: 3.19 m wide × 2.17 m high. Dimensions of surviving ancient plaster: 3.07 m wide × 2.00 m high. The main areas of modern restoration are the lower part of the dado, and in the main zone the middle and right half of the right-hand field and the upper half of the left-hand field.

The decoration is almost identical to B above, even as regards the variations in width between the central and side-fields of the main zone and the different treatment of the garlands in each case. The main novelty is that the base-line of the one surviving bird turns upwards to form a T-shaped element at either end.

On the decoration of the dado this piece is more informative than B. Although the lower part is entirely lost (the panels have been restored to a height of 43 to 45 cm), there are traces of ornamentation within the panels; vertical yellowish green stems at the sides of the right-hand purple panel and an indecipherable whitish-yellow element at the middle; yellow traces in the other purple panel; and a horizontal yellow line in the central black panel.

The measurements show minor variations from those of B. In the dado the purple panels are 29 cm wide and the central black one 85 cm. In the main zone the one complete red field is 1.02 m wide (the full height is not preserved), and the black intervals vary from 26 to 28.5 cm. The horizontal black band below the fields is 11 cm high.

(D) Part of the ceiling of the same corridor, found (1956) collapsed face downwards beneath the wall-plaster.

2.08 m × 2.00 m. An all-over pattern in yellow on a purple-red ground. Squares formed by stalks with series of little side-shoots are linked at the corners by intersecting diagonal lines decorated with ears of barley; a roundel masks the points of intersection. Within this scheme are set floral ornaments, birds and panther's heads.

In the interstices between the square panels, parallel to their sides, run lines of three bluish-green 'flowers' (the same tambourine-like medallions as appear on the walls) linked by yellow stalks with side-shoots. Within fourteen of the sixteen surviving squares are set birds (probably

Photo: Verulamium Museum

LXXXVI   No. 41 (C)   Verulamium XXI, 2, second section of red wall in Corridor 3.

Photo: Verulamium Museum

LXXXVII   No. 41 (C)   Verulamium XXI, 2, bird at centre of red wall.

LXXXVIII No. 41 (D)
Verulamium XXI, 2, restored
ceiling with barley-stalk pattern.
Photo: M.B. Cookson

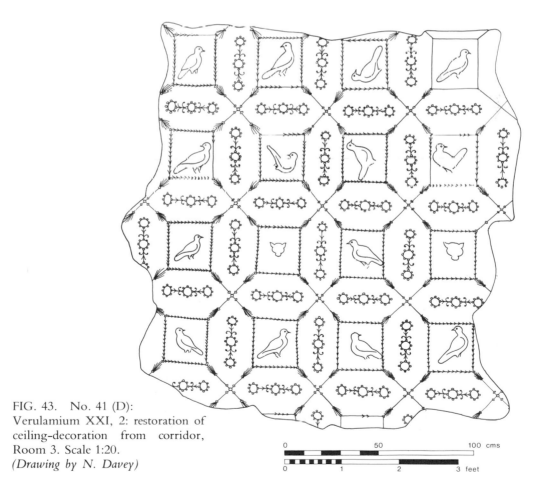

FIG. 43. No. 41 (D):
Verulamium XXI, 2: restoration of
ceiling-decoration from corridor,
Room 3. Scale 1:20.
(Drawing by N. Davey)

doves), their plumage painted in pale blue, white and yellow. They are oriented in various directions, reflecting the changing viewpoint of the spectator on the floor below, and are represented in various poses, now in profile to the left, now in profile to the right, now with head forward, now with head turned back, now with tail raised, now with tail lowered. The remaining two squares, the second and fourth in the second row from the edge of the ceiling, are occupied by frontal panthers' heads painted in yellow. One of the animals has a green 'ruff' beneath its muzzle, a reminiscence of the acanthus calyces from which animals' heads or foreparts are frequently shown emerging in Roman art.[5] The muzzle of this creature is in fact rather long for a panther, but we should best attribute this to lack of skill on the part of the painter.

This decoration, like that of the walls, belongs to the realms of jobwork rather than art. Even allowing for inevitable slight distortions in the reconstruction, the panels seems to have varied in shape and size, the sides of the 'squares' ranging from 21.5 to 25 cm. The birds, too, vary in size, as well as in spacing; sometimes they fill their fields adequately, sometimes they are uncomfortably crammed in the top half. These variations are not, like the changes in orientation and posture, a deliberate device to enliven the decoration but rather the vagaries of an inexpert craftsman translating a master's instructions or a pattern in a copy-book.

The ceiling-pattern continued in Room 2, the perpendicular extension of the corridor, with the sole difference that the background colour was a lighter red. The motifs painted here included more birds and a winged human mask (PL. CXII).

The affinity with the wall-decorations of the corridor and courtyard is obvious. The 'flowers' and foliate stalks recall the ornaments in the red fields; the birds and animal-heads recall the creatures in the peopled scroll. There is also a reminiscence of a probable ceiling-decoration or decorations from Silchester, where barley-heads again formed linking-elements in a repeating pattern on a red-purple ground (No. 33); the resemblance, however, stops there, since the Silchester paintings were much finer in quality and much more naturalistic in their treatment of fruit and foliage.

★(E) Wall-decoration from the end (south-west) wall of the perpendicular extension of the same corridor. The lower part of the decoration was found (1959-60) adhering to the wall, while the rest had collapsed on to the floor.

Total dimensions of restored area: 2.49 m wide × 2.59 m high. Up to 50 cm of the lower part of the dado is original, but the parts above are mostly modern restoration; there seems to be no independent check on the height and width of the fields in the main zone. The dado originally projected slightly; it has mistakenly been forced back into the plane of the remaining decoration.

The dado consists of three marbled panels, each with an independently coloured marble surround. The central panel, which has a pale blue surround, is orange-brown with fine white and black stippling; and the two side-panels present a variegated surface of red, yellow and pale blue, set in one of them in a black surround, in the other in an orange-brown one. The scheme is articulated by four vertical fasciae, arranged in alternation with the panels. Each is painted in red and yellow washes with grey veining. A vague suggestion that the panels and fasciae are in relief is created by the black and white stripes which separate the different-coloured marbles; but the effect is not consistently carried out, since the lighting seems to come now from the right, now from the left; the four vertical fasciae, for instance, have white and black stripes on alternate sides. The three main panels are respectively, from left to right, 52 cm, 49 cm and 49 cm wide; the side-panels are restored to a height of 60 cm and the central one, which is set lower within its frame, to a height of 66 cm. The fasciae are each 10 or 11 cm wide.

Crowning the dado and forming the transition to the main zone was a series of white bands reinforced by yellow stripes and red lines, the whole set between a pair of yellow bands. The effect of the colouring is to suggest a group of mouldings in relief — an effect curiously at variance with the real architectural surface, which here formed an offset between the projecting plinth and the main zone above. Not only was the decoration inappropriate but it was also unevenly applied, since the lower angle of the bevel came at a higher level in the sequence of 'mouldings' at the left than at the centre of the wall.

Photo: Verulamium Museum

LXXXIX No. 41 (E) Verulamium XXI, 2, restored end-wall of Corridor 2.

The main zone was coloured entirely red apart from the narrow bands of colour 2.5 cm wide which were used to mark out two large rectangular fields. These coloured bands, edged as usual with white lines, have faded so that the original tones cannot be identified with certainty; that at the left was probably yellow, that at the right a darker colour (purple?). Each of the two fields had inner border-lines of yellow at the sides. The carelessness of the execution is vividly demonstrated at the point where the continuous horizontal band which runs along the foot of the panels meets one of the vertical panel-frames; its upper edge has been traced from opposite sides, resulting in a striking disparity, which the painter has clumsily tried to rectify by carrying the right-hand line on into the left-hand band.

Further white and yellow stripes run along the top of the main zone.

A reconstruction-drawing carried out at the time of the excavation shows the two fields in the main zone as being rather narrower, with the red ground bisected by a central interval containing vertical fasciae of green, purple and yellow. This drawing, in conjunction with the published photograph,[6] also reveals that there was a quarter-round moulding, painted purple, at the foot of the wall and remains of another marbled panel (here white-ground) on the lower part of the adjacent, north-west wall.

★(F) Remains of a green panel-decoration discovered (1959-60) in the room of the lion mosaic (Room 4). The large restored piece in Verulamium Museum, produced at the Institute of Archaeology by the *strappo* method, takes no account of the remains of the dado and is of little real value. An idea of the decorative scheme must be gained from the excavation-records, from original fragments discernible in the restored panel, and from further fragments in storage.

Remains of the dado were found in position on the south-west wall. A measured sketch in the excavation-notebook shows an area of plaster about 4 feet (1.20 m) long and 1 foot 8 inches (50 cm) high, in which a zone described as 'dark red with terrazzo effect' (17 in. = 43 cm) was surmounted by a dark red band between blue-green stripes.[7] The main zone seems to have been painted entirely light green apart from panel-framings formed by red bands (2.5 cm wide)

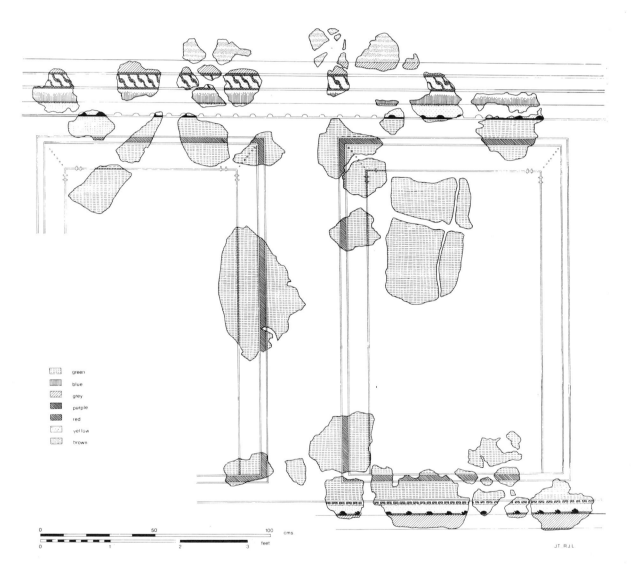

FIG. 44   No. 41 (F): Verulamium XXI, 2: reconstruction of decorative scheme in Room 4, based on fragments in store. Scale, 1:15.

(Drawing by J. Thorn, adapted by R.J. Ling)

between white lines; the decorative scheme was therefore similar to that of the south-west wall of corridor 2 (E above), only the colours being different. The excavation-notebook suggests that there were four panels on one wall (the north-west? or the exposed part of the south-west?) of which the inner pair were wider than the outer. As in wall E, the panels had inner border-lines, this time red.

A gap of about 8 cm separated the upper edges of the panels from the frieze, in which the first and most striking element was a series of shallow, delicately painted modillions shown in perspective from the right; their basic colour was yellow, with two white lines indicating mouldings in relief and purple used for the undersides and the arched interspaces. There is some evidence that this motif was repeated at the foot of the main zone.

Other elements which appear to have featured in the frieze are an imitation torus moulding decorated with a guilloche (purple on a yellow ground with white highlights and brown shadows) and a series of brown and white horizontal stripes suggesting plain mouldings, rather like the series of white and yellow stripes in wall E.

References: S.S. Frere, *Antiq. Journ.* xxxvii (1957), p. 13 f., pls. III *a*, IV *a* V; xxxix (1959), p. 17 f., pl. I; xl (1960), p. 17, pl. III *a*; xli (1961), pl. XXII *a*; Toynbee 1962, pp. 193 f. (nos. 169–171), pls. 195–198, 202; Toynbee 1964, pp. 214 f., 215 f., 218, 219, pl. LI; J. Liversidge, 'Wall paintings from Verulamium', *British Museum Quarterly* xxxv (1971), pp. 87–93, pls. XXVI–XXIX; Davey 1972, pp. 254 ff., figs. 2–4; Liversidge 1977, p. 79, fig. 5.1 *b*; S.S. Frere, *Verulamium Excavations* ii (forthcoming).

Excavator: S.S. Frere, Verulamium Excavation Committee.

[1]J.M.C. Toynbee and J.B. Ward-Perkins, 'Peopled scrolls: a Hellenistic motif in Imperial art', *PBSR* xviii (1950), pp. 1–43, pls. I–XXVI.

[2]See Toynbee 1964, p. 215 and the bibliography there cited. Cf. RCHM, *Dorset* ii, 3 (1970), frontispiece; A. Down, *Chichester Excavations*, ii (1974), pls. 13, 14, fig. 8.30.

[3]Cunliffe, i, pls. XLVII, LII, LIII *b*.

[4]Cf. Barbet *et al.* 1977, pp. 191–5.

[5]Both within peopled scrolls (Toynbee and Ward-Perkins, *art. cit.* (note 1), *passim*) and as isolated ornaments, e.g. in the atrium of the House of the Menander at Pompeii (A. Maiuri, *La Casa del Menandro* (1933), fig. 9, pl. III: black panel below 'Durchblick').

[6]*Antiq. Journ.* xl (1960), pl. III *a*.

[7]According to the notebook, fallen plaster in the vicinity of the north-west wall suggested that the decoration of the dado had changed: there were traces of yellow panelling divided by red lines and the corner of a red panel bordered by a black key-pattern on a yellow background.

No. 42. VERULAMIUM (St. Albans), Herts. Insula XXII, Building 1. Third century or first half of fourth. Now in Verulamium Museum (in storage). PL. XC. FIG. 45.

Large piece of wall-decoration restored from fragments fallen face downwards in the corridor along the south-east side of the building (1955 excavations).

Overall dimensions: 2.75 m wide × 2.99 m high.

Panel-decoration. Above a baseboard of purple with pinkish-white splashes (at least 17 cm high) comes a dado of alternate yellow and white rectangular panels set on a purple background speckled white. The yellow panels take the form of long rectangles under the large fields of the main zone and carry traces of orange brush-marks simulating marbling; the white panels, which carry grey brush-marks, are virtually square and lie beneath the intervening narrow panels of the main zone. All are framed by black and white stripes and have inner border-lines, orange in the yellow panels, pale green in the white ones.

In the main zone large red fields, one of which has been restored, alternated with yellow pilaster-like panels. The red fields were each surrounded by a grey border 7 to 7.5 cm wide (between white stripes), and in the surviving example there is a pair of inner yellow border-stripes from which rows of diagonal spots diverge at the corners. At the centre have been set the restored remains of a short candelabrum with yellow stem and green leaves. The yellow panels have three orange border-lines with diagonal spots at the top corners; and in one of the two surviving examples the surface is bisected by a vertical orange foliated rod. Traces of a similar rod may be seen in the other panel.

Crowning the main zone is a white frieze 7.5 cm wide painted with greenish-grey stripes to suggest a profiled cornice-moulding. Above this are remains of an upper zone in which the most striking feature is the rectangular panel set above each of the red fields of the main zone; this is grey, is set within a broad yellow surround, and contains a delicate yellow trellis fence across the bottom.

Photo: Verulamium Museum

XC   No. 42   Verulamium, restored wall-plaster from Insula XXII, 1.

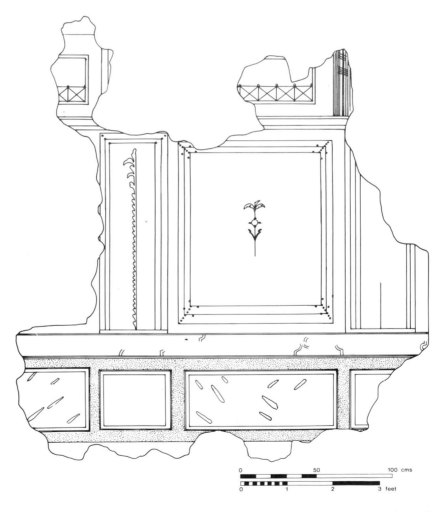

FIG. 45   No. 42: Verulamium XXII, 1: restoration of wall-decoration from the
north-west wall of the corridor (Room 5). Scale, 1:25.
(Drawing by N. Davey)

The main interest in this very fragmentary decoration is the presence of a decorated upper zone, a feature which is regular in Italian wall-painting, but which is rare (other than in the form of a scroll: cf. Nos. 41, A–B; 44, A) in the northern provinces (see Introduction). Italian examples of the upper zone frequently contain fences, at least from the mid first century to the end of the second, conveying the idea of balconies within architectural or semi-architectural schemes.[1] There, however, the 'balconies' often have a light background, suggestive of space, while in our decoration, in the third century, the background is dark and the whole effect more schematic.

References: S.S. Frere, in *Antiq. Journ.* xxxvi (1956), p. 2; Davey 1972, p. 253 f., fig. 1; S.S. Frere, *Verulamium Excavations* ii (forthcoming).

Excavator: S.S. Frere, Verulamium Excavation Committee.

[1]See the examples cited under Rudston (No. 31), n. 2. Cf. also Schefold, pls. 48, 108 (Pompeii, late Third and Fourth Styles).

No. 43. VERULAMIUM (St. Albans), Herts.   Insula XXVIII, building beneath Building 1, Room 6. Mid second century (before *c.* 155–160). Now (1979) in London, Fortress House (in storage). PL. XCI. FIG. 46.

Photo: Oxford University Institute of Archaeology

XCI   No. 43   Verulamium, restored marble panelling from Insula XXVIII.

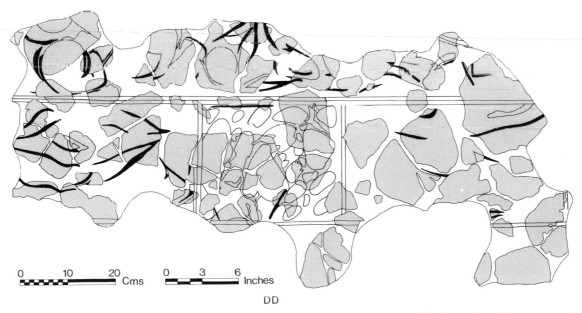

DD

FIG. 46   No. 43: Verulamium XXVIII, restoration of imitation marbling from building beneath Room 6 in Building 1. Diagram showing position of original fragments. Scale, 1:8.

(Drawing by Diane Dixon)

Piece restored from fragments of wall-plaster found lying face downwards in the remains of a timber building destroyed by the Antonine fire of *c.* 155-160; sealed beneath Room 6 of the subsequent House XXVIII, 1 (1957 excavations).

Overall dimensions: 1.18 m long × 59.5 cm high. A decoration of imitation marble veneering; series of panels between continuous maroon and purple zones: (a) green with yellow and black veins, (b) reddish purple with yellow streaks and large pools producing the appearance of a breccia (restored 29.5 cm long), (c) white with green mottling and yellow and black streaks (restored 46 cm long). The panels, which form a zone 25 cm high, are bordered by white stripes, sometimes reinforced by a black one; the effect may have been slightly reminiscent of the dado-panels in corridor 2 of Verulamium XXI, 2 (No. 41, E).

The maroon zone below carried tiny white splashes; the purple zone above is painted in a reddish tinge over a darker purple so as to leave streaks and whorls suggestive of marbling.

Below Room 2 of House XXVIII, 1 was found plaster in red panels separated by white stripes.

Unpublished. See S.S. Frere, *Verulamium Excavations* ii (forthcoming).
Excavator: S.S. Frere, Verulamium Excavation Committee.

No. 44. VERULAMIUM (St. Albans), Herts. Insula XXVIII, Building 3. Mid second century (between *c.* 150 and *c.* 155-160). Now in Verulamium Museum. PLS. XCII-XCIV, CXVII.

Pieces restored from collapsed fragments of wall-plaster found (1958) in Rooms 3 and 9 of a timber-framed house destroyed in the fire of *c* 155-160.

(A) Pieces from the south-west wall of Room 3 (corridor).

(i) Dado and main zone (collapsed in a sheet face downwards; the plaster is almost complete apart from restored areas at the right end).

Overall dimensions: 3.72 m wide × 2.07 m high. A system of panels imitating different types of breccia and alabaster, all set against a continuous background of dark purple.

FIG. 47   No. 44 (A i): Verulamium XXVIII, 3: restoration of wall-decoration from Room 3. Diagram showing position of original fragments. Scale, 1:25.

(Drawing by Yvonne Brown)

Photo: M.B. Cookson

XCII No. 44 (A) Verulamium XXVIII, 3, restored wall with columns and marble panelling. Scale in feet.

In the dado long rectangular panels alternate with narrow vertical ones, the two types lying respectively beneath the large fields and beneath the intervals in the main zone. All the panels are framed by white stripes (up to 1 cm wide), and the dividing purple bands are 7.5 cm wide above and 8 to 9 cm wide between them; the purple background also extended downwards for at least 14 cm at the base of the wall. Of the long panels two are complete (measurements 1.10 to 1.11 m by 42 cm) and one (at the left) half complete. Each contained a breccia pattern, with pools of light colour on a darker ground. The colours, all reddened by the effect of the fire, seem originally to have been, from left to right: (a) reddish brown on purple; (b) pale green and white on black; (c) pink and red on reddish brown. The intervening vertical panels (19 to 20 cm by 42 cm) were purple, slightly lighter in tone than the surrounding bands.

In the main zone large fields alternate with narrow intervals each carrying, on the purple ground, a painted column. None of the fields is preserved to its full height, but, as in the dado, two retain their full width (1.11 m) and a third at the left survives partially. The patterns are: (a) breccia, pale and dark purple on black; (b) alabaster, 'flowers' in pink, red and reddish purple; (c) breccia, pale green and white on black (as in the middle panel of the dado). The fields are outlined in white, like the dado panels, and the two more complete ones have an additional black line inside the white.

The treatment of the columns in the intervening spaces is fully plastic, volume being achieved by the use of red shading and white highlights on a basically pink surface; further relief is achieved by a black frame 2 cm wide which hugs the contours. The base is of the familiar double-torus type found in western provincial architecture and represented also in the painted wall-decoration in the *principia* at York (No. 52); the shaft is covered with purple lines forming a network-pattern. The latter at first sight recalls the leaf- or scale-decoration of monumental architecture (cf. Lullingstone, No. 27, A), but the 'scales' here have wavy outlines, unlike the majority of those on real columns, and they seem to be combined with fluting (indicated by vertical pink lines on the central white highlight), a totally anomalous circumstance. The painter seems to have played freely with accepted decorative forms. Only part of one capital is preserved; it shows purple acanthus leaves with pink and white highlights and black shadows.

Whatever the peculiarities in the treatment of the columns, the manner in which they are used in the decoration is doubly peculiar. For all their apparent strength and three-dimensionality, they seem to have had no architectural role to play but merely floated on their purple grounds within an otherwise two-dimensional scheme. It is, of course, possible that they supported an entablature in the missing area above the main fields, but there is no trace of this in the plaster from the upper zone (see below), and the absence of a podium tends to argue against it. This uneasy combination of a flat-surface scheme with a single illusionistic detail is, to the best of our knowledge, unparalleled in Roman painting.

(ii) Upper zone (smashed against the opposite wall of the corridor).
Overall dimensions: 1.37 m wide × 1.06 m high.
Owing to the shattered nature of the fragments much of the piece is restored. It shows a frieze carrying a scroll which probably consisted of a series of volutes spiralling alternately above and below a continuous stem, like the peopled scroll from Verulamium XXI, 2 (No. 41, A). The colour-scheme too was similar to that of the XXI, 2 scroll: the background was originally yellow, though now scorched red and orange, the stems of the volutes, along with the nodes and buds, were black, and the leaves pale green. There are also traces of calyx-ornaments like those in the forks of the other scroll, though the examples here seem to have been crowned by a white, red and purple bar outlined in black and not with the distinctive yellow and purple triple-'flame' crests.

But the main difference from the scroll in XXI, 2 is that the volutes here spiral much more tightly and probably contained no animal forms. They were constructed, as in a similar scroll from Alesia in France,[1] with the aid of compass-drawn guide-lines, part of one of which is visible where the left-hand volute diverges from it. The frieze is restored to a height of 82 cm and is framed by a white stripe, beyond which there is a continuous purple zone.

Photo: M.B. Cookson

XCIII   No. 44 (A ii)   Verulamium XXVIII, 3, restored fragments of scroll from above marbled wall.

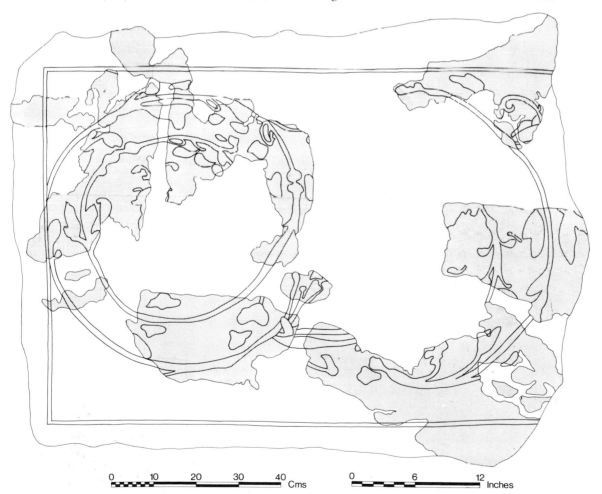

FIG. 48   No. 44 (A ii): Verulamium XXVIII, 3: restoration of part of scroll from upper part of wall in Room 3.
Diagram showing position of original fragments. Scale, 1:9.

(Drawing by Yvonne Brown)

(B) Pieces from Room 9 (see also PL. CXVII)

(i) Upper part of dado and lower part of main zone (restorations at lower left and right and middle right).

Overall dimensions: 74 cm wide × 1.25 m high. In the dado the upper right corner of a purplish-red panel with a white border-stripe and part of a surrounding band of purple (6 cm wide above). Above this a white band 5.5 cm wide separates the dado from the main zone. This contains the bottom right corner of a red field with the usual green border (2.8 cm wide) between white lines and, outside it, a black surround (8 cm wide at the bottom). Traces of an elaborate candelabrum in pink and purple (cf. ii below) survive in the vertical part of the black surround.

FIG. 49   No. 44 (B i): Verulamium XXVIII, 3: restoration of upper part of dado and lower part of main zone in Room 9. Diagram showing position of original fragments. Scale, 1:8.
(Drawing by Yvonne Brown)

Photo: M.B. Cookson

XCIV No. 44 (B) Verulamium XXVIII, 3, restored fragments of wall-decoration from Room 9.

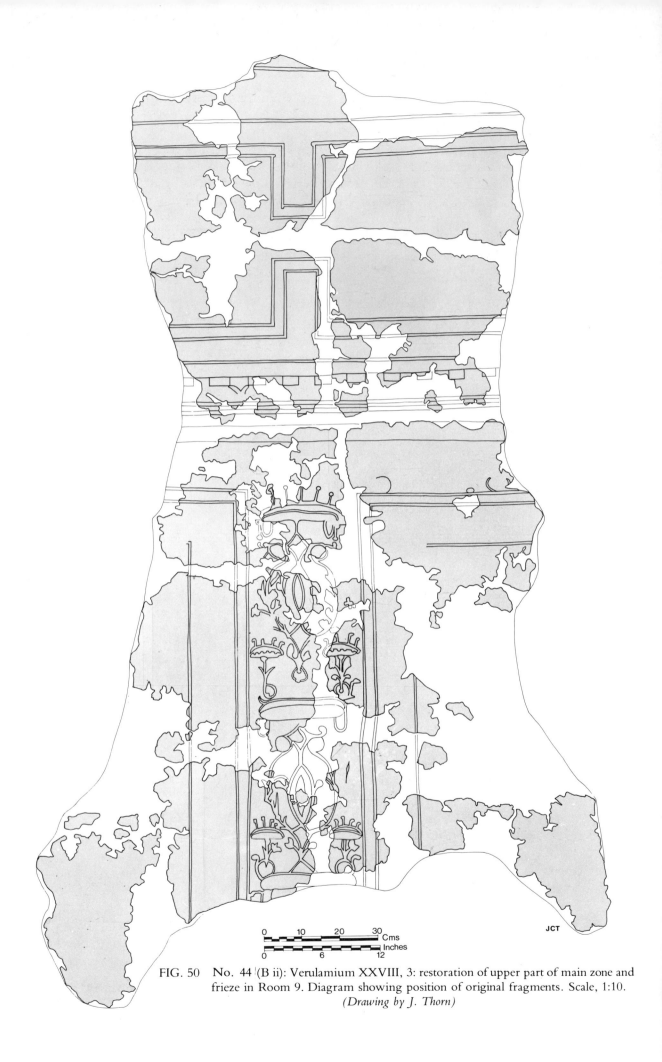

FIG. 50   No. 44 (B ii): Verulamium XXVIII, 3: restoration of upper part of main zone and
frieze in Room 9. Diagram showing position of original fragments. Scale, 1:10.
(Drawing by J. Thorn)

(ii) Upper part of main zone and frieze (virtually complete apart from restorations within the red areas).

Overall dimensions: 1.52 m wide × 2.52 m high.

In the main zone the upper corners of two red panels with green borders and the upper part of the intervening black strip (29 to 30 cm wide). In the latter there is an elaborate candelabrum painted mainly in pink, purple and blue, whose elements include broad cushion-like plates and tendrils enclosing almond-shaped motifs, the whole being crowned by a plate embellished with vertical purple prongs. The black bands above the red fields (about 11 cm wide) show traces of pink volutes, some at least filled with blue. As a result of the fire and subsequent deterioration, the black of the background has faded to grey or pinkish white; it is also possible that the pink of the candelabrum results from the scorching of a yellow pigment, the more normal colour for such ornamentation.

The frieze begins with a deep red band 5 cm wide, above which comes a narrower yellow band and a series of lines and bands in pink, purple and white, evidently intended to suggest profiled cornice-mouldings (compare some of the decorations in Verulamium XXI, 2: No. 41, E, F); these are surmounted by a series of illusionistic dentils painted white with purple shadows round them (for the motif compare a piece at Lincoln: No. 25, D). A narrow black band separates the dentils from the upper zone, which is red, 63 cm high, and contains two inner borders of black which project inwards to form rectangular bays immediately above the candelabrum of the main zone. The red zone itself and the black borders are set between white stripes.

At the top of the piece comes a black zone 13 cm wide and a glimpse of a purple zone above.

References: S.S. Frere, in *Antiq. Journ.*, xxxix (1959), p. 13; Toynbee 1962, p. 194 f. (no. 172), pl. 201; Toynbee 1964, pp. 217, 218, pl. LII, *a*; Liversidge 1977, p. 79 f., fig. 5.3; S.S. Frere, *Verulamium Excavations* ii (forthcoming).
Excavator: S.S. Frere, Verulamium Excavation Committee.

[1]Barbet *et al.* 1977, pp. 175-184, figs. 2-10.

No. 45. *WANBOROUGH, Wilts. Residual material. Dating uncertain. Now in Swindon, Borough of Thamesdown Museum and Art Gallery. FIG. 51.

Various pieces restored from fragments of wall-plaster found in a dump overlying the main Roman road-ditch. The reconstructions were carried out by Mr. Bryn Walters.

Dimensions of the five largest pieces (in cm): 74 × 77; 45 × 97; 72 × 91; 51 × 84; 32 × 41.

The original fragments are of a coarse plaster and are much damaged, the colours being faded almost beyond recognition. The reconstruction therefore posed serious difficulties and is not everywhere certain. But there can be no doubt that the plaster derived from a scheme based on the familiar formula of red fields and black intervals; the red fields, as frequently elsewhere (Nos. 2; 8; 28; 41, A), were framed by green or yellow bands between white lines and had inner yellow border-lines; the black intervals contained yellow candelabra, more free-flowing and organic than in other decorations, but possibly not so irregular as the restoration suggests. In at least one piece the candelabrum is restored in a black band above the red field, as well as in the vertical interval at the side; but this is questionable, since it results in the 'grain' of the plaster of one candelabrum running perpendicular to that of the other.

Unpublished.
Excavator: B. Walters, Swindon Archaeological Society.

No. 46. WIGGINTON, Oxon. Villa. (A) Third century? (B) First half of fourth century. (A) Now (1979) in London, Fortress House (in storage), (B) Now in Potterne (in storage). PLS XCV-XCVI. FIG. 52.

(A) Room 19 (part of third-century house). Part of a painted ceiling restored from fragments (1966 excavation).

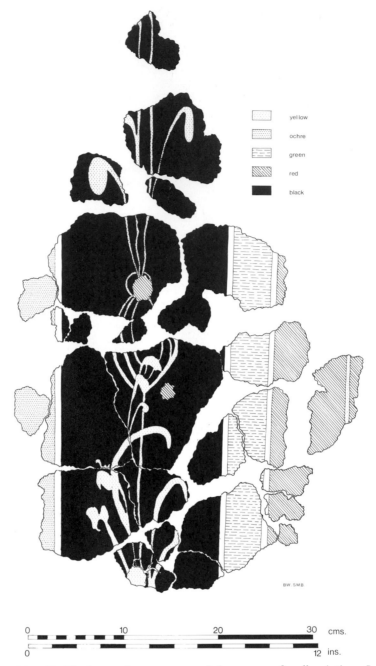

yellow

ochre

green

red

black

FIG. 51   No. 45: Wanborough, reconstructed fragments of wall painting. Scale, 1:4.
(Drawing by Bryn Walters, adapted by Tina Baddeley)

Overall dimensions: 84.5 cm × 85 cm.

On a white ground a large roundel (inner diam. 68 to 69 cm; outer diam. 77 cm) is formed by broad contiguous bands of green and purplish-red. Outside and concentric with these runs a pale green line (diam. approx. 81.5 cm), from which diverge further lines of the same colour; two of the junctions, marked by green blobs, survive. At the centre of the roundel is a floral motif formed by a reddish-purple wavy line describing a circle with four sets of three large green leaves growing round it.

The painting is rather careless, despite the use of guide-lines, one of which can be seen marking out the diameter of the roundel.

To judge from its size and from the traces of subsidiary lines leading off its outer border-line, the roundel did not form part of an all-over pattern but rather occupied the centre of a radiating design of the type familiar in metropolitan ceiling-painting of the third and fourth centuries, especially that of the catacombs.[1] Indeed, our painting, with its scheme of red and green frames

Photo: Department of the Environment: Crown Copyright reserved
XCV   No. 46 (A)   Wigginton, restored area of ceiling-decoration.

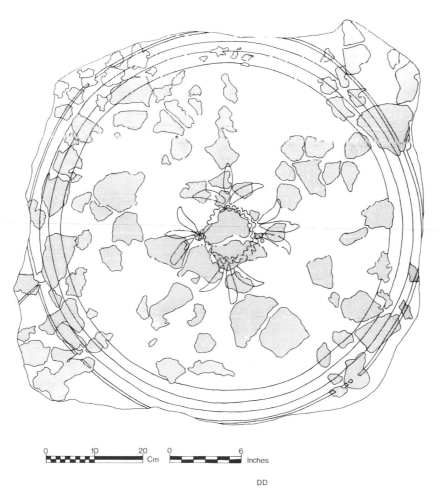

FIG. 52   No. 46 (A): Wigginton, restoration of part of a painted ceiling. Diagram
showing position of original fragments. Scale, 1:8.
(Drawing by Diane Dixon)

on a white ground, looks like a provincial variant of the so-called Striped and Linear Styles, which were popular in Rome from the Severan period onwards.[2]

(B) Room 4. Fragments of wall-plaster found in the filling of the hypocaust (1965 excavation) included part of a winged cupid and details of architectural perspectives. Two pieces have been restored showing the corner of a columnar structure viewed from the left (upper piece 18 cm × 22 cm; lower piece 10.5 cm × 12 cm). The painting is carried out in a skilful, impressionistic style, mainly in light and dark browns and yellows; only the intercolumniation at the right, which is painted with blue frit, significantly varies the colour-scheme. Interesting details are the way in which the corner-capital, apparently Ionic, casts its shadows upwards on to the architrave, indicating that the light comes from below and from the left, and the way in which the receding architrave seems to bend slightly upwards, as if the painter intended to suggest a curving exedra or recess.

Photo: R.J. Ling

XCVI   No. 46 (B)   Wigginton, restored details of architectural perspective.

Unpublished: see *JRS* lvi (1966), p. 208.
Excavator: E. Greenfield, Department of the Environment.

[1]E.g. Borda, figs. on pp. 124, 129, 134, 136.
[2]Wirth, pp. 134 ff., 165 ff.; Mielsch 1975b, pp. 127-9.

No. 47. ★WINCHESTER, Hants. Building of unknown function. Dating uncertain (perhaps second century). Now in Winchester, City Museum. PLS. XCVII, CXXIII.

Fragments of a fine wall-decoration recovered in salvage operations on the site of the Woolworth extension (1958). The most interesting show remains of delicate candelabra, yellow with white and grey detail and pale green leaves, on a red ground (PL. CXXII). Three pieces larger than the rest have been reconstructed at the Institute of Archaeology, London.

(A) 27.5 cm wide × 20.5 cm high. At the left a black zone, separated from the red area by a yellow band 2.7 cm wide carrying two narrow white stripes, one down the centre, the other along the right edge. The stem of the candelabrum is about 7 cm from this edge. Crowned by a trident-like umbel, it is also decorated with a pair of volutes, from whose eyes grow vertical-stemmed yellow flowers, and with a green calyx from which springs a pair of short-stemmed green leaves (PL. CXXIII).

(B) Approx. 20 cm wide × 27.5 cm high. At the left the framing band apparently consisted of grey, pale green, and yellow-white stripes but is now heavily restored. The visible part of the candelabrum consists of two calyx-ornaments and a double-volute-ornament somewhat similar to that in Piece A. The calyces differ from the example in A by being grey in colour; the lower one also has a white fringe with bobbles round it (PL. CXXIII).

(C) Approx. 25 cm wide × 39.5 cm high. The red ground at the left has worn away, leaving the plaster greyish-yellow in colour;[1] traces of a candelabrum, 9 cm from the framing band, include more green leaves and calyx-ornaments, one of which is lyre-shaped with a bobbled white fringe. The colours of the framing band, here 3.3 cm wide, have disappeared. Beyond it is a black ground with remains of delicately painted honeysuckle tendrils, one growing from below, one hanging from above; their stems are whitish-cream and their leaves green.

Photo: Winchester City Museum
XCVII   No. 47 (C)   Winchester, fragment of plaster with honeysuckle.

The remaining candelabrum fragments include the same basic ornamental elements, though treated with great spontaneity and showing variations of detail; the most significant intruder in the repertoire is a grey onion-shaped swelling with short yellow volutes growing from it.
Although the remains are very fragmentary, there is enough to suggest that the decorative

scheme was similar to second-century examples at Leicester (Blue Boar Lane: No. 22) and Verulamium (XXI, 2: No. 41, A-C); large red fields with candelabra at the sides and horizontal foliate rods and garlands at the top alternated with black intervals containing more elaborate candelabra. Some of the intervals also contained, as Piece C demonstrates, spiralling plants like the one which encircled the column in one of the Leicester aediculae (No. 22, A (ii)).

But the vegetation within the red-ground candelabra is rather more spontaneous and more luxuriant than at Leicester or Verulamium (in feeling, if not in their colour-scheme, the candelabra have something in common with fragments from Bern-Bümpliz in Switzerland, perhaps datable to the second half of the second century).[2] The borders of the fields too are different from those at Leicester and Verulamium: at Leicester the black intervals were replaced by 'Durchblicke' with columnar aediculae which overlapped on to the fields, and at Verulamium the fields were framed either by a single white line (Corridor 3) or by a green band between white lines (courtyard). The Winchester decoration is obviously a local or regional version of a much more widespread scheme.[3] Fragments from probably similar schemes, more closely related in style to the Leicester and Verulamium examples, have been found at Colchester (unpublished: excavations at Balkerne Lane in 1962) and Scampton, Lincs (No. 32).

Fragments of white panels with yellow surrounds may perhaps be ascribed to the dado below the red and black schemes.

Reference: Liversidge 1977, pp. 76, 79, pl. 5.II.
Excavator: F. Cottrill, Winchester City Museum.

[1]Miss Liversidge (see bibliography) mistakenly thinks that this is a different-coloured panel.
[2]Drack, pp. 60-62, pls. XXXV-XXXVII.
[3]Similar fragments were found in the building south of the Forum at Winchester (see No. 48).

No. 48. WINCHESTER, Hants. Building added to south side of Forum. Late second or early third century. Now (1979) with the Winchester Research Unit, 13 Parchment Street (in storage). PL. CXVIII.

Large areas of painted wall-plaster were found (1968) collapsed on the floor. The best pre-served and most interesting piece (37 cm wide × 50.5 cm high) shows part of a perspectival architectural scheme (PL. CXVIII). A jutting entablature painted yellow, white, green and grey-black supports a vertical frame to the left of which, on a red ground, floats a patera rendered in yellow with cream highlights and purple shadows. Further to the left are traces of swirling grey fillets. The architecture is represented as if the viewer is looking up at it from the right, and it is possible to interpret it as the left wing of an aedicula set in an interval between red fields, rather like the aediculae in the walls from Blue Boar Lane at Leicester (No. 22, A-B). The patera, though otherwise unknown in British paintings, had a long history as a decorative motif in classical art, going back to Hellenistic architectural carvings and Roman paintings of the Second Pompeian Style.[1]

Further fragments from the building show traces of candelabra and garlands on a red ground, like the fragments from the Woolworth site (No. 47); yellow, white and blue stripes on a red ground; grey and green stripes on white; and an architectural scheme similar to that of the best-preserved piece, but barely decipherable. One fragment, which carried elements in pale green and purple, evidently with white highlights, may derive from a representational scene.

References: M. Biddle, in *Antiq. Journ.* xlix (1969), p. 315; Liversidge 1977, pp. 79, 80.
Excavator: M. Biddle, Winchester Excavations Committee.

[1]De Vos 1969, p. 155 f.

No. 49. WINTERTON, Lincs. Villa, Building F (bath-house). Third or first half of fourth century. (A) Now in Scunthorpe, Borough Museum and Art Gallery. (B) Now (1979) in London, Fortress House (in storage). PLS: XCVIII, A,B. FIG. 53.

Wall-plaster collapsed on the floor of Room 6, possibly an addition to the original building (constructed *c* 180), included fragments of pink and purple fish and of figure-scenes on a green ground. Two pieces attributed to the east wall, one large and one small, have been restored. Excavated 1963.

(A) 1.22 m wide × 79 cm high. Fragments of a figure-scene above a purple zone. At the left, on a grey-green background, the lower part of a female figure stepping with her right foot raised in three-quarters view to our left. Beside her, against a column or pilaster rendered in

Photo: Department of the Environment: Crown Copyright reserved.
XCVIII A No. 49 (A) Winterton, restored figure-scene.

FIG. 53 No. 49 (A): Winterton, restored figure-scene from bath-house. Diagram showing position of original fragments. Scale, 1:8.

(Drawing by Frank Gardiner and Diane Dixon)

stripes of dark red, pink, grey, and orange, stands a child or wingless Cupid,[1] turned to the right with his head and right arm upraised. The broad, somewhat ugly face, shown in three-quarters view, is painted in pink with deep purple shadows under the jaw and, curiously, along the upturned forehead and cheek; the hair is yellow with looping purple outlines. The body may perhaps have been less broad and frontal than it has been restored; the feet, along with the left foot of the female figure, should possibly be set a little further to the left.

The upstretched arm of the child passes over a yellow fascia and into a green area where it touches one of a pair of lowered hands (or wing-tips?). Beyond this the restoration is problematic: it shows what appear to be the legs of a figure standing in a tub or well-head resting on a coiled support.

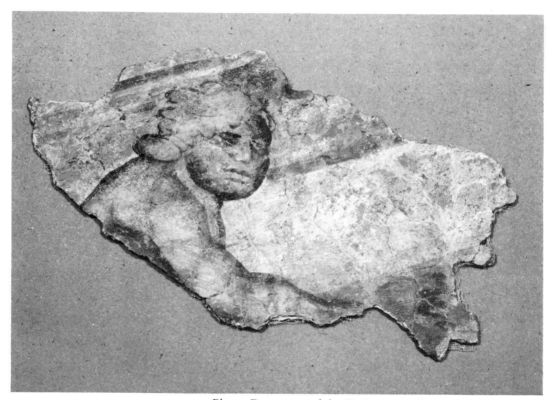

Photo: Department of the Environment: Crown Copyright reserved

XCVIII B   Detail of No. 49 (A). Scale, 1:3.

(B) 26.5 cm wide × 25 cm high. The upper part of the head and right side of the face of a child or Cupid. The flesh is pinkish-red with pinkish-white highlights on the forehead and cheekbone, and a deep purple shadow along the side of the face; the thick, tousled hair is indicated by purple curls filled with yellow. The whole head is framed by a strong purple contour. Above the head the background is coloured the same pinkish red as the face, but this grades to purple at the right and is fringed by the same colour at the left, before giving way along a curving edge to a surface of pale green. It is possible that this pinkish-red background is part of a billowing cloak. Although the head is frontal, the turn of the one surviving eye shows that the figure is looking to its left.

Given the fragmentary condition of the material from Room 6, little discussion is possible. The room was perhaps a plunge-bath, and the fragments with fish would therefore fit in with a well-established tradition (see Southwell, No. 34, and the parallels cited there). But no conclusions can be drawn about the role or subject-matter of the figure-scene or scenes.

In style the paintings suggest a fourth-century date. The heavy, dark contours call to mind paintings such as those of boating Cupids from the Palazzo della Farnesina ai Baullari in Rome, dated to the second quarter of the century;[2] and the wide, semicircular eye of the second child is also appropriate to the Constantinan period. It can be compared with the eyes of the figures in the ceiling of the palace below the cathedral in Trier.[3]

References: Davey, p. 268, fig. 16; Liversidge 1968, pl. 17 *a*; Liversidge 1976, pp. 276–280, figs. 139–141, pls. XXVIII, XXIX.

Excavator: I.M. Stead, Department of the Environment.

[1] For Cupids without wings on sarcophagi, N. Himmelmann-Wildschütz, in *Marburger Winckelmann-Programm*, 1959, pp. 29–31.

[2] H. Mielsch, in *Affreschi*, pp. 49–52, pls. XXVII, XXVIII; Mielsch 1978, pp. 182–4, pls. 94 (3), 95 (2).

[3] T. Kempf, in Reusch, pp. 236–43. Datable to the 320s or 330s: Mielsch 1978, p. 174.

No. 50. WITCOMBE, Glos. Villa. Third or fourth century. Now (1979) in London, Fortress House (in storage). PL. XCIX. FIG. 54.

Piece of ceiling-plaster restored from fragments found in a drain in the courtyard (1960 excavations).

90 cm × 89.5 cm. On a white ground a pattern of square panels (sides 29 to 33 cm) framed by garlands with little sprigs and groups of three berries growing from the sides. Alternate panels are restored to contain roundels, each of which has an outer border-stripe of purple (diam. approx. 27 cm) and an inner one of pale green (diam. approx. 22 cm). The colours of the garlands framing the panels with roundels are alternately pale green and ochre.

Of the ornaments within the roundels the clearest is a rosette with eight wedge-shaped, triple-pointed petals, alternately ochre and pale green. Two other fragmentary ornaments have been restored to form the centres of plant-whorls in purple and green. In the panels which lack roundels there were evidently heterogeneous objects, two of which have been restored: a green bowl (?) or shield (?), and a mysterious object which may have been intended to suggest a *ballista*.[1]

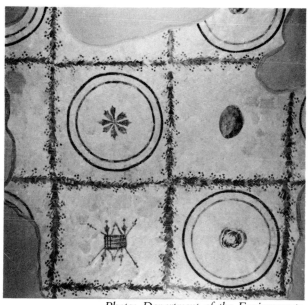

Photo: Department of the Environment:
Crown Copyright reserved

XCIX   No. 50   Witcombe, restored ceiling-plaster.

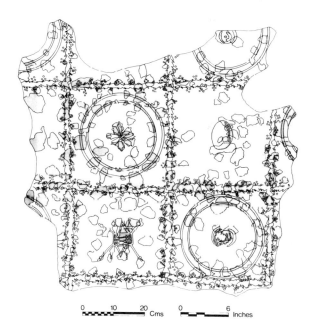

0 10 20 Cms   0   6 Inches

FIG. 54   No. 50: Witcombe, restored area of ceiling-decoration. Diagram showing position of original fragments. Scale, 1:12.
(Drawing by Diane Dixon)

Traces of guide-lines converging at the centres of some of the ornaments confirm their position in the panels, and a hole in the eye of the rosette was presumably made by the point of the compasses with which the enclosing roundel was marked out.

From the same or a matching decoration must come the fragment of intersecting garlands excavated by Mrs. Clifford in 1938.

Ceiling-patterns based on intersecting garlands or similar vegetal forms were popular in Roman painting at least from the time of Nero's Golden House onwards.[2] The motif was also transferred to walls, where the intersecting grid was set diagonally, and to floors, where it appears in mosaic pavements in Africa and the east.[3] Particularly interesting from our point of view are fragments of painted plaster from Building G of the Roman villa at Winterton, Lincs. Bluish-green garlands identical with ours, even down to the sprigs and berries at the sides, separate panels containing roundels of pink or blue.[4] Though on a much smaller scale and more finely rendered than our decoration, the Winterton pieces suggest a common source of inspiration, presumably a pattern-book in circulation in the province. Another similar pattern, this time with red roundels, is attested by fragments from Cirencester.[5]

In the 1962 excavations at the Witcombe villa fragments of plaster with painted fish were recovered from cracks in the floor of the cold plunge-bath (Room 7a). For this common motif see Southwell (No. 34).

See further Appendix, No. 12.

Reference: Liversidge 1969, pp. 143, 147, fig. 4.7e (the 1938 fragment).
Excavator: E. Greenfield, Department of the Environment.

[1] Cf. the reliefs illustrated in Dar.-Sag. v, s.v. 'Tormentum', p. 370, figs. 7022-3 (= *Arch. Anz.* 1979, p. 71, figs. 4, 5); and a stucco relief in the House of the Cryptoportico at Pompeii: *PBSR* xl (1973), pl. IX, *a*.

[2] Nero's Golden House: *Ant. Denkm.* iii, 2 (1912-13), pls. 16, 18; Dacos, figs. 23, 29, 38, 40.

[3] Stabiae: Elia, pls. XXXVII, XXXVIII (Vespasianic).Sabratha and Asgfa (Cyrenaica): G. Pesce, in *Boll. d'Arte* xxxvi (1951), p. 162 f., figs. 8, 10 (fourth century). Mosaics in Africa: *Inv. mos.*, iii. M.F.G. de Pachtère, *Afrique proconsulaire, Numidie, Maurétanie (Algérie)* (1911), no. 3; *Corpus des Mosaïques de Tunisie*, i, 1. *Utique, insulae I-II-III* (1973), pls. XXXVI, XXXVII; K.M.D. Dunbabin, *The Mosaics of Roman North Africa* (1978), pl. XLVII. Mosaics at Antioch: Levi, pls. CXXVI (a, b, d, e), CXXXI (b, d), CXXXVII (c), CXLI (a).

[4] Liversidge, 1976, p. 281 f., pl. XXXI, *d*, *e*. Ceiling-patterns formed by garlands, either green or half yellow and half red, also occurred at Caerwent in House VII N, Room 8 (unpublished drawing in Newport Museum).

[5] Liversidge 1962, p. 48, fig. 7.3, 4.

No. 51. WROXETER, Shropshire. Insula V, Baths. Second half of second or third century. Now in Wroxeter, Museum. PL. C. FIG. 55.

Piece of vault-decoration from *caldarium* (Room 15), restored from scattered fragments. Over-all dimensions: 1.21 m × 1.76 m.

A pattern of large octagons containing roundels, rendered mainly in black on a white ground. The main dividing frames are formed by a white band 4.5 cm to 6 cm wide bisected by a narrow black stripe and set between a pair of broader, grey-yellow stripes decorated with black spots 2 to 3 cm apart. A further narrow black stripe forms an inner border in both the octagons and the square interspaces. The roundels consist of two concentric rings, the outer one 58 cm in diameter, the inner 31 cm; the latter is a plain stripe, while the former has a serrated inner edge with a little spike emerging from every third notch.

Within this basic pattern additional interest is provided by clusters of large and small spots. At the centres of the roundels and the square interspaces are ornaments focused round five large spots arranged to form, as it were, a four-petalled rosette: in the squares two small spots continue the line of the petals towards the corners, while in the roundels the line is prolonged by a pyramid of four spots, two medium-sized ones side by side and two small ones in series. Further ornaments consisting of superposed pyramids of three large and three small spots decorate the circumference of the inner ring of the roundel at four equidistant points. Finally a single small spot floats near the tip of each spike in the outer frame of the roundel.

The scheme was painted with the aid of a grid of incised guide-lines, traces of which are visible on some of the fragments of original plaster; the lines apparently intersected at the mid-points of roundels and squares. The roundels themselves were marked out with compasses, the point of which left a depression in the eye of the central rosette.

Octagonal schemes are favourites in Roman ceiling-decoration: our version, in which octagons contain roundels, is paralleled in painted ceilings from Collingham, Yorks., and various continental sites (see No. 12 and the parallels cited there). As at Collingham, there may be some debt to work in relief. Our main frame, in which a black line bisects a white band, recalls a common type of coffer-frame found in stucco vaults and reflected in mosaic pavements, the inspiration in both coming perhaps ultimately from wooden ceiling-panelling.[1]

Particularly interesting are the possible hints of local or regional motifs. Diagonal and pyramidal groupings of spots are common at the corners of panels, but the particular form of our pyramids, with distinct large and small spots, their use as an external embellishment of a continuous line (in the roundels), and their dark colouring on a white ground — all are strongly reminiscent of spot-ornaments on fragments of plaster from a villa at Acton Scott, little more than 13 miles (21 km) south-west of Wroxeter (Introduction, FIG. 1).[2] The unusual motif of a light-coloured (grey-yellow) stripe carrying dark (black) spots is paralleled, to our knowledge, only at Droitwich (Worcestershire: No. 15, D), Caerwent (Monmouthshire), and Frocester Court (Gloucestershire) (Introduction, FIG. 3).[3] In these three more southerly sites the stripe and spots are in light and dark green or in light and dark brown (Frocester Court), but the general form of the motif is still sufficiently individual to suggest a community of ideas, especially as the Caerwent and Frocester stripes too may have been used for octagons. We may suspect an interchange of motifs between workshops based, broadly speaking, along the Severn valley.

Further painted fragments, showing roundels containing stylized flowers, are ascribed to the Baths Basilica.[4]

Unpublished.
Excavator: G. Webster, Wroxeter Training School.

[1] See e.g. Ling, pp. 24 ff., esp. 48, pls. VII *b*, VIII, IX, XI, XII, XIII, XIV *b*. Mosaic reflections: Morricone Matini.

[2] Mentioned by F.S. Acton in *Archaeologia* xxxi (1846), p. 342; F. Haverfield in VCH *Shropshire*, i (1908), p. 260; G. Webster, *The Cornovii* (1975), p. 85 f. The present writers owe their knowledge of the fragments to water-colour drawings in an excavation-notebook in the Local Studies Library, Shrewsbury (MS. 6007).

[3] Caerwent, House II S: unpublished water-colour in Newport Museum (dating uncertain). Frocester Court: *TBGAS* lxxxix (1970), pp. 78–80 and figs. 17, 18 (mid fourth century?).

[4] P.A. Barker, in *Britannia* vi (1975), p. 110; cf. p. 248.

No. 52. YORK. Fortress, *principia*. Early fourth century. Now in York Minster, Undercroft (piece B in storage). PLS. CI-CIII, CXXIV. FIG. 56.

Remains of wall-decoration from the north-west wall of a room added over a pre-existing road on the north-west side of the *principia* in the early fourth century.[1] One large and one small area reconstructed, the latter from plaster found *in situ*, the former from scattered fragments (collected according to a grid system). 1968 excavation.

(A) (i) Lower part of the wall (5.62 m wide × 1.01 m high). Above a pink baseboard comes a dado of long rectangular panels imitating different coloured marbles, the whole series enclosed between two horizontal purple bands. The panels, from left to right, are (a) white with irregular purple veins (streaks and curves) and a pale purple surround; (b) yellow with 'fried egg' decoration (purple blob enclosed by wavy purple lines) and a pale green surround with dark streaks; (c) dark red with black and white splashes and a yellow surround containing wavy purple streaks; (d) dark green with light green spirtling and a surround of the same colour. The dark red panel contains an inset lozenge with its acute angles truncated, while the upper part of the frame of the dark green panel is replaced by a black band decorated with white and pale green leaves. The total height of the dado, including the baseboard, is about 80 cm. Above the dado is an orange-red surface forming the background to architectural elements. At two points, corresponding to the white and dark red panels of the dado, stand pairs of columns, each with schematised double torus bases rendered in white, pale purple, and dark purple with a strong black outline. A purple ski-like form beneath each base is presumably a shadow. In the middle of each pair of columns is what seems to be a perspectival pillar-base, white with purple shadows and black outlines; and in the space between the two pairs, corresponding to the yellow panel of the dado, is the lower part of a pale blue field.

(ii) Upper part of the wall (5.57 m wide × 1.88 m high). The top of the main zone can be divided into four sections, again corresponding to the panels of the dado. (a) A pale purple surface with architectural elements in white and purplish brown: at left and right, column-shafts; at the centre, an arch; at the top, passing behind the columns, is a series of modillions in perspective as if seen from the right. (b) The upper part of a field with a blue background

C No. 51 Wroxeter, restored piece of ceiling-decoration.

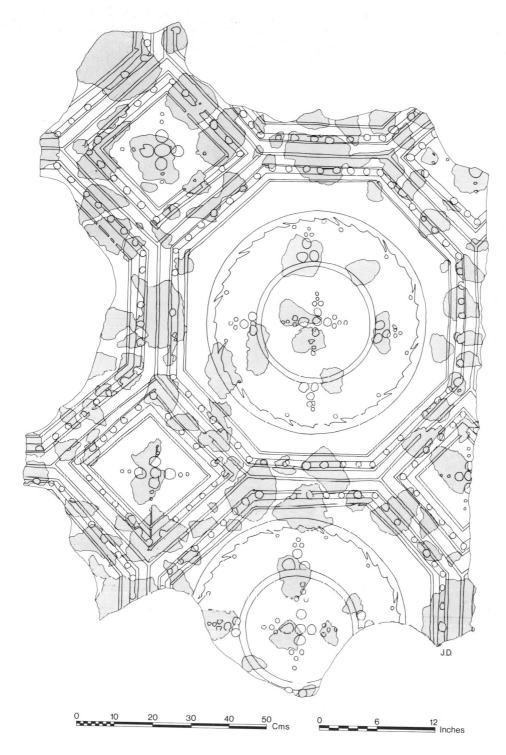

J.D.

FIG. 55 No. 51: Wroxeter, restoration of ceiling-plaster from caldarium in Baths. Diagram showing position of original fragments. Scale, 1:10.

(Drawing by Judith Dobie)

CI No. 52 (A) York, general view of restored wall-plaster.

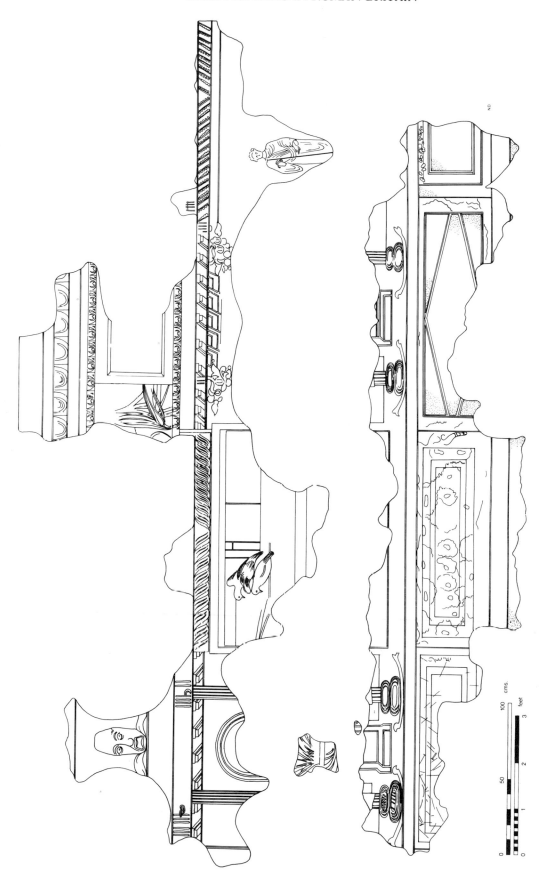

FIG. 56 No. 52 (A): York, restoration of painted plaster from room on north-west side of *principia*. Scale, 1:25.
(Drawing by N. Davey)

CII   No. 52 (A)   York, detail with theatrical mask.

CIII   No. 52 (A)   York, detail of column-base.

grading to greenish blue and pale yellowish green. Within the field, to left of centre, are three birds, creamy-yellow in colour with purple outlines, perched one above the other; while in the top right corner is set a yellow panel punctuated by a few vertical purple lines. Above runs a kind of simplified guilloche in black, green, yellow and orange, changing direction at the central point. (c) On a red ground two clusters of leaves in pale green and white, evidently meant to represent the capitals of the columns whose bases rest immediately above the dado. Between them a series of five purple ceiling-coffers in perspective as if seen from the left; and above them a series of modillions in pink, purple and white, also seen from the left. (d) On a red ground a standing figure, the details of which are uncertain. Above this section runs a border of oblique strokes, purple, green, or creamy-white, all on a pale purple ground; the strokes change direction at the centre and normally have lobes projecting along one side.

Of the upper zone there are tracts above the first and third sections of the main zone. Above the first, the main feature is a tragic(?) mask against a pale blue background. Skilfully rendered in purple, brown, and orange, the mask has large staring eyes and a saddle-shaped mouth-opening and rests on volutes growing left and right from beneath the chin; the *onkos* is missing. Above the third section, there is a rectangular window-opening framed in red and orange and set between a pair of horizontal bands with illusionistic egg-and-dart mouldings, each rendered in yellow, white and purple. A further, larger egg-and-dart, rendered solely in pale greenish yellow on a white ground, runs at a higher level.

(B) 97 cm wide × 87 cm high. The right-hand extremity of the dado of the same wall. An oblong panel painted creamy-white and orange with purple streaks indicating veins[2] is enclosed by pale and dark purple borders respectively 5 cm and 9 cm wide. Above the corner, on a pinkish-orange ground, is a curving purple form, the remnant of another column-base, which straddled the angle in the wall. Photographs taken at the time of the excavation (PL. CXXIV) show the end of another dado-panel on the adjacent wall, apparently pink with blue and dark purple borders.

The restoration of (A) is problematical. A number of features seem anomalous: notably the violent dislocations of colour and decorative scheme in the main zone, the fact that the left-hand pair of columns lack capitals, and the way in which one set of modillions passes behind the columns and the other above. The asymmetrical arrangement of different coloured panels in the dado is also unusual, but the five panels surviving do not represent the whole length of wall exposed, still less the whole length of the wall (which extended south-westwards beyond the excavated area), so some symmetry may have been achieved in the missing part of the decoration.

The garish and unrealistic colouring of the marbled dado[3] and the strong, dark contours of the columns, of the birds and of the features of the mask are typical of fourth-century painting (although the style is not yet as schematized as that of the Christian paintings from Lullingstone, No. 27). The double-torus form of the column-bases is a stylisation of what is a familiar type in western provincial architecture, occurring in York itself as well as in many other towns and rural settlements,[4] and there are parallels in a painted scheme at Verulamium dated to the mid second century (No. 44, A i) and in fragments of wall-painting found in the Rue de l'Abbé de l'Epée in Paris (first half of the second century ?).[5] For the use of an inset lozenge in an oblong panel in the dado compare decorations from Aldborough (Appendix, No. 1), Catterick (No. 5, C), Malton (No. 28), and Winterton.[6]

References: Davey 1972, p. 265 and fig. 13; *Britannia* vi (1975), p. 290, pl. XXII, B; R. Cant, *The Undercroft, York Minster* (guide-book, n.d.), pp. 3, 7.
Excavator: D. Phillips, York Minster Archaeology Office.

[1] Since this was written, Dr. Brenda Heywood has informed me that sealed pottery beneath the only floor in the room suggests a date in the second half of the fourth century. We must accept the possibility, therefore, that the paintings are later than hitherto believed.
[2] The idea that these represent letters (*Britannia* vi (1975), p. 290) is unconvincing.
[3] The type of marbling in Piece B, to judge from the photographs, was a very rare combination of oblique bands

and a superimposed tracery of purple scribbles: a parallel occurs in a bath-suite outside the eastern defences of the fortress of Vindonissa, Switzerland (unpublished: information from Alix Barbet).

[4] Blagg, pp. 56–60. A type found in military contexts, including York itself, is close to our painted version (cf. *ibid.*, fig. 4.4, though this particular example has a moulding above the upper torus, a feature lacking in the painting). We are grateful to Mr. Blagg for information on column-bases.

[5] We are deeply indebted for photographs and information to Mlle. Hélène Eristov. Cf. *Gallia* xxxv (1977), p. 323; *Cahiers de la Rotonde* ii (1969), pp. 21–4, fig. 8.

[6] Liversidge 1976, p. 282 f., fig. 143, pl. XXXIV, *c, d.*

No. 53. YORK. Fortress, centurion's quarters north-west of *principia*. Between second and fourth centuries. Now (1980) in York Minster (in storage).

A small piece from the base of a timber-framed clay partition, which formed the south-west wall of a room excavated outside the north-west tower of the Minster. Each face of the wall carried a series of successive plaster facings. 1971 excavation.

Overall dimensions 1.42 m wide × 86 cm high.

The second-phase plaster on the north-east face preserved remains of painted marbling (1.41 m wide × 50 cm high). Above a dark red baseboard about 16 cm high comes a series of panels and vertical bands side by side. From left to right: a vertical band of green; a vertical band (12 cm wide) of yellow with black and red splashes; a panel (61 cm wide) of yellow with diagonal red zig-zags; a panel containing a square set diagonally (about 53 cm from corner to corner). The interior of the inset square, which is framed with a red line, is pale green with red, yellow and black splashes; the triangular spaces round it have a white ground carrying leaf-like forms in red, yellow and green with black and red splashes.

The painting is crude; for the motif of an inset lozenge or diagonally set square in a marbled dado see the examples cited under No. 52.

Unpublished.
Excavator: D. Phillips, York Minster Archaeology Office.

APPENDIX I

Appendix No. 1. ALDBOROUGH, Yorks.   Baths inside west wall. Second century ? (the paintings evidently belong to the earlier phase of the building, which yielded coins of the second century). PL. CIV.

Excavations in 1830 yielded fragments of painted plaster, some still adhering to the walls. Drawings published by H.E. Smith show three motifs:

(A) A rectangular field framed by a pink border and enclosing a grey lozenge which in turn contains a yellow roundel with a white square set in it. The yellow part of the medallion and the triangular spaces round the lozenge, which are also yellow, carry foliate designs with blue leaves and red stems and veining.

Photo after H.E. Smith, *Reliquiae Isurianae*

CIV   Aldborough, fragments of painted wall-plaster from Baths.

(B) A rectangular field framed by a grey border and white line enclosing a yellow lozenge decorated with a similar blue-leaved and red-stemmed foliate design. The triangular areas round the lozenges have yellow and red foliate motifs on a grey ground.

(C) Above a grey horizontal stripe come, at the left, a vertical pink band and next to it two pale blue fields containing each a geometric figure. The first is a lozenge, pink in the top half, yellow in the bottom. The second is a grey roundel with pink inner and white outer frame.

References: H.E. Smith, *Reliquiae Isurianae* (1852), pl. IV; Liversidge 1958, p. 374 and fig. 3; Liversidge 1968, p. 88 and fig. 33.

Appendix, No. 2. ALDBOROUGH, Yorks.   Building immediately inside south-west part of defences. Second or early third century? (the building evidently antedates the city-walls, which are not earlier than the Severan period).[1] PL. CV.

Remains of wall-paintings, evidently on the lower parts of the walls, were exposed in excavations of the late 1840s and published by H.E. Smith. Four main areas are illustrated:

(A) A pink socle with red flecks, surmounted by a white panel framed with a pale yellow border; at the middle of the white panel is the lower part of a lozenge formed by grey stripes.

(B) The lower part of a pink panel and, adjacent to it at the right, vertical bands of pink and pale yellow and what is probably the bottom left corner of another pink panel. All the areas, whether pink or yellow, are splashed with black. The left-hand panel contains a yellow rectangle displaced to the left of centre and again splashed black. All the divisions are effected by white stripes, and a diagonal stripe links the lower left corner of the left-hand panel and its inset rectangle.

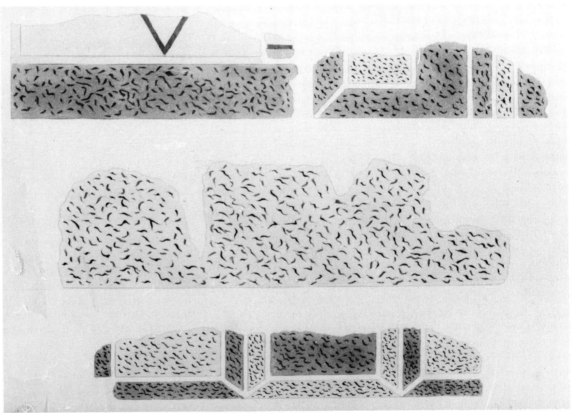

Photo after H.E. Smith, *Reliquiae Isurianae*

CV   Aldborough, fragments of painted wall-plaster from building inside south-west defences.

(C) A large area of white with black and red splashes.

(D) An alternating system of pale yellow panels set within pink surrounds and pink panels set within pale yellow surrounds. Each colour is splashed with black, and divided from its neighbour by white stripes, which are also used diagonally to link the lower angles of the inset panels and the surrounding colour-bands.

References: H.E. Smith, *Reliquiae Isurianae* (1852), pl. VI; Liversidge 1958, p. 374 and fig. 1; Liversidge 1968, p. 88 and fig. 32.

[1] A coin found in the footings of the city-wall has a die probably of Julia Domna: *YAJ* xl (1959–62), p. 60.

Appendix, No. 3. BIGNOR, Sussex.   Villa.   Late third or fourth century.

Remains of wall-plaster found in the first excavations (1811-17) are known from drawings published by Lysons.

(A) On the lower part of the west wall of Room 33 plaster was preserved *in situ*. Above a dark brown dado were tall fields separated by pink fasciae; the central field was yellow with white borders, and the four remaining fields (two at each side) were pale blue.

(B) Fragments from the baths showed parts of panels in pale yellow, pale blue and other colours, and a broad zone of red with white speckling. Three pieces were painted in imitation of mosaic tesserae, two of them with a guilloche coloured white, blue, red, yellow, and two shades of grey (Introduction FIG. 2; cf. Sparsholt, No. 35).

References: S. Lysons 1813-17, iii, pl. XXXII and vignette at end of List of Plates; Liversidge 1969, pp. 130, 133, 134, fig. 4.1 *(a-c)*, pl. 4.2.

Appendix, No. 4. CAERWENT, Monmouthshire (Gwent).   House VII S, Rooms 6 and 7. Middle or third quarter of fourth century.[1] FIGS. 57, 58.

The lower part of an architectural wall-decoration excavated in 1901 and recorded in full-size water-colours. One of these (torn off at the right-hand end) is preserved in Newport Museum; a detail from another (by A.E. Hudd) is published in the excavation-report in *Archaeologia* (see bibliography). The rest have not been found.

The architecture rested directly on the edge of a continuous dado or baseboard, at least 10 or 12 cm high, painted pink with red and white splashes. Above this a series of illusionistic recesses alternated with projecting piers, each with a bevelled base-moulding. This scheme was marked out in very basic fashion, each angle or other structural division being indicated by a strong brown stripe, often reinformed by a white stripe, and each intervening surface being coloured in a flat wash of yellow, pale orange or ochre, orange-red, pale green, or pink.

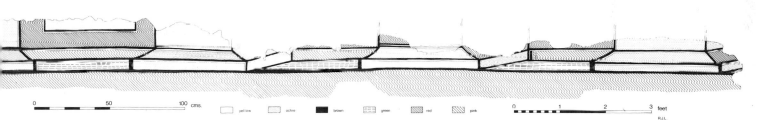

FIG. 57   Appendix, No. 4: Caerwent, House VII S, Room 7. Remains of wall-painting found in position (after water-colour drawing in Newport Museum). Scale, 1:25.
(Drawing by R.J. Ling)

Neither perspective nor colouring were entirely consistent. In the Newport water-colour (FIG. 57) the left-most of the three complete recesses included is shown head-on, without a hint of perspective (the side-walls are not visible), whereas the next two are each shown from the right, the left side-wall being represented perspectively, the right hidden. All the recesses have pale green floors and, on the back-walls, a pink wainscoting surmounted by a red zone (which, in the best preserved (left) example, acts as a border for a yellow panel). But the colours of piers and side-walls vary. The first two piers are yellow, apart from the bevel of the base-moulding, which is ochre; while the third has a yellow base and a red surface above, and the fourth is something between yellow and ochre. In the side-wall of the second recess the vertical part of the base moulding is yellow, and the bevel ochre (the water colorist as elsewhere has continued the colour upwards above the break in the plaster); in the side-wall of the third recess, and in the remaining fragment of that of the fourth, the vertical part of the moulding is ochre and the bevel red.

The other water-colour (FIG. 58) shows a similar recess, this time with centralised perspective. Both piers and side-walls are uniformly ochre-coloured (white stripes are added to the vertical parts of the front faces), and the left side shows a crowning moulding which is more or less the reverse of the base-moulding. On the back-wall the red surface above the pink wainscoting continues uninterrupted, apart from a single horizontal white stripe, up to a level immediately below the crowning-moulding of the side-wall. Here it gives way to another pink band, above which there is a trace of green.

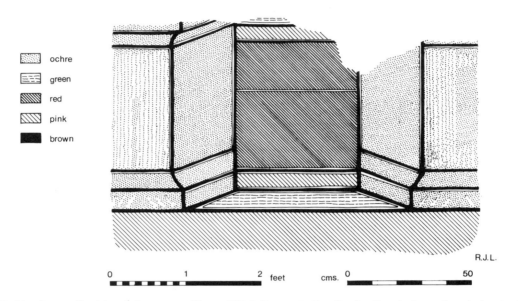

FIG. 58   Appendix, No. 4: Caerwent, House VII S, Room 7. Detail of wall-painting, after *Archaeologia* lviii. The dado is speckled red, purple and white. Scale, 1:15.
(Drawing by R.J. Ling)

The position of the recorded areas within the room is problematic. Both are ascribed to the north wall of Room 7,[2] but it is difficult to accommodate them in the space available. The Newport water-colour would seem, from its perspective, to represent an area to the left of the central part of its wall, but it is 5.12 m (16 ft. 10 ins.) long, well over half the length of the north (longest) wall, which is about 7.92 m (26 ft.). Moreover the *Archaeologia* recess (FIG. 58), which logically belongs to the mid-point of a wall, cannot be identical with that of which a fragment remains at the right extremity of the Newport water-colour, since the break in the plaster comes much lower in the latter than in the former. One must conclude that the two drawings represent parts of different walls. It is also possible that the anomalous left-hand niche in the Newport water-colour belongs to the end of the adjacent wall: i.e. that the drawing shows the north end of the west wall and the west part of the north wall.

Whatever the true arrangements of perspective and colouring (and in the latter case the water-colorist may have been misled in places by fading or discoloration of the original plaster) the scheme was illusionistic in only the most superficial sense. The colouring was schematic; there was no shading; and the linear modelling was carried out in confused fashion: for instance the projecting base-mouldings were not echoed in the back corners of the recesses, where all the receding lines ended flush against a vertical one. The effect was a pattern-like abstraction loosely based on architectural forms — the same effect in fact as seen in the west wall of the Lullingstone chapel, a decoration of very similar date (No. 27, A).

From the upper part of the wall are said to have come fragments with green foliage on a purple ground.

References: T. Ashby, A.E. Hudd and A.T. Martin, in *Archaeologia* lviii (1902–03), p. 141 and pl. XII, fig. 2; Liversidge 1968, p. 88 and fig. 34 *b*.

[1]Cf. D.J. Smith's dating of the Seasons mosaic, which seems to have been contemporary with our paintings: Smith 1977, p. 129 f. An earlier pavement in Room 7 was associated with earlier layers of wall-painting.

[2]This is presumably the meaning of the label of the *Archaeologia* plate, which mistakenly reads 'north wall of House No. 7'.

Appendix, No. 5. CAERWENT, Monmouthshire.   House XVI N, Room 3. Late third or early fourth century? (coins found stratified above the floor (a hoard?) range from Gallienus to Licinius). FIG. 59.

The south wall of the room, preserved to a height of 13 ft. 9 in. (4.19 m) carried painted plaster in two phases, the first hacked to provide a purchase for the second. The earlier layer is recorded in a drawing by F.G. Newton. Excavated in 1905.

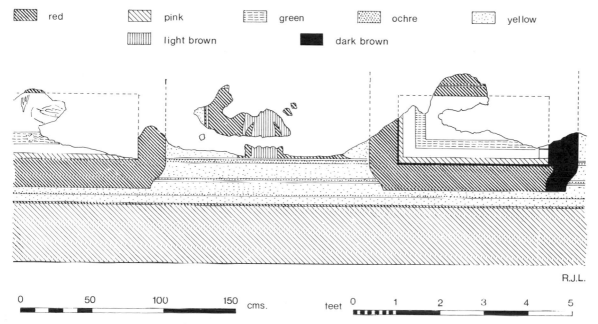

FIG. 59   Appendix, No. 5: Caerwent, House XVI N, Room 3. Wall-painting found *in situ* (after F.G. Newton). The dado was painted with veins imitating marbling; the background of the panels was blue. Scale, 1:26. *(Drawing by R.J. Ling)*

A pale brown (pink?) dado with dark brown veining, surmounted by a yellow band, carried yellow pilasters; a complete example 4 ft. 8 in. (1.42 m) wide is shown at the centre, and the edge of another at the right. A dark brown area in the central pilaster seems to indicate some form of decorated panel. Between the pilasters, framed by chestnut-brown (red?) surrounds, are small rectangular panels with a fawn or pink outer frame (at least at the bottom and the left), a green inner frame (again at the bottom and left), and a greyish-blue ground. The panel to the left of the central pilaster carries brown and white traces which may indicate a representational subject.

The edge of the right-hand pilaster casts a shadow, but the central pilaster casts none. The dado, including the crowning band, is 1 ft. 7 in. (48 cm) high.

Reference: T. Ashby, in *Archaeologia* lx (1906–07), p. 128, pl. XIX.

Appendix, No. 6. CIRENCESTER, Glos.   Insula XVII, Building 1. Dating uncertain.

Remains of wall-painting found in 1849 in a house lying obliquely across Dyer Street, in front of the Ship Inn, are recorded in a drawing published by Buckman and Newmarch.

On the south-west wall of Room B the painted plaster remained in position to a height of about 20 in. (51 cm). Above a projecting podium and a white dado came the lower parts of coloured panels: at the centre a pink panel containing a medallion formed by a black bead-and-reel; at the left a yellow panel with wavy green diagonal lines; at the right a yellow panel with

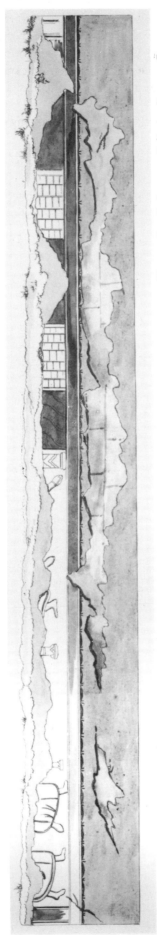

Photo after S. Lysons, *Reliquiae Britanico-Romanae.*

CVI   Comb End, stretch of wall-painting found in position.

red scallops and green strokes. The wavy lines, scallops etc. are clearly designed to suggest variegated marble; the pink panel carries black and dark pink splashes. In the interstices are (a) at the left a black fascia 11 in. (28 cm) wide with a sprig of green, a dark green band 4 in. (10 cm) wide, and a yellow band 1½ in. (4 cm) wide between black lines; (b) at the right a dark green fascia 16½ in. (42 cm) wide between two yellow bands 1½ in. (4 cm) wide, each enclosed between black lines.

A further coloured drawing shows variously-coloured framing-elements from Rooms A and B.

Reference: J. Buckman and C.H. Newmarch, *Illustrations of the Remains of Roman Art in Cirencester* (1850), pp. 71-74, pl. VI (3).

Appendix, No. 7. COMB END, Glos. Villa. Dating uncertain (fourth century?). PL. CVI.

A stretch of wall-painting about 20 feet (6 m) in length, found *in situ* in 1794 (?) and recorded in a drawing by Lysons.

The yellow ochre dado is represented like a curtain pinned at regular intervals to the underside of a purple band bordered by white above and below. The main zone shows the bottom of a large-scale figure-scene, of columns, of brown panels, and of a design of black-outlined white rectangles possibly intended to indicate masonry. At the left, after a vertical brown band, two long-skirted figures move to the right on a white ground; then comes a pair of small columns, separated by a broad gap, and the feet of two further figures, running (?) to the left. A thicker column concludes the figural part of the decoration; then come three brown panels alternating with two panels of 'masonry', and finally the remains of some vertical stripes. It is possible to argue that a figure-scene is taking place in front of a large building (the sequence at the right), but there is too little evidence to justify an interpretation.

If Lysons's drawing accurately reflects the style of the original figures, their strong purple contours and two-dimensional treatment might suggest a fourth-century, and more specifically late fourth-century, date (cf. Lullingstone, No. 27).[1]

References: S. Lysons, in *Archaeologia* xviii (1817), p. 113; Lysons 1813-17, ii, pl. I; Liversidge 1958, pp. 380, 383, fig. 10; Toynbee 1964, p. 219 f., pl. LII *b*; Liversidge 1968, p. 276, fig. 117; Liversidge 1969, p. 145, pl. 4.4

[1]There was probably no later re-decoration: what Miss Liversidge regards as such (see bibliography) is surely the masonry of the wall showing through where the plaster has fallen away.

Appendix, No. 8. GREETWELL, Lincs. Villa. Dating uncertain. PL. CVII.

Fragments of wall-paintings are known from a drawing by B. Ramsden (about 1890), now in Lincoln City and County Museum. These show mainly floral and foliate motifs, probably from a ceiling-decoration or decorations: included are a rosette with eight green and blue triple-pointed petals round a red and yellow centre; a rosette with four triple petals of red round a green and blue centre; a yellow leaf with three prongs and red markings; and concentric red, blue and black circles with green leaf-forms growing from the circumference. A fragment with white lettering on a red ground, shown in another drawing, is preserved in the museum.

Accounts of the villa also mention a piece with 'the figure of a swallow'.

References: E. Venables, in *Associated Architectural Societies' Reports and papers* xxi (1891), p. 49; *idem*, in *Arch. Journ.* xlix (1892), pp. 259, 262; Liversidge 1958, p. 378, fig. 5 *a-g*; Liversidge 1969, pp. 139 f., 145, pl. 4.8.

Appendix, No. 9. HADSTOCK, Essex. Villa. Dating uncertain.

Fragments of wall-paintings excavated in 1850 are known from water-colours by J. Youngman. Of thirty-six pieces illustrated four can be identified in Cambridge, Museum of Archaeology and Ethnology.

Most pieces carry merely framing stripes in red, black and yellow, but some show roundels and stylised floral forms. One has a yellow quatrefoil in a red circle (diam. approx. 5 cm) within a blue circle (diam. approx. 12.5 cm), and nearby a red leaf-shaped motif outlined in yellow, part of a chain of such motifs running past the circles. Another has a green quatrefoil surrounded by a yellow circle within a red one. To judge from the remains of guide-lines we can postulate a repeating pattern, perhaps from a ceiling, in which the roundels were set within squares formed by chains of leaf-motifs.

References: J.C. Buckler, *Arch. Journ.*, viii (1851), p. 31; J. Liversidge, in *Proceedings of the Cambridge Antiquarian Society* xliv (1950), pp. 13 f., pls. I, II; Liversidge 1958, p. 378 and fig. 4; Liversidge 1969, pp. 137, 146, fig. 4.4 *a, b*.

PLATE IX

Scale 6 Inch to one Foot

Photo: *Lincolnshire Museum*

CVII   Greetwell, fragments of wall-painting drawn by B. Ramsden.

Appendix, No. 10. IWERNE MINSTER, Dorset.   Villa, Building B. Fourth century. PL.
CVIII.

Photo: H. St. George Gray (copyright Dorset Natural History and Archaeological Society)
CVIII   Iwerne Minster, south-west angle of 'Painted Room'.

The westernmost room had walls decorated with painted plaster; photographs of 1897, taken
by H. St. George Gray, show the dado and the lower part of a panel-system *in situ* (Dorchester,
Dorset County Museum). Gray's notebooks, now dispersed, also contained coloured drawings.
The dado was white with small pink spots and was surmounted by a horizontal red band; the
panels were also white and were framed by lines and stripes of yellow, red and green. Traces of
a green leaf-design were observed on the vertical strips between the panels.

Fragments of plaster from the villa were formerly in the Pitt-Rivers Museum at Farnham, the
contents of which have now been dispersed.

References: C.F.C. Hawkes, in *Arch. Journ,* civ (1947), pp. 50, 51, 59; Liversidge 1969, p. 130,
pl. 4.1; RCHM, *Dorset* iv (1972), p. 41, pl. 48 (below).

Appendix, No. 11. WATER NEWTON, Hunts.   Bath-building north-east of modern
village. Dating uncertain. PL. CIX.

Wall-decoration from a building in Normangate Field drawn by Artis in 1826. It shows large
red fields separated by thick columns illusionistically painted in dark blue and yellow. Each field
has a yellow inner border-line and a pale blue outer border, as well as a general framing band of
sea-green which also acts as a kind of background for the columns. The columns are given dark
brown bases and capitals and rest on a dark brown plinth with a white stripe along the top.
Between the column-bases run a light mauve band between brown stripes and, above this, a
brown stripe and a band of yellow ochre. Across the top of the column-capitals, sagging over
the red panels, runs an awning painted in different shades of brown, and above this runs a
continuous horizontal red band.

Reference: E.T. Artis, *The Durobrivae of Antoninus* (1828), pl. XXXII; cf. pl. XXVI, 4.

Photo after E.T. Artis, *The Durobrivae of Antoninus*

CIX   Water Newton, wall-decoration found in bath-building in Normangate Field.

Appendix, No. 12 WITCOMBE, Glos.   Villa. Third or fourth centuries? FIG. 60.

At the time of the villa's discovery (1818) several rooms retained painted wall-plaster, which was described by Lysons and recorded in water-colour drawings, now preserved in the Red Portfolio of the Society of Antiquaries of London. The walls of Room 1 survived to a height of from 5 ft. 4 in. to 6 ft. (1.60 to 1.80 m) and were decorated with a pink dado and white panels framed by red bands. The walls of Corridor 2 stood nearly as high and again had a decoration of white panels, this time framed by bands of light blue and orange (or yellow?) and separated by intervals carrying delicate ivy-leaf candelabra. The walls of Room 5 stood 4 ft. to 5 ft. 4 in. (1.20 to 1.60 m); the panel-decoration mentioned by Lysons, which is barely visible in his

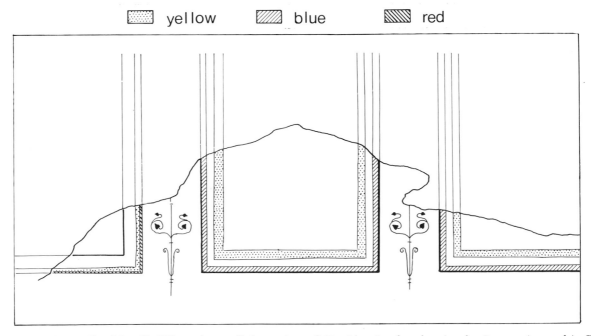

FIG. 60   Appendix, No. 12: Witcombe, wall-decoration of Corridor 2, after drawing by Lysons (no scale). By courtesy of the Society of Antiquaries of London.

(Drawing by R.J. Ling)

general drawing of the remains, was evidently white-ground and had a dado of red surmounted by a green band.

An isolated fragment drawn by Lysons shows a lozenge (?) framed by two shades of grey and containing pink and white marbling. No provenance is given.

In an account of more recent excavations by Mrs. E.M. Clifford (1938–39) the plastered walls of Corridor 2 are described as 'coloured pink, yellow and green, with pink, red, yellow and white stripes'. The disparity from Lysons's description and drawing is difficult to explain: possibly what Mrs. Clifford saw was part of the dado, not mentioned by Lysons; possibly she is referring to loose fragments (in which case their derivation from the corridor, apparently fully cleared by Lysons, must be questionable). In the same excavation the walls of Room 4 were found to be 'pinkish-purple'; other plaster fragments from the room were 'white and cream with a red stripe'.

See also No. 50.

References: S. Lysons, in *Archaeologia* xix (1821), pp. 178, 179, 181; Society of Antiquaries of London, Red Portfolio, Gloucestershire W–Z, pp. 25, 26, 28; E.M. Clifford, in *TBGAS* lxxiii (1954), pp. 17, 21; cf. 22, 60.

APPENDIX II

PIGMENTS

By Leo Biek

It was thought worth while to include a list of pigment identifications (Table I) made recently at and for the Ancient Monuments Laboratory. This has been compiled by Justine Bayley who carried out the work at the Laboratory. The analyses of Nos. 1-4, 6-11, 16 and 19 were done by Rebecca Wetzel in Ashland, Mass., USA, and those of Nos. 5, 12 and 13 by S. Wyles at the Laboratory of the Government Chemist to whom we are also grateful for useful discussion. No. 29 was identified by D.T. Moore at the British Museum (Natural History).

The work is current and the list is no more than a reflection of material now in the Laboratory; it is presented without special arrangement or comment and nearly all the material is as yet unpublished. Apart from the absence of yellow ochre and green earth, the range of colours seems to be fairly typical when compared with published data collected by one of the authors (RL), and arranged as bare quotes in Table II.

The pellets of Egyptian blue are fairly coarse-grained and of overall diameter varying from 5 to 10 mm. A comprehensive account by W.T. Chase of the common use and unusual nature of this material appeared in 1971 in *Science and Archaeology* edited by R.H. Brill (Cambridge, Mass.: MIT Press; pp. 80-90).

Identifications preceded by this symbol (‡) are by comparative visual inspection at the Ancient Monuments Laboratory only and have not been confirmed analytically. (D) indicates a relatively darker pattern than (F) = fainter, and hence suggests a major component. The quartz, so often found, may be a deliberately-added dilutent or an accidental contaminant.

The Munsell number assigned to each pigment is given only as a guide since the colour is never totally homogeneous.

No. 5 is probably not a pigment but contains material which suggests some kind of association with storage or preparation of pigments. Major amounts of lead and minor quantities of calcium and phosphorus have been detected, but the material is largely amorphous and difficult to interpret precisely.

TABLE I. RECENT PIGMENT ANALYSES

Serial number	Site	Colour	Munsell No.	AMLab No.	Compounds detected by X-ray diffraction analysis	Physical description.
1.	Water Newton	white		590224	calcium carbonate	lumpy deposit (up to 5 mm) in pot base
2.	,,	red	10R4/6	590229	haematite (D), calcium carbonate (F), quartz (F)	fairly fine deposit in pot base
3.	,,	yellow/ green	5Y7/6	590230	calcium carbonate (D), quartz (D)	fairly coarse deposit in pot base
4.	,,	pale red	2.5YR6/6	590225	haematite (D), calcium carbonate (D), quartz (F)	fine deposit in pot base
5.	,,	buff/ white		590231	see note (p. 220)	hard deposit inside pot base
6.	,,	,,	10YR6/3	590228	calcium carbonate, quartz	fine-grained deposit in pot base
7.	,,	red	10R4/6	590223	haematite (D), quartz (D)	lump of fairly coarse pigment from a pot base
8.	,,	reddish	2.5YR5/2	590226	haematite (D), calcium carbonate (D)	coarse powder
9.	,,	blue	2.5PB6/8	590222	Egyptian blue	pellet
10.	,,	,,	2.5PB6/8	590227	,,	two pellets stuck together
11.	Alice Holt	red	10R6/8→2.5YR5/8		haematite (D), calcium carbonate (D), quartz (F)	coarse pigment in pot base
12.	Chichester	blue	10B8/4	743000	Egyptian blue	pot base containing fine pigment
13.	Rudston	,,	5PB6/10	660027	,, ,,	pellet
14.	Hayton	,,	10B7/6	752308	(‡Egyptian blue)	potsherd containing blue powder
15.	Wroxeter	pink	7.5R7/6	780034	haematite, calcium carbonate, quartz	fairly fine-textured pigment in pot base
16.	Braintree	purple/ red	10R4/2→10R2.5/2	749430	haematite (D), quartz (D)	pot base containing fine pigment
17.	Lincoln	pale red	10R5/8	7310340	(‡haematite)	pot rim sherd with both fine-textured pigments overlying each other, white under and over red
18.	,,	white		,,		
19.	,,	purple/ red	10R4/4	7310341	haematite	pot base containing coarse pigment
20.	Tower of London	blue	2.5PB5/8→7/8	791216	(‡Egyptian blue)	several pellets stuck together
21.	Braintree	purple/ red	10R4/6→10R4/8		(‡haematite)	traces of colour on a Purbeck Marble palette
22.	Tower of London	blue	10B6/8	768427A	(‡Egyptian blue)	lump
23.	Chelmsford	pink	7.5R8/4	7716438	haematite, calcium carbonate, quartz	fine deposit on potsherd
24.	Southwark	pink	7.5R7/6	790634	,, ,,	fairly fine-textured lumps, with white spots
25.	Colchester	red	7.5R4/8	722288	(‡haematite)	fairly fine-textured lumps
26.	,,	blue	2.5PB5/8	722286	(‡Egyptian blue)	two pellets
			2.5PB6/6	722287	,, ,,	
27.	Richborough	,,	5PB5/10		,, ,,	massive lump c. 12 x 8 x 5 cm
28.	,,	purple/ red	7.5R3/6		(‡haematite)	parts of two lumps c. 1-2 cm across of fine-grained pigment
29.	Catsgore	blue	2.5PB7/6		Egyptian blue, quartz	lump

TABLE II. PUBLISHED PIGMENT IDENTIFICATION

Site	Reference	Identification[1] white	black	pink	red	yellow	green	blue	Comment
Downton	J. Plesters *Wilts. Archaeol. N.H. Mag.* lviii (1961–3), 337–41	calcium carbonate	carbon black		iron oxide	iron oxide	iron magnesium silicate	Egyptian blue	also brown and orange iron oxides, and mixtures
Verulamium	"	"	"	ochre & chalk primer	" also as primer	"	"	"	previously examined at National Gallery Lab.
Stanton Low	"	"	"		iron oxide	"	"	"	2 samples (dark purple–red) had small amount of extractable, glue-like protein.
Hucclecote	in E. Clifford *Trans. Bristol & Glos. Archaeol. Soc.* lv (1933), 348				haematite	limonite	"		
Witcombe[2]	A.A. Moss *Trans. Bristol & Glos. Archaeol. Soc.* lxxiii (1954), 17, 60	",[p]		haematite,[p] calcium carbonate[p] +	+[a]		",[p]		
Darenth	F.C.J. Spurrell *Arch. Journ.* lii (1895), 236							Egyptian blue	
Woodeaton	E.M. Jope & G. Huse *Nature* cxlvi (1940), 26							Egyptian blue ",[a,c]	
Silchester	cf. F.C.J. Spurrell *Arch. Journ.* lii (1895), 236							Egyptian blue[c]	
"	in Boon 1974, 211, nn 2 and 4[2]				(ochre[a,m]) +[r]	+[r]	+[r]	+[r] (Egyptian blue[c])	incl. rubber with residues of 4 colours. presumably same as Jope's
Wroxeter	A.P. Laurie *et al Proc. Roy. Soc.,* A, 39 (1913–4), 418 ff.							Egyptian blue[c]	
Northchurch	E. Holland in *Britannia* vi (1975), 257			haematite,[p] chalk[p]					
Lullingstone[2]	in Meates 1955, 154							+[m]	
York	R.E. Wetzel forthcoming	calcium carbonate	carbon black		haematite vermilion (cinnabar)	goethite	glauconite celadonite	Egyptian blue	green (earth) is combination of 2 hydrous iron magnesium silicates containing aluminium and potassium; also mixtures.

1 all in painted plaster except where superscripted: [a] = palette, [c] = pellet, [m] = mortarium, [p] = pot, [r] = rubber   2   + = colour described but no details given.

PLATES

Above
CX   No. 13 (B)   Dorchester (Poundbury), fragments of figure-frieze
from Mausoleum R 8, before restoration. See also PL. XL.
Photo: Dorchester Excavation Committee.

Below
CXI   No. 38 (B)   Tarrant Hinton, head and shoulders of figure in
mythological scene.   *Photo: G.E. Gray.*

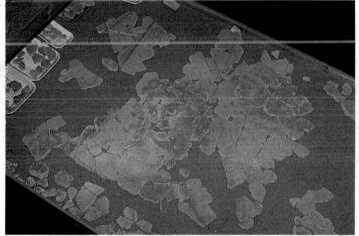

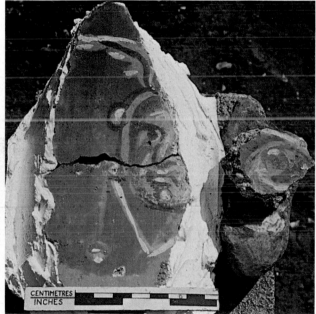

Above
CXII   No. 41 (D)   Verulamium XXI, 2, mask from ceiling in
Corridor 2.
Photo: M.B. Cookson.

Left
CXIII   No. 17   Fishbourne, fragments of candelabrum from
early palace.
Photo: R.J. Ling.

Above
CXIV   No. 10 (B)   Colchester, gladiator.
Photo: Alison Colchester, Colchester Archaeological Trust.

Right
CXV   No. 40 (A)   Verulamium XIX, fragments of still
life.
Photo: Verulamium Museum.

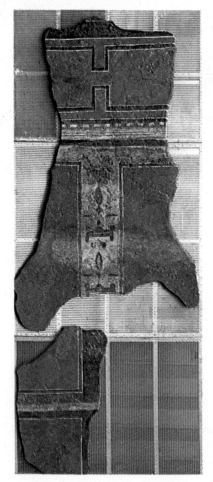

Above
CXVI   No. 40 (D)   Verulamium XIX, fragments of cornice and frieze with S-modillions.
Photo: Verulamium Museum.

Left
CXVII   No. 44 (B)   Verulamium XXVIII, 3, restored pieces of
wall-decoration from Room 9.
Photo: M.B. Cookson.

Above
CXVIII   No. 48   Winchester, fragments of architectural
perspective from building south of forum.
Photo: R.J. Ling.

Right
CXIX   No. 34 (A)   Southwell, detail of Cupid.
Photo: Department of the Environment: Crown Copyright reserved.

Below
CXX   No. 21   Kingscote, restored areas of mythological
scene.   *Photo: B. Cavill.*

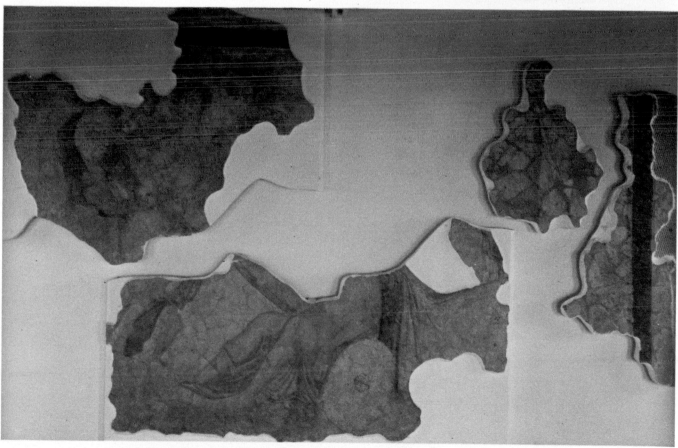

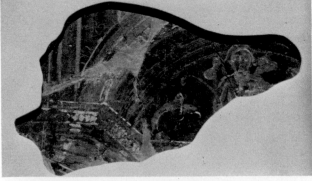

INDEX

INDEX

Numerals in **bold type** indicate the main catalogue-discussions. The authors are grateful to Hilary Barr for compiling this index.

(C) **Names and subjects**